本书献给 所有支持我们的人们，
尤其是我们的家人和朋友们，
他们的无私爱心帮助我们走过了这段旅程。

特别感谢凯普赖斯·霍恩 (Caprice Horn)
对出版本书抱有的愿景和作出的承诺
以及她的深厚友情。

衷心感谢卡尔·米德尔顿 (Carl Middleton of Neat)
的耐心和慷慨，以及他所作的精美装帧设计。

感谢尤金·布卢姆 (Eugen Blume)
充满洞察力、精斟细酌的文稿。

最后，由衷地感谢爱德华·路希—史密斯
(Edward Lucie-Smith)，
不仅因为他优美动人的话语，而且
还有他真诚的友谊，
将永远积极地、久远地影响着我们的生活。

In the creation of this book we would like to
pay tribute to the many people who have supported
us, especially our family and friends whose
unconditional love has helped us along our journey.

We would particularly like to thank Caprice Horn,
not only for her vision and commitment to this project,
but also for her friendship.

Carl Middleton of Neat deserves our appreciation
for his patience, generosity and brilliant book design.

We are grateful to Eugen Blume for his insightful
and considered text.

Finally, we shall be forever indebted to Edward
Lucie-Smith, not only for his eloquent words but also,
for his friendship, which has affected our lives in
such a positive and profound way.

MASLEN & MEHRA

CONTENTS
目录

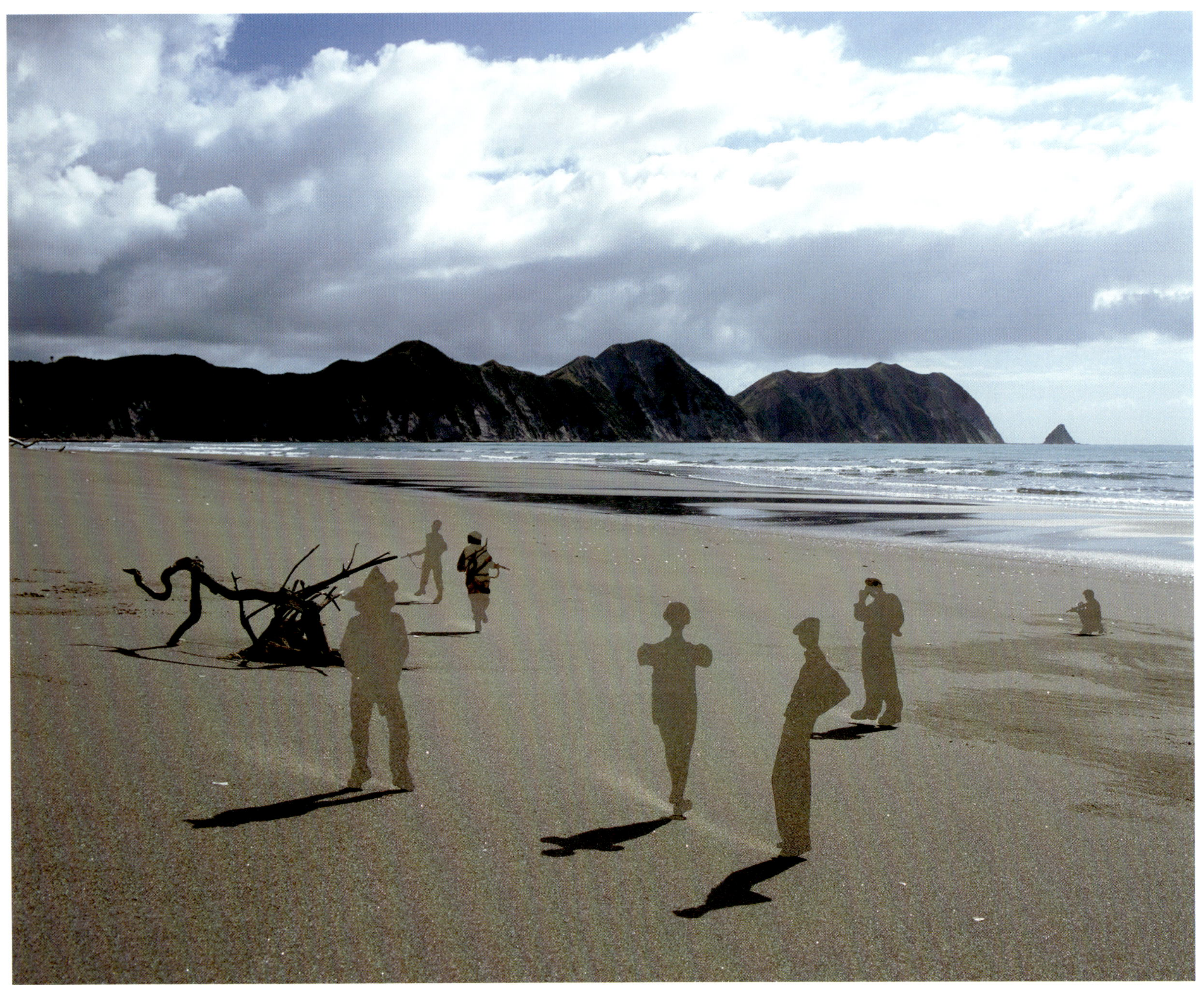

Tolaga Bay New Zealand II

2006
Durst Lambda print
120x160см

EUGEN BLUME

尤金·布卢姆的评论文章

The pair of artists Tim Maslen and Jennifer Mehra attained international recognition through their large-format colour photography, which most often presents landscapes. For these photographs, they have developed special lightboxes which, in contrast to the backlit photographs of Jeff Wall, for instance, mostly stand upon the ground and extend the perspective of the picture, as if in an extension of the pictorial space, right into these landscapes. Through their metal framing and rounded corners, they clearly recall the framed pictures of fine art, the discipline of painting which was the first to free itself from the wall and to lay claim to a frame for the demarcation which was henceforth deemed to be necessary. These details, however, constitute only incidental aspects in the works of Maslen and Mehra. It is in the silhouetted figures placed directly into the landscape that these artists, each still less than forty years old, have found their distinctive language. These figures, whose outlines render human shapes exactly, possess no interior structure but are cut in two dimensions out of mirrored aluminium. With their approximately halfway life-sized proportions, they are positioned within the landscape in such a manner as to convey the impression that it is a matter of full-sized figures which, by means of their clothing, pay homage to a special camouflage technique. Of course the aluminium mirror takes on those aspects of the landscape which are reflected upon it but which, because of the degree of inclination assumed by the two-dimensional figures, do not necessarily correspond to that which surrounds them in the landscape. From time to time, the blue sky is mirrored within an expanse of green grass, so that the figures emerge crisply out of their surroundings, in their colouration as well.

蒂姆·马斯伦 (Tim Maslen) 和詹妮弗·梅赫拉 (Jennifer Mehra) 两位艺术家拍摄的全画幅彩色照片，常以自然景色为背景，赢得了国际摄影界的一致好评。他们在创作中发现了灯箱的特殊光线效果，与杰夫·沃尔 (Jeff Wall) 的逆光摄影不同。例如，灯箱大多放置在地面上，扩大了画面的透视效果，镜像空间似乎在伸展，自然地融入背景景色。金属框架和圆角容易让人联想到画框里的美术作品，其表现风格首先是摆脱墙面的约束，依赖框架来作为不可或缺的限界。然而，这些细节仅是马斯伦和梅赫拉作品中的附属元素。这一批年龄不到四十岁的艺术家们，正是从放入恰当背景的廓影中，找到了他们独具特色的艺术语言。这些镜射的人影逼真地凸现出人的体态。轮廓内并没有内容，而是插入的铝镜二维图像。将人影缩小大约一半的比例，置于画面环境中，再借助"衣服"这一特殊的伪装技法，给人们造成"正常身高比例"的印象。当然，铝镜显示的是从周围环境折射上去的自然景色，因为二维图像设定的倾斜角度不同，所以，镜像不一定与周围的环境完全吻合。蓝天经常被镜射为绿草的延伸，因此，着色的人影就会活生生地突显在所处的环境之中。这些廓影让人们想起传统剪影的平面形象，然而，借助与铝镜互补的黑色调，便可刺激观看者在大脑中想象出轮廓人影的内部实体。令人惊讶的是，这种黑色调产生的效果与铝镜非常相似。即使单调的表面空无一物，观看者也能联想起所有的相关细节。因此，用轮廓线勾画的贫寒国王也会带来一种身着盛装的印象。人们甚至会想象国王的长袍上镶衬着貂皮。二十世纪二十年代兴起的动画电影，就运用了镜像——如果想要扩展表达空间——虽然主旨为叙事，仍然会在本质上与现代主义的精神维度标记密切相关，如马列维奇 (Malevich) 的黑色方块。黑颜色以及黑色空间在精神意义上的作用都是欧洲和亚洲神秘主义者所描述的"神圣的空无"(Divine Void)。

马斯伦和梅赫拉的镜像人物与人的投影有着相似的效果。尽管只是将自然景色的片断折射到轮廓内部，观看者也会产生这样的幻觉：人影穿着衣服。例如，从剪影中武器和制服的形状可辨认出是士兵。为什么人的视觉会作出这样的反应，这一点并不难解释。根据人的意识中存在的一般概念，认为投射在人影上的景象并不是真实的。这个景象会被内部结构自动替换，因而与外部轮廓更为协调。人们的想象力打破了自身的局限性，融入了多样化的、甚至是极其壮观的景色。人的视觉会

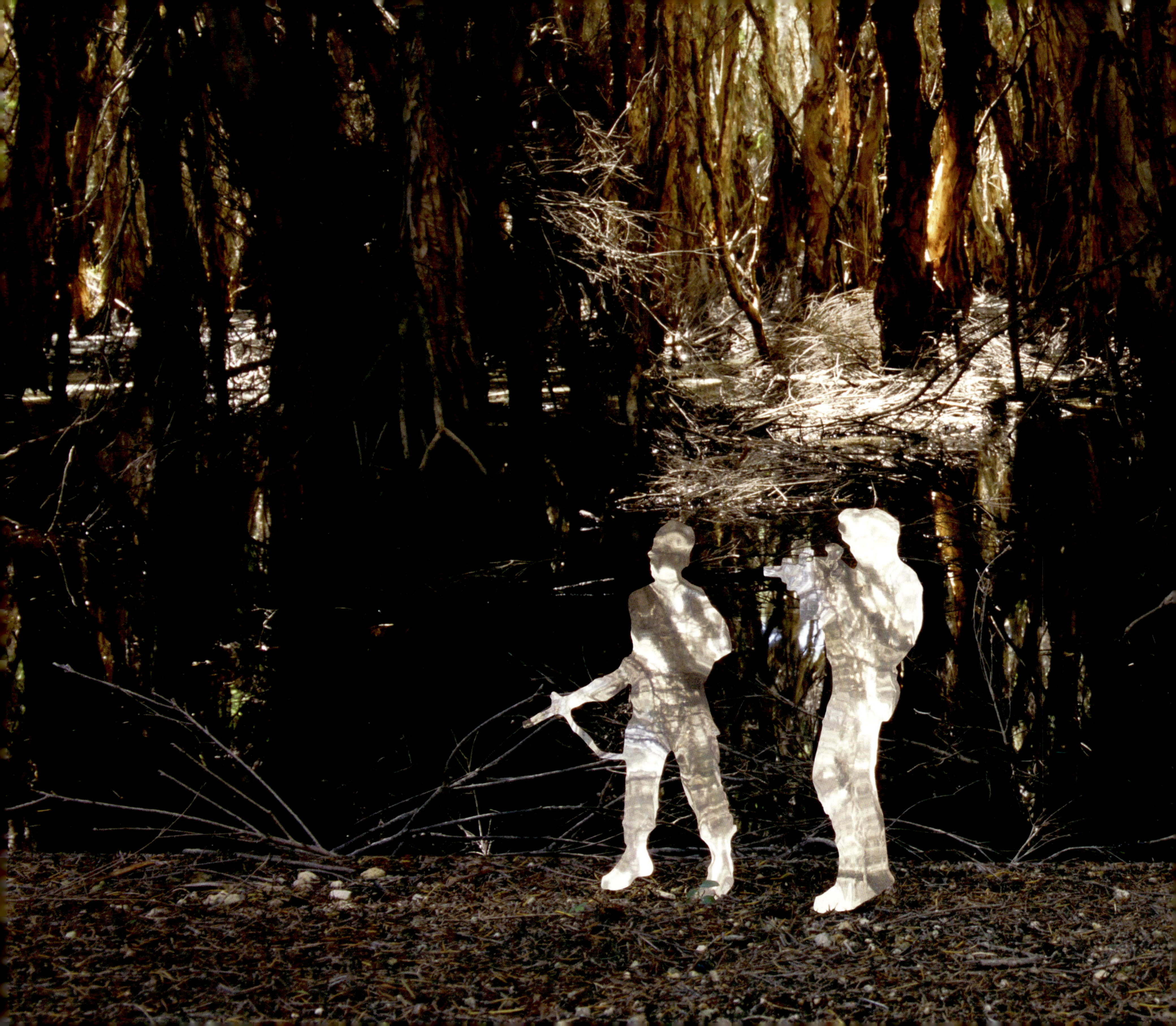

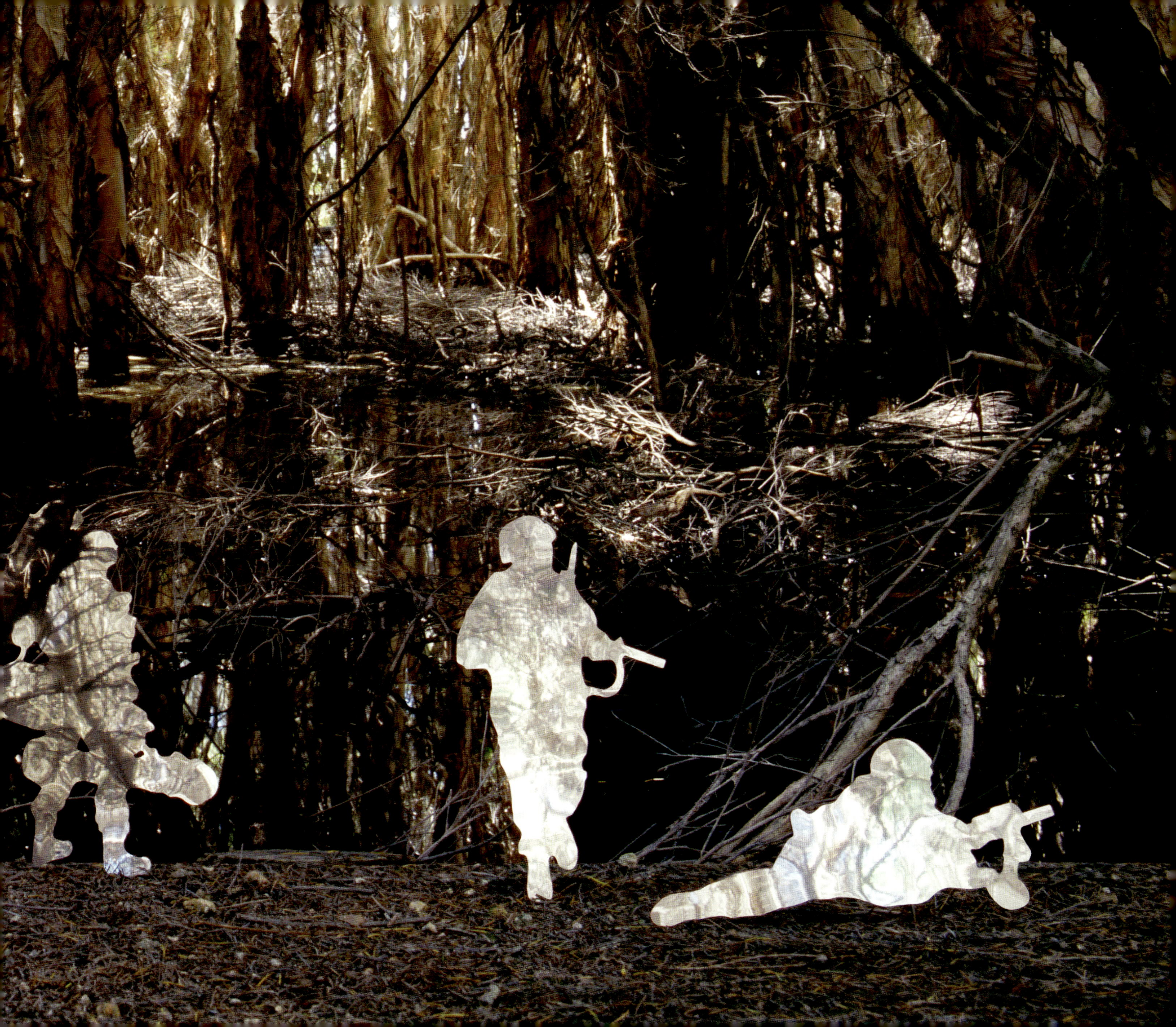

Herdsman Lake Perth Western Australia

2006
Durst Lambda print
120x160cm

They issue a reminder of the flat shapes of traditional silhouettes which, however, by means of a black hue that is complementary to the mirroring aluminium, induce the viewer to reconstruct mentally the interior reality of the delineated figures. Strangely enough, this black hue functions in a manner similar to that of the mirrored aluminium. Even though nothing was represented upon its dull surface, still the viewer's memory associated all the pertinent details, so that a poor king limned in silhouette was nevertheless richly attired. One could even surmise his robe lined with ermine. In the animated films developed during the 1920s, there was mirrored - if one were inclined to range far afield - albeit with narrative intention, but closely related on an essential level, the spiritual dimension of an icon of Modernism, the black square of Malevich. This black colour functioned as well as a blank space, in a spiritual sense as the Divine Void, which has been described by both European and Asian mystics. The mirroring figures of Maslen and Mehra play a role similar to that of these shadowy figures, even if the reflected segments of nature impart an interior delineation to them and the viewer comes to fantasize real clothing for them, for example the weapons and uniforms of the figures which are often thereby made recognizable as sol-diers. There is a simple explanation for the reason why human vision reacts in this way. The landscape reflected upon the shape is not considered to be real by the normative criteria stored in our consciousness. It is automatically replaced by an interior structure, which is more appropriate to the exterior figuration. The human being flows out of his natural limitation, as it were, into these diverse, occasionally magnificent landscapes. He is completely assimilated by the reflecting surface,

被镜像完全同化，从而获得原先受到排斥的信息。隐喻的镜像人物唤起的正是以完整无缺的形式将最初的渴望与本能再一次联系起来。置身于自然环境的人是文学艺术史上最常见的创作主题。在认识善良与邪恶的过程中，经常会涉及"人类最原始的场景"，提到"被逐出天堂乐园"。从此，人类始终在努力减少时空的干扰，通过心智和认知再一次返回了已经变得疏远的精神家园。然而，当代批评家尚未得出结论。人类正在以同样的尺度逐步了解自己的本性和灵魂。人类对自然环境造成了严重的破坏。在以完全毁灭自然界作为对被逐出乐园的报复行为中，人类似乎一直在试图建立一种无偏见的概观。人类放纵自己的整个过程，尤其是二十世纪全世界的工业生产，对环境造成了全方位的破坏。尽管有着各种各样的反对运动，都无法制止这个过程。反而，破坏的速度越发加快了。人类并没有从自身去反省其产生的原因，而是将一切归咎于大自然，较少审视人类自己。在马斯伦和梅赫拉拍摄的超自然的风景画面上出现全副武装的士兵绝非偶然，若没有这些士兵的出现，便不能够明确的体现他们孜孜不倦追求的目标。也可以用毫无特征的景色来镜射人影。投射在人形轮廓上的镜像不带有主观意念。即便墨守着这样一种错误观念：是他们将人类的影像投射在自然景色之上的，但轮廓表面附着的却是大自然赐予的景色。面对不可抗拒的自然变迁过程，一切军事目的均是次要的。这些人影使得人们联想起征服者、胜利者、外籍军团和士兵，他们起到了支撑欧洲列强和美国的殖民地野心。这种以武装暴力为目的的外国人入侵别国领土，如约瑟夫·康拉德 (Joseph Conrad) 在他的小说《黑暗的心》(Heart of Darkness) 中所描述的对比属刚果 (Belgian Congo) 施行的残暴。其结果都将注定是失败的。这正是镜像人影隐喻的含义所在。自然 界广袤无际，大自然力量无穷，是人类赖以生存的王国，而并非反之。

当然，在这些沉重内容之外，马斯伦和梅赫拉的作品可以被看作为无拘无束、纯美学的杰作，甚至 可以诠释为超现实主义的摄影作品。萨尔瓦多·达利 (Salvador Dali) 和雷尼·马格里特 (René Magritte) 的绘画中都曾经有相似的映射，人物与自然环境背景难以区分。尤其是马格里特，画面中人物的剪影与环境景色融为一体。镜像是马格里特重要的象征性手法，他是第一位勾勒出人物剪影、再将环境景象折射在轮廓表面的艺术家。然而，在他的绘画中是一种梦幻般的意象，

absorbed into something out of which he was originally driven. The metaphor
of a mirror-man awakens nothing other than the primal longing to be connected
once again in an integral manner to nature. Human beings in the landscape
are a quite common topos, which extends throughout art history. They refer to
the primal scene, to the banishment from the paradisiacal garden through the
knowledge of good and evil. Ever since this original exile, humanity has striven to
reduce the intervening distance, to attain once again the homeland from which it
became alienated through the mind, through cognition. A critical observation of
the present era does not, however, lead to the uplifting conclusion that humanity
is currently embarked upon the path of coming to understand itself as both nature
and spirit in equal measure. The human violations of nature are too severe. It is
as if humanity were attempting to establish an objective overview in the very
act of retaliating for its banishment by means of a total annihilation of nature.
The fundamental process, which has been unleashed, especially by the
global industrializing endeavors of the twentieth century, is an all-encompassing
destruction of the environment. In spite of various oppositional movements, this
process cannot be stopped, but on the contrary it is speeding up more and more.
Humanity has begun, instead of recalling in a productive manner its origin within
nature, to transform itself into a nature-less mirror-mankind. It is not by chance
that armed soldiers arise in the magically photographed landscapes of Maslen
and Mehra, without it ever becoming clear what goals they are pursuing.
They as well are occupied by the landscape in an utter lack of distinction.
They lose their subjectivity in a reflection, which is projected onto the figures.

超现实主义的表现。而对马斯伦和梅赫拉来说，更需潜心研究的是如何让这些轮廓本身产生作用。其效果惊人，映射的人物与雷尼·马格里特的绘画人物极为相似，折射周围的部分景物，例如，河岸上出现一片碎石。我们不妨可以将这些联想延续到路易斯·卡洛尔 (Lewis Carroll) 的《镜中缘》(Through the Looking Glass)，爱丽丝穿过镜子进入了魔法世界，所有一切的顺序、比例都似乎彻底颠倒了。但是，这里的人物并没有穿越那面镜子而进入另一个空间，而让人物本身作为一面镜子，透过这面镜子或在这面镜子的表面折射出景物。人类在如此的瞬间融入镜像，变得难以从周围环境中分辨出来。伪装手法最为成功。人影中明显可见的武器喻指士兵，特别适合用来突出伪装的创意。士兵将自己伪装起来而不被敌人看到。镜子似乎可以用作理想的伪装，因为镜子仅仅反射周围的环境。然而，人物形象仍然令人惊讶地清晰，镜射出意想不到的景象，但只有在极为少数的情形下，才会镜射出军事意义上的伪装效果，这对袭击得以成功是必不可少的。军事题材让我们想起泰伦斯·马立克 (Terrence Malick) 拍摄的电影，特别是战争片《红色警戒 (Thin Red Line)》大部分为外景拍摄，士兵在绿叶繁茂的草地上行进，好似是镂空的剪影在移动。

尤金·布卢姆现任德国汉堡火车站博物馆总策展人

By means of the fixed delineation of their surface they are at the mercy of nature, even while they cling to the mistaken belief that it is they who project their image onto nature. All military goals remain secondary in the face of the omnipotence of natural processes. The figures summon up reminiscences of the conquerors, the conquistadores, the foreign legionnaires and soldiers whose role it was to shore up the colonial ambitions of the European and American powers. This penetration of strangers into a strange land for the purpose of violence, such as was described so forcefully for the Belgian Congo by Joseph Conrad in his book The Heart of Darkness, is doomed to failure, as is announced metaphorically by the mirrored images. Nature is much more vast and mighty. It marks the human beings living within its realm, and not the other way around. Of course the works of Maslen & Mehra may be read, beyond these sombre considerations, as un-constricted, aesthetic play, even as a photographic paraphrase of Surrealism. Salvador Dali and René Magritte once painted similar reflecting figures, which could not be distinguished from the nature to which they belong. Especially with Magritte, there are pictures in which the silhouette of a figure merges with the surrounding landscape. The mirror is an especially important metaphor for Magritte. He was the first artist to cut out figures and to project the surrounding landscape into their interior surface. In his case, however, it is a matter of a fantasized image of painting, a surreal action. Maslen and Mehra, on the other hand, are much more concerned with investigating the ways in which such shapes could function in reality itself. The effects are astounding there where, within the reflecting figures in a manner quite similar to that of René Magritte, that which surrounds them is

DETAIL ON FOLLOWING PAGE:
下页图片：

Lightbox installation London - 2006
Recycled advertising lightboxes
131x190x16cm each

灯箱装置，伦敦- 2006
广告灯箱使用再生材料制作
每只尺寸：131x190x16厘米

mirrored halfway, for example a field of debris on the bank of a river. We could extend the sequence of associations even further to Lewis Carroll's Through the Looking Glass, where Alice passes through a mirror to enter into an enchanted world in which all relationships and proportions seem to have been inverted. But here the figures placed within the landscape do not pass through a mirror into another space but are instead themselves a mirror, through which or upon which the landscape is reflected. The human being dissolves at the most intense instant of reflection and becomes indistinguishable from that which surrounds him. The camouflage is a perfect success. The figures, whose visible weapons suggest soldiers, are of course particularly suitable for allowing the idea of camouflage to emerge into prominence. Soldiers camouflage themselves in order no longer to be seen by the enemy. The mirror seems to provide an ideal camouflage, inasmuch as it reflects nothing other than that which surrounds it. And yet the figures remain strangely visible, mirroring something incalculable and only in the most rare cases reflecting that which, with camouflage in a military sense, would be necessary for a successful attack. It is especially this military aspect which calls to mind the films of Terrence Malick, especially The Thin Red Line, a war film which takes place mostly out in the landscape of nature, in high verdant grass through which soldiers move as if they were mere vacant mirrorings.

Eugen Blume is chief curator at Hamburger Bahnhof Museum Berlin.
Originally translated from German.

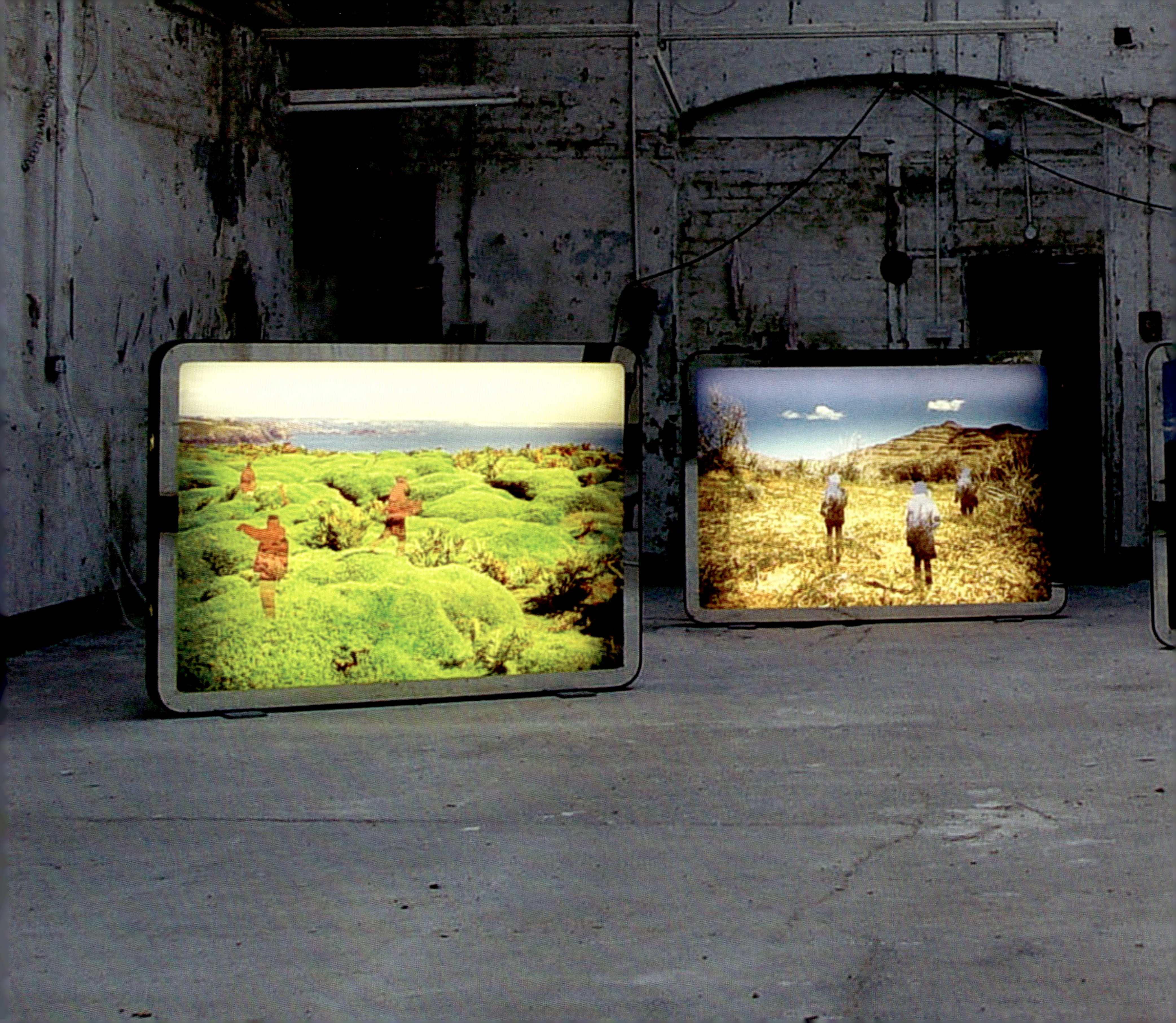

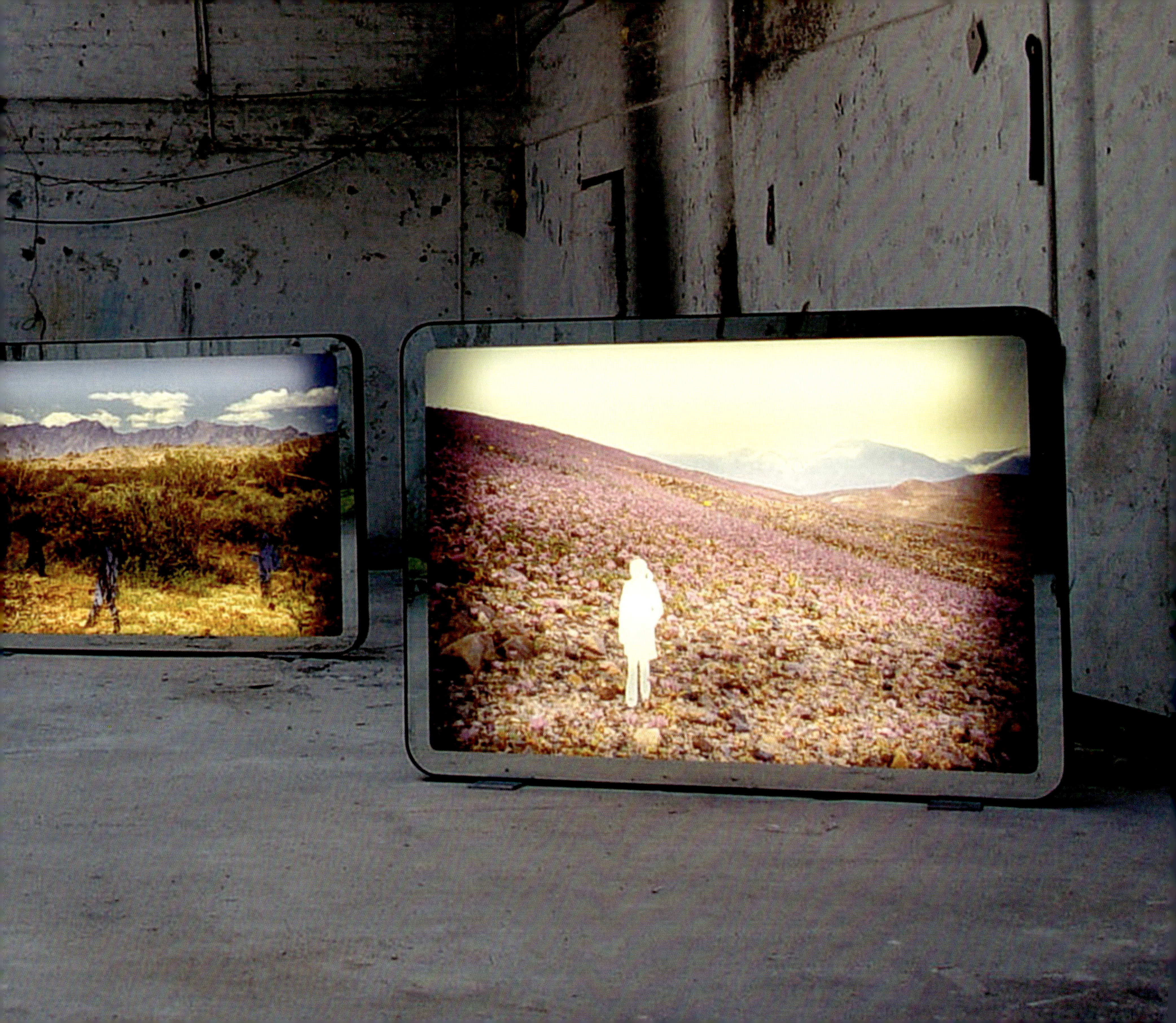

MIRRORED

《镜像》

Xouria Sporades Marine Park I

2007
Durst Lambda print
72x52см

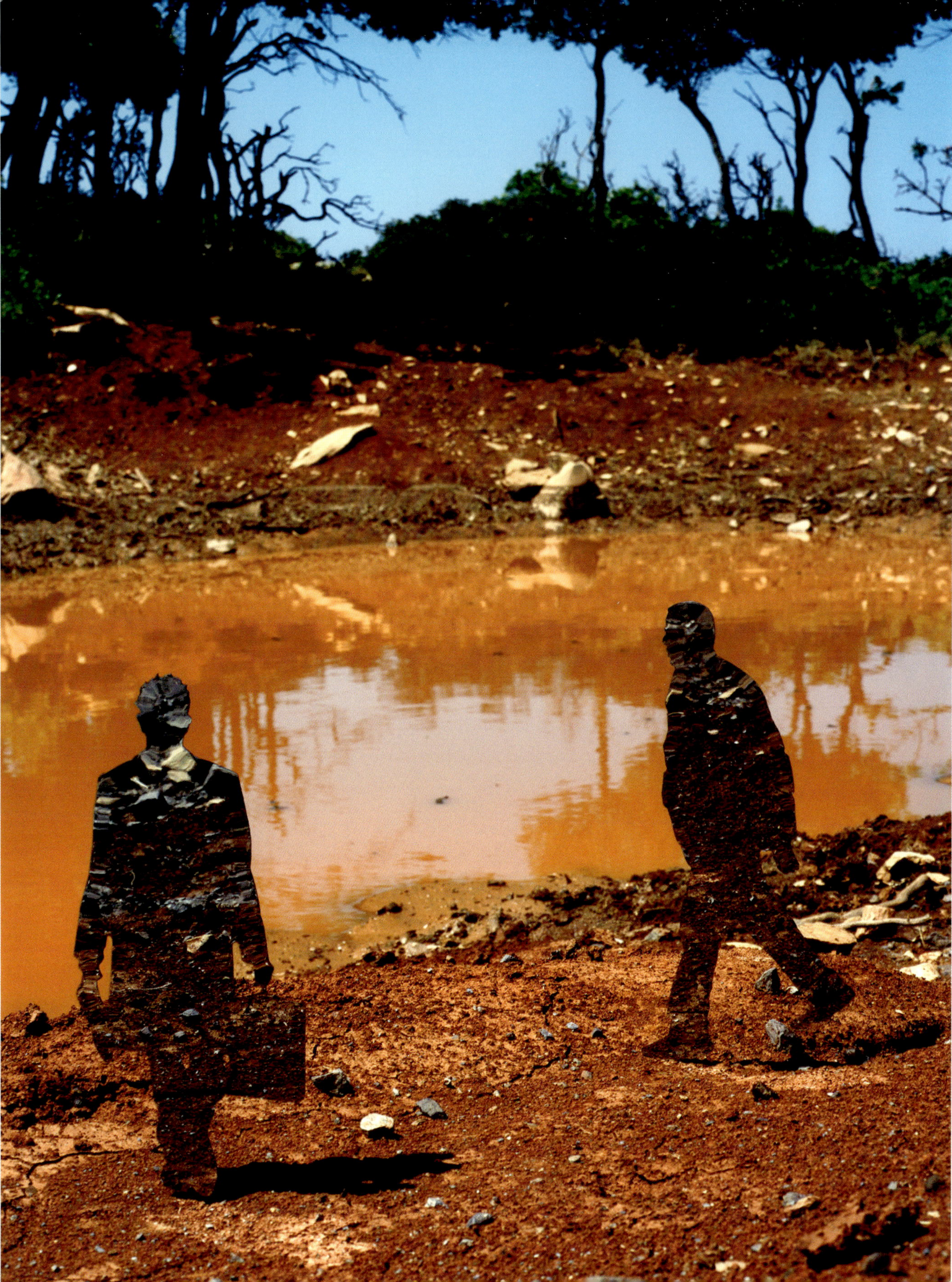

Alonissos Sporades Marine Park II

2007
Durst Lambda print
52x72cm

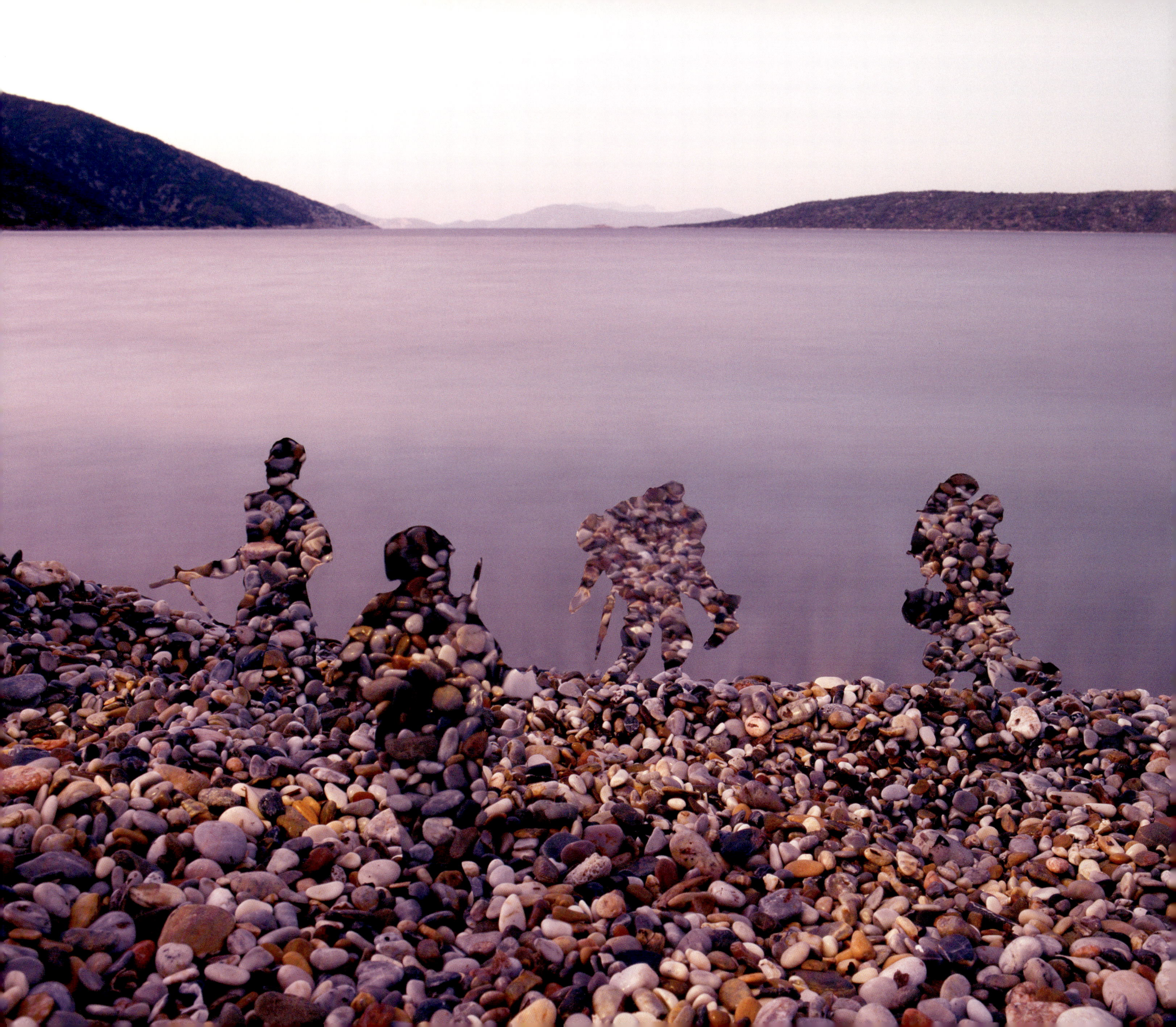

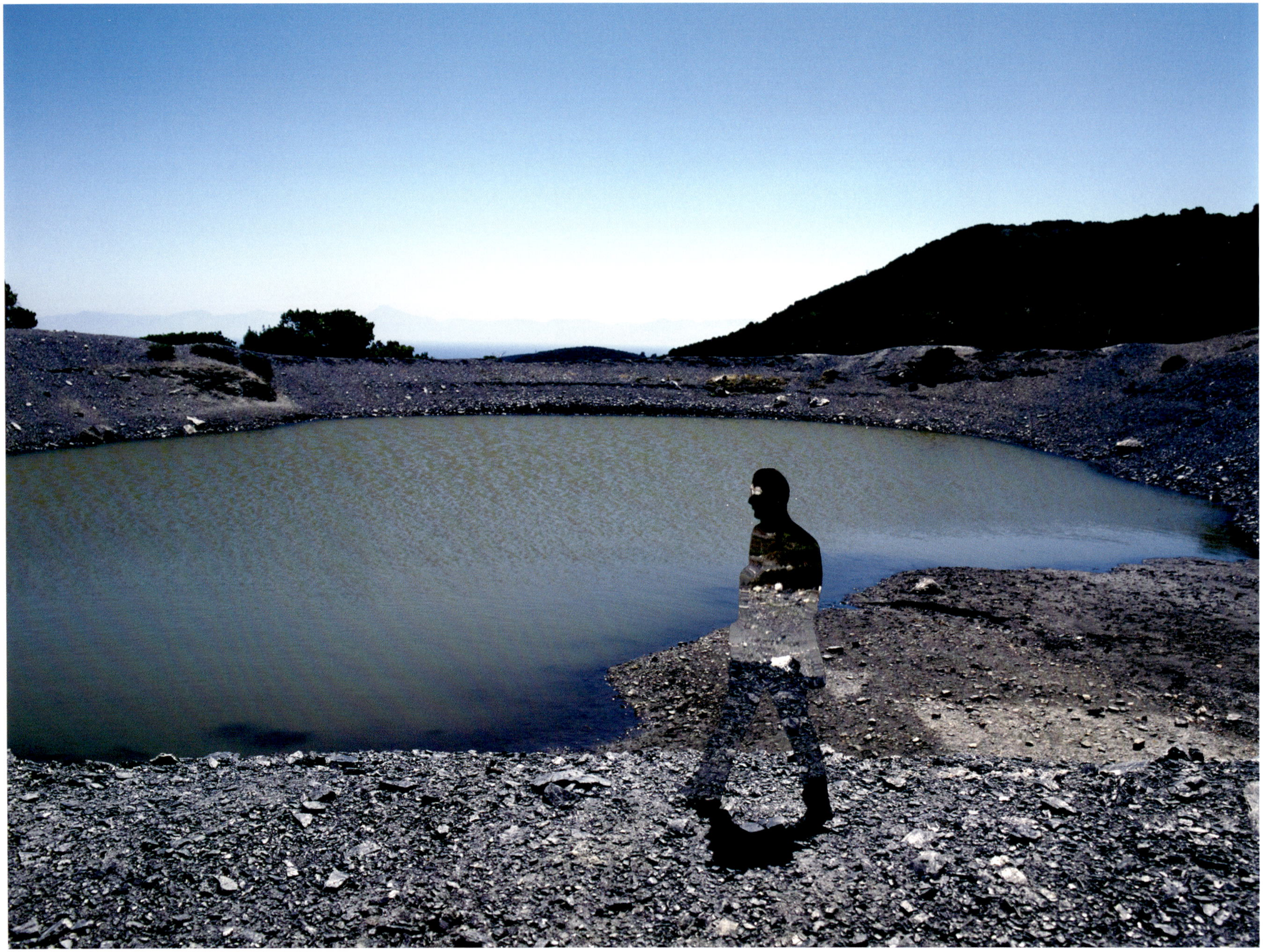

Kavakia Sporades Marine Park

2007
Durst Lambda print
52x72см

Aghios Konstantinos Sporades Marine Park I

2007
Durst Lambda print
52x72cm

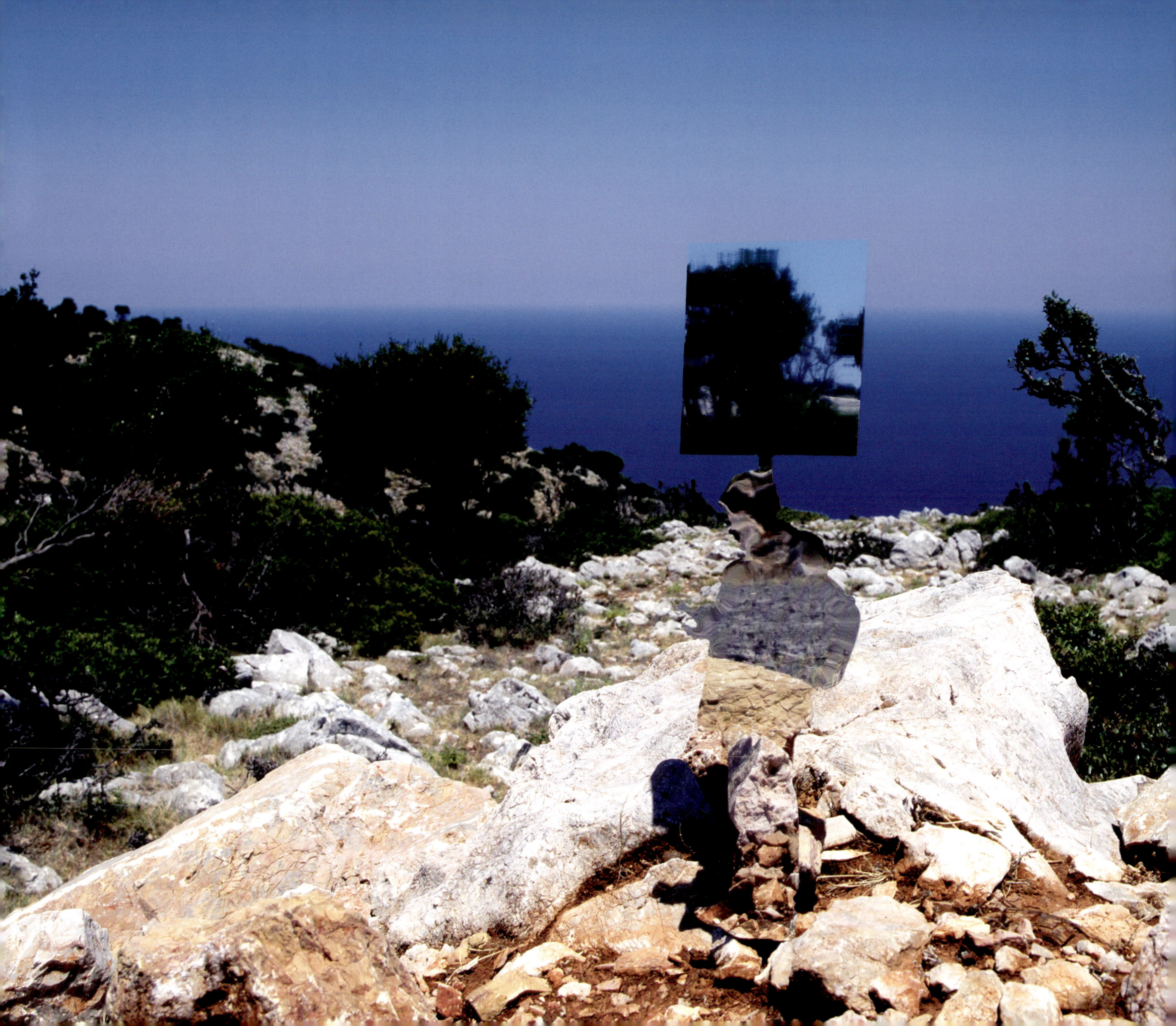

Pink Hutt Lagoon Western Australia I

2006
Durst Lambda print
120x160см

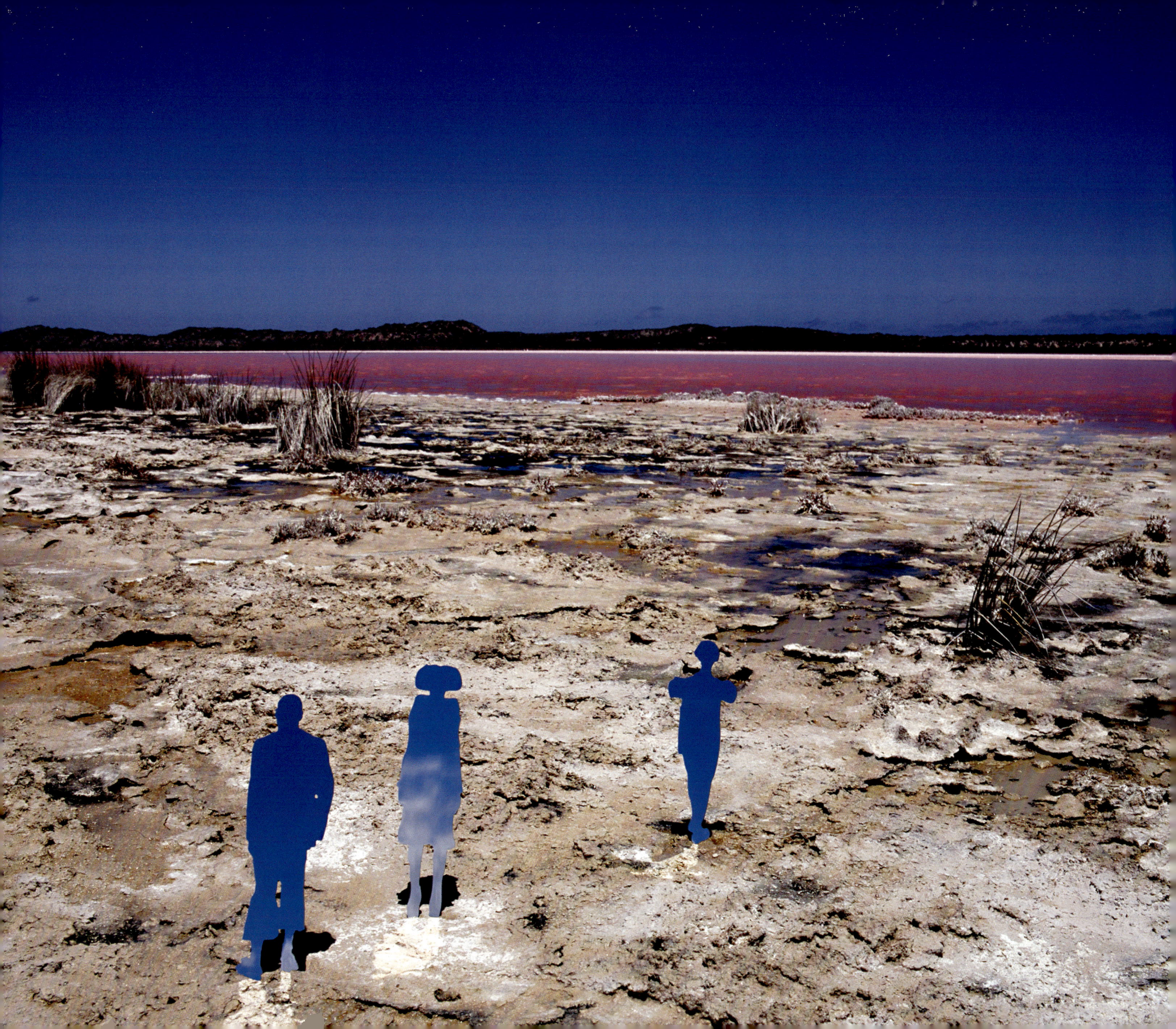

Inferno Crater Waimangu New Zealand

2006
Durst Lambda print
120x160cm

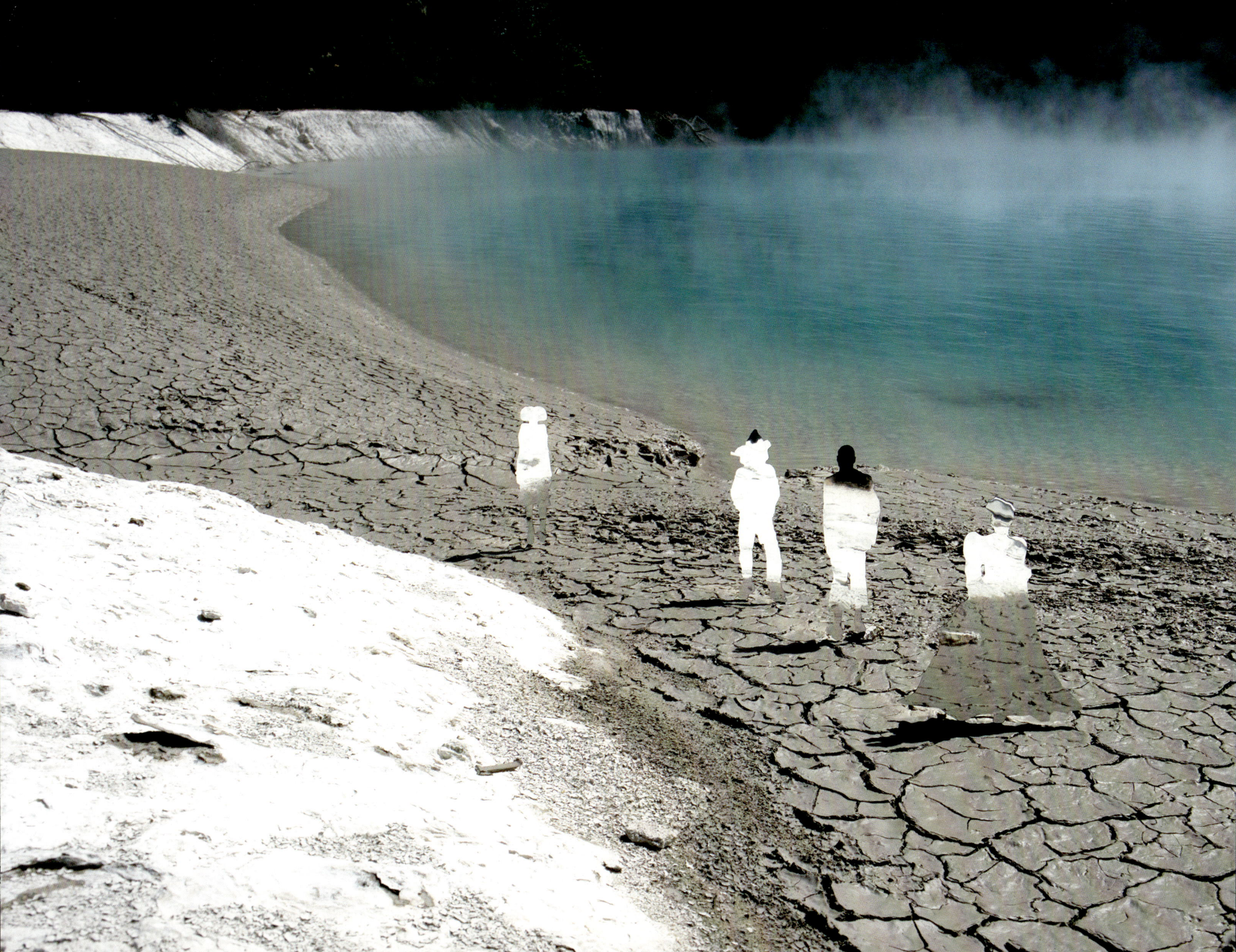

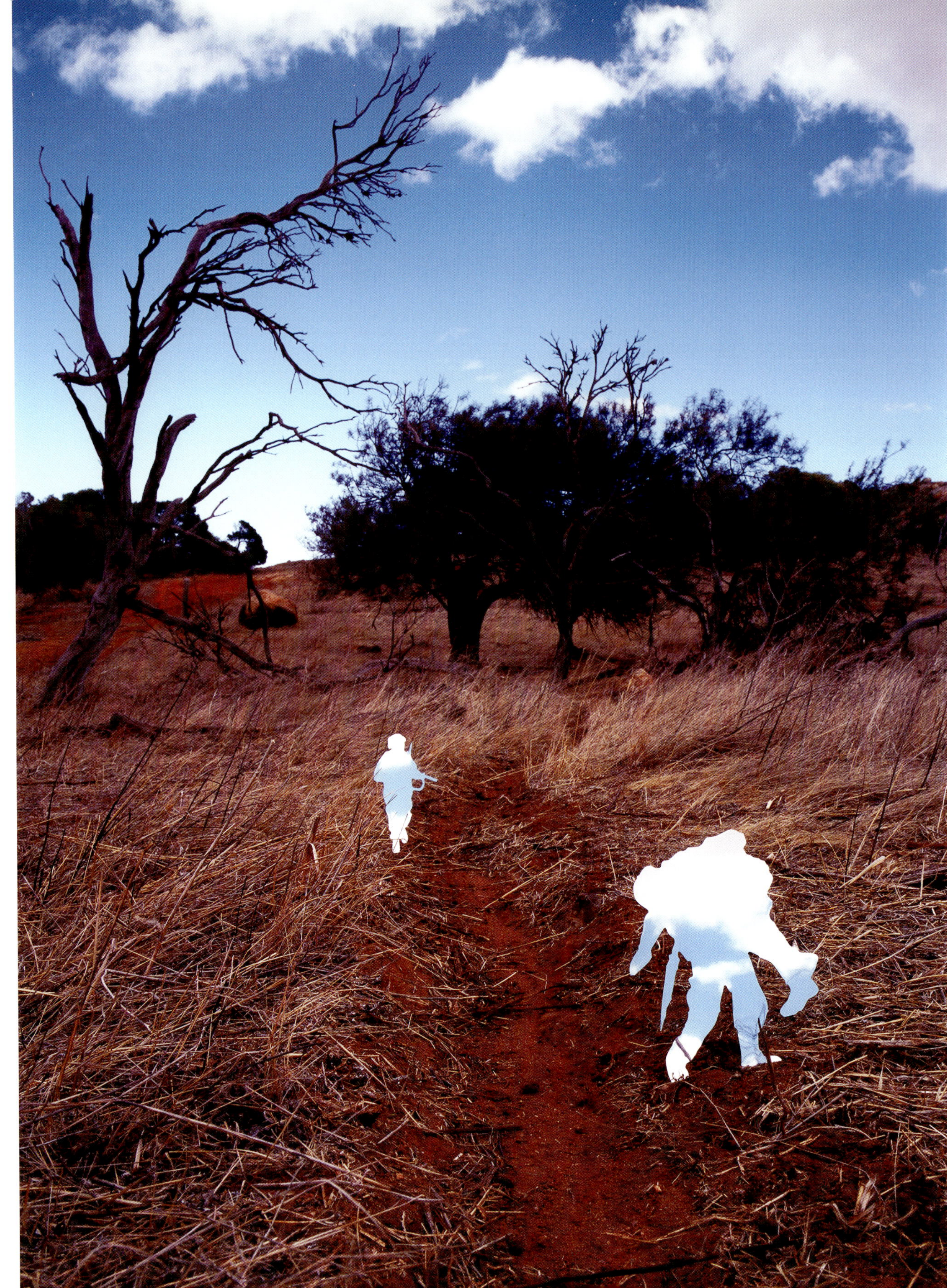

Horrocks Beach Rd Western Australia III

2006
Durst Lambda print
160x120cm

River Walk Okura River New Zealand

2006
Durst Lambda print
120x160см

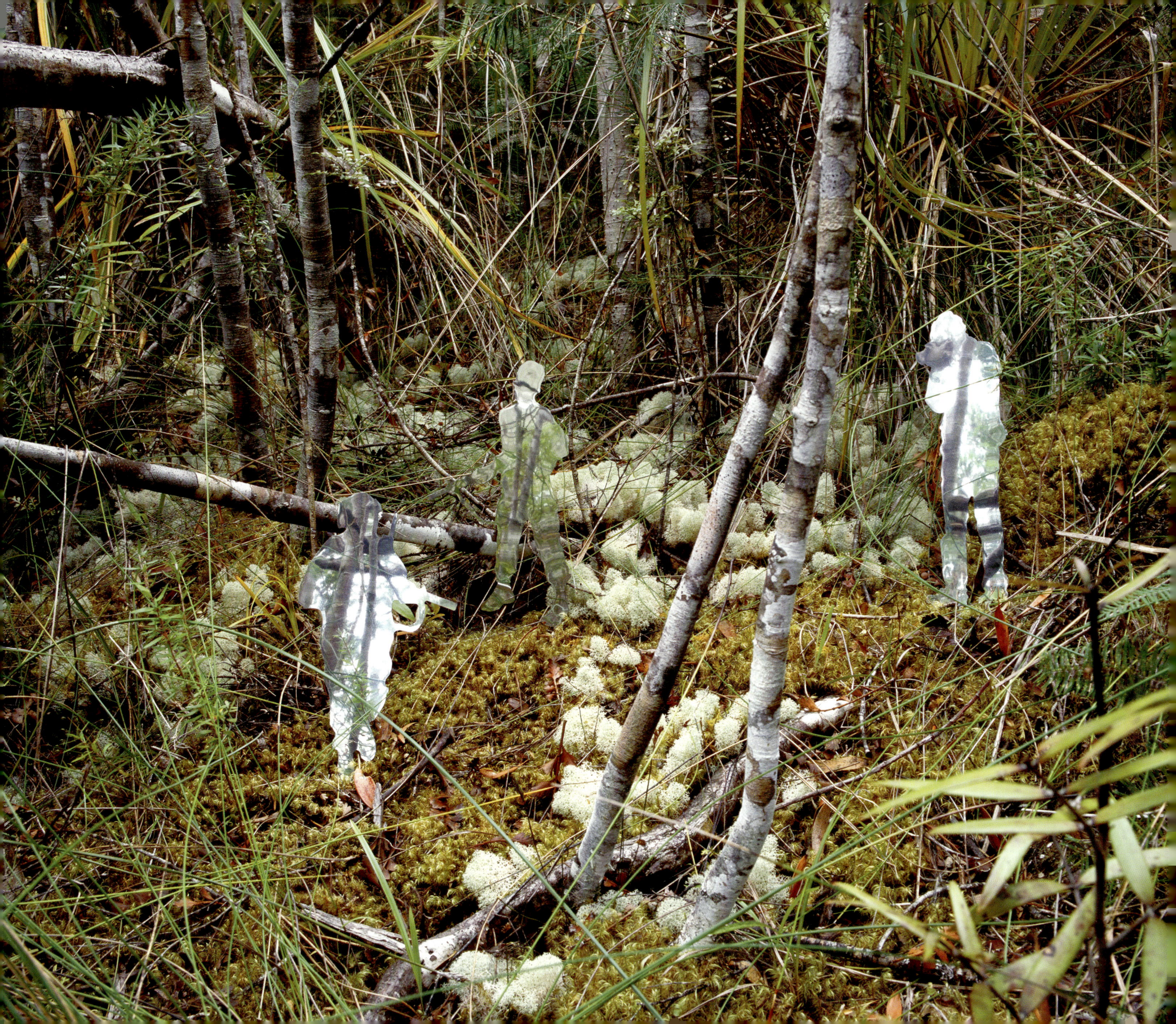

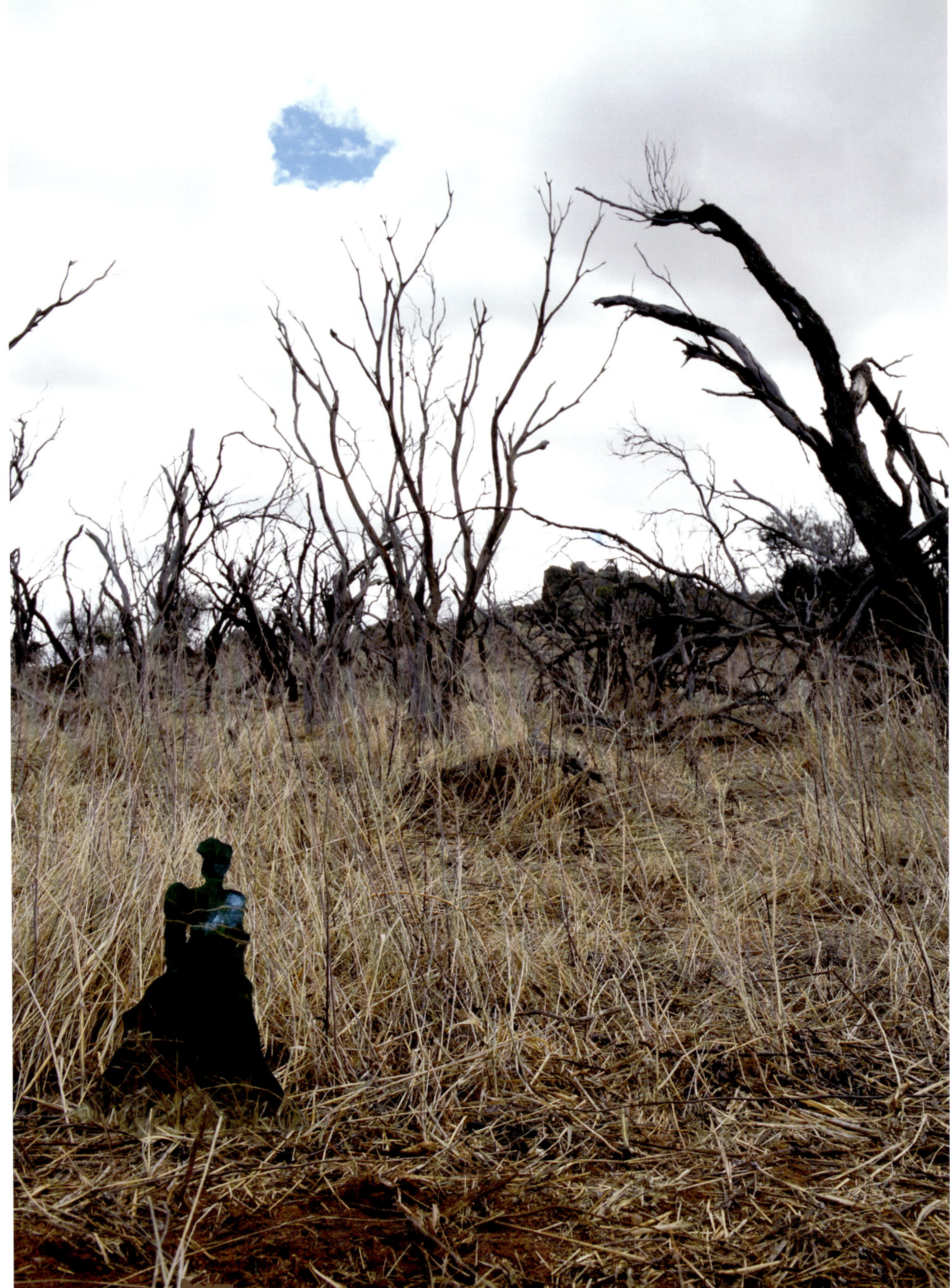

Horrocks Beach Rd Western Australia II

2006
Durst Lambda print
72x52cm

Brand Highway Badgingarra Western Australia

2006
Durst Lambda print
120x160cm

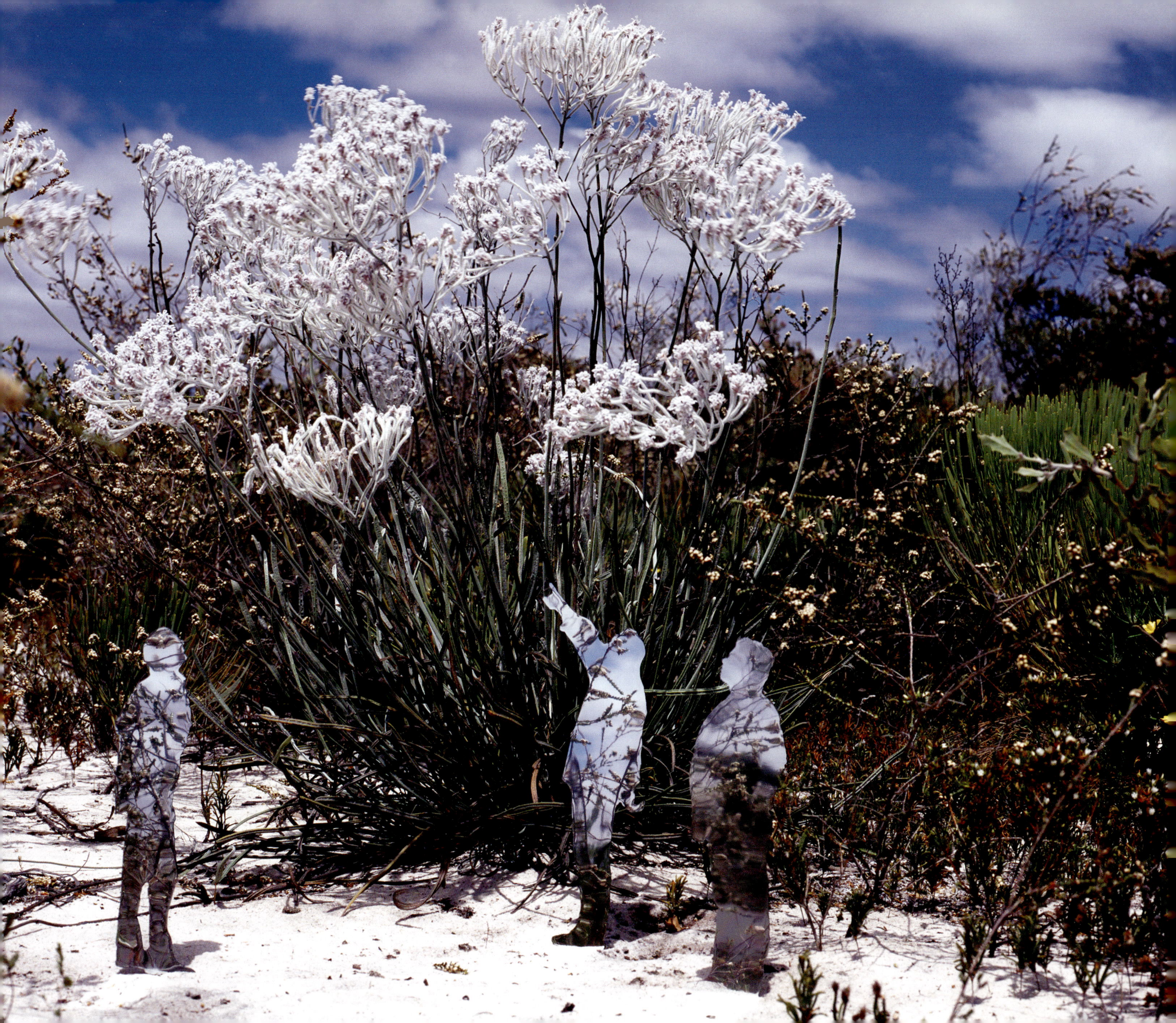

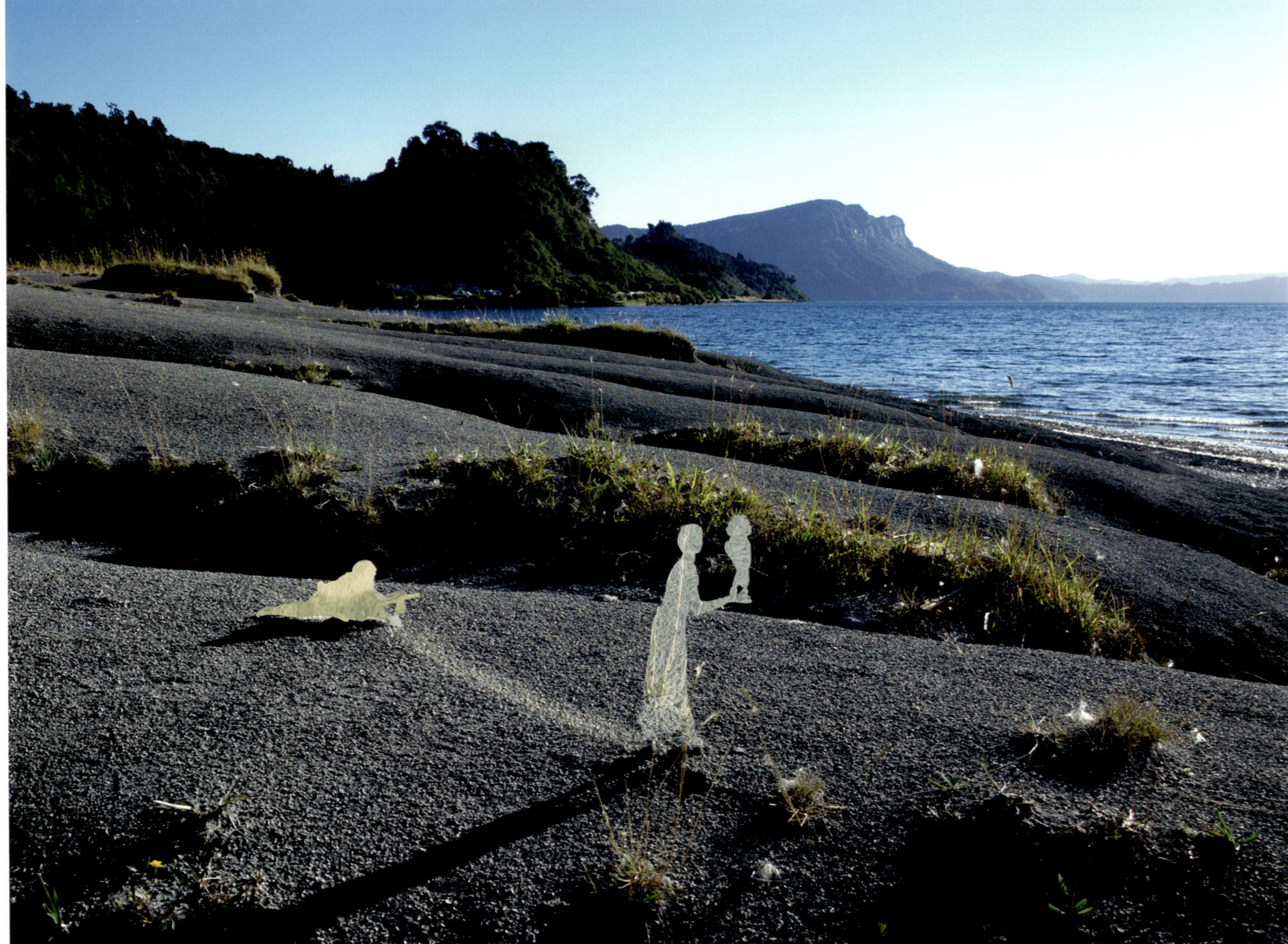

DETAIL ON FOLLOWING PAGE:
下页图片:

Waikanae Beach Gisbourne New Zealand
2006
Recycled advertising lightbox
广告灯箱使用再生材料制作
131x190x16cm

39

Lake Waikaremoana New Zealand
2006
Durst Lambda print
52x72cm

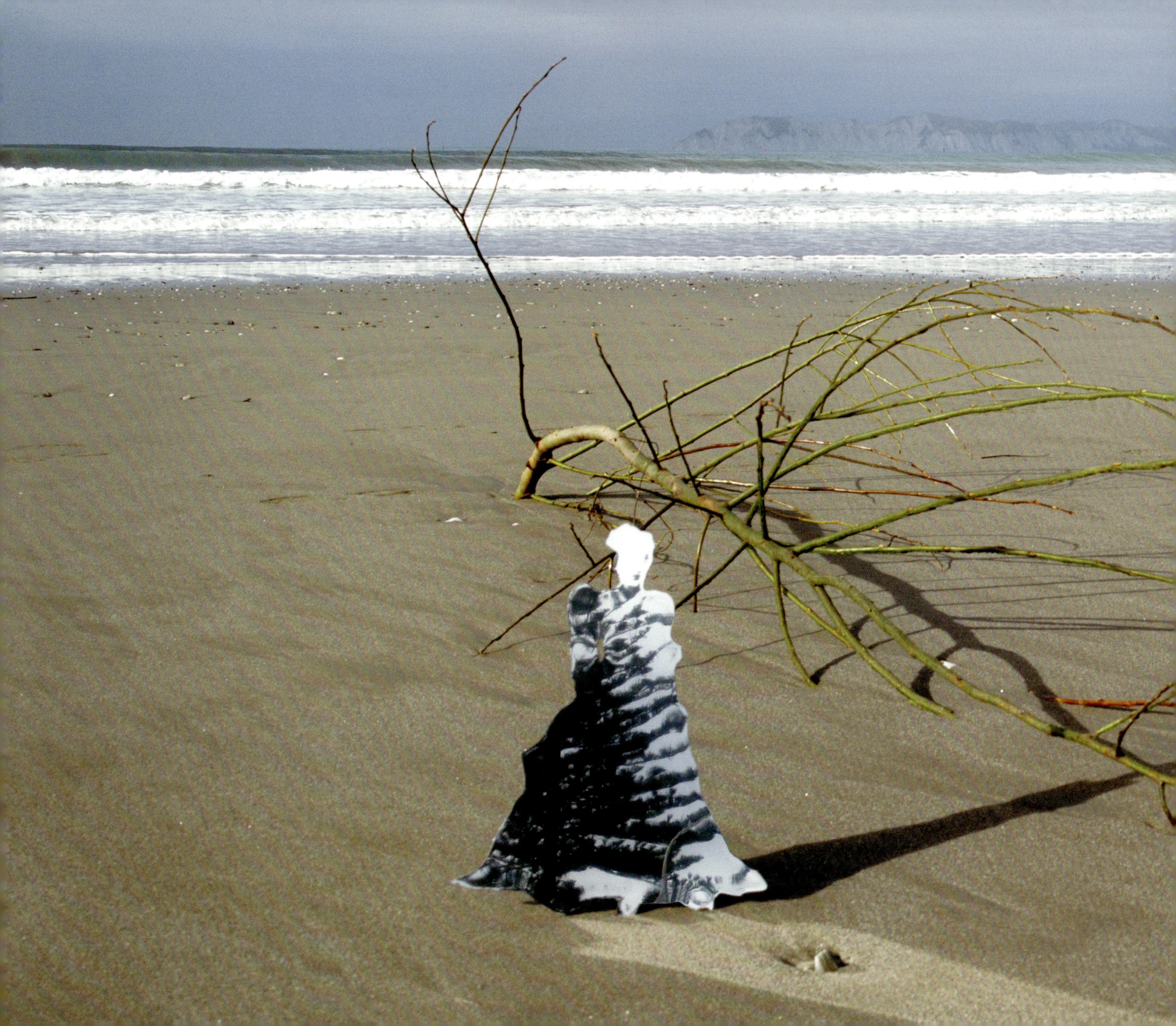

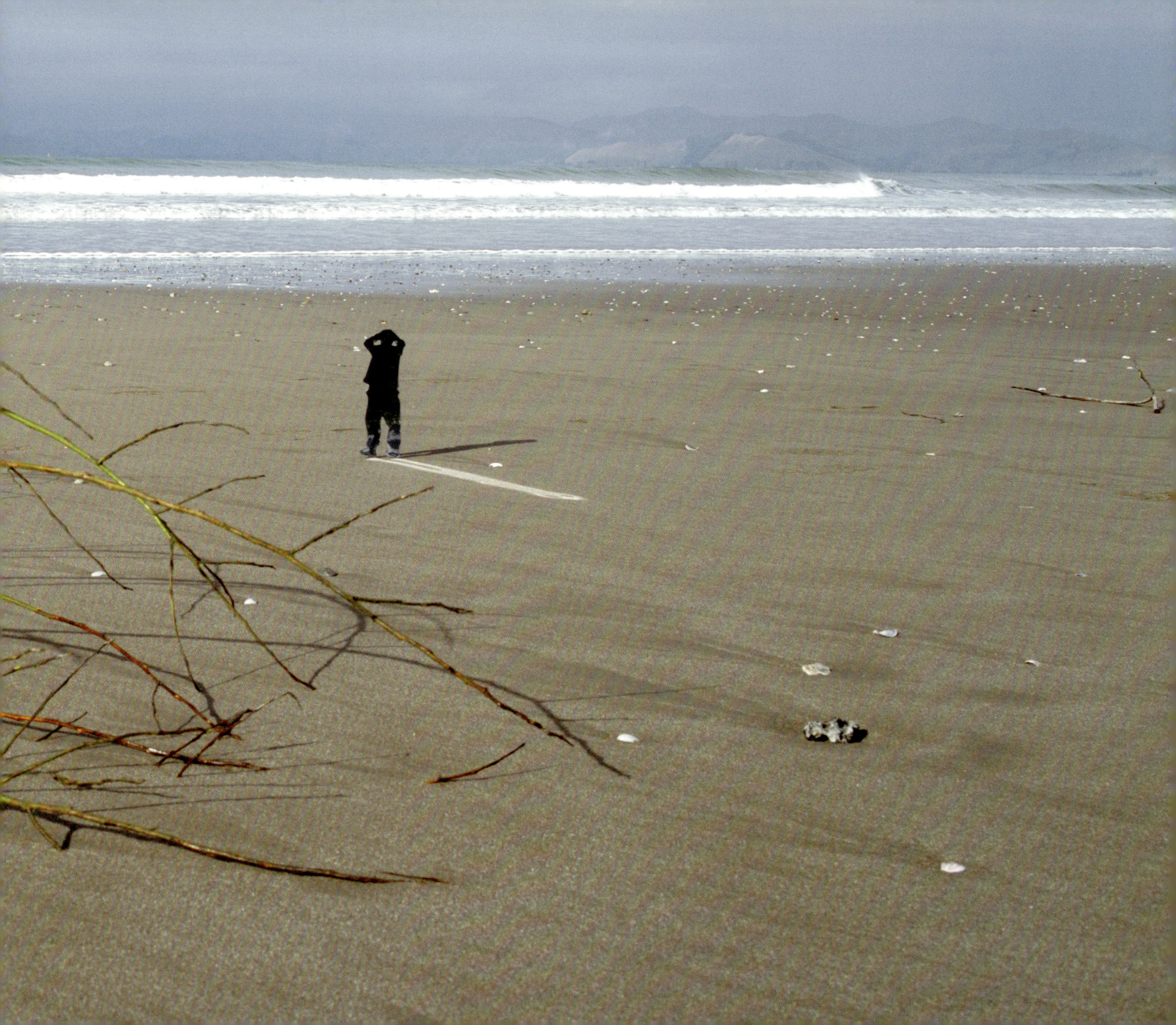

Ikawhenua Range Urewera Park New Zealand

2006
Durst Lambda print
120x160см

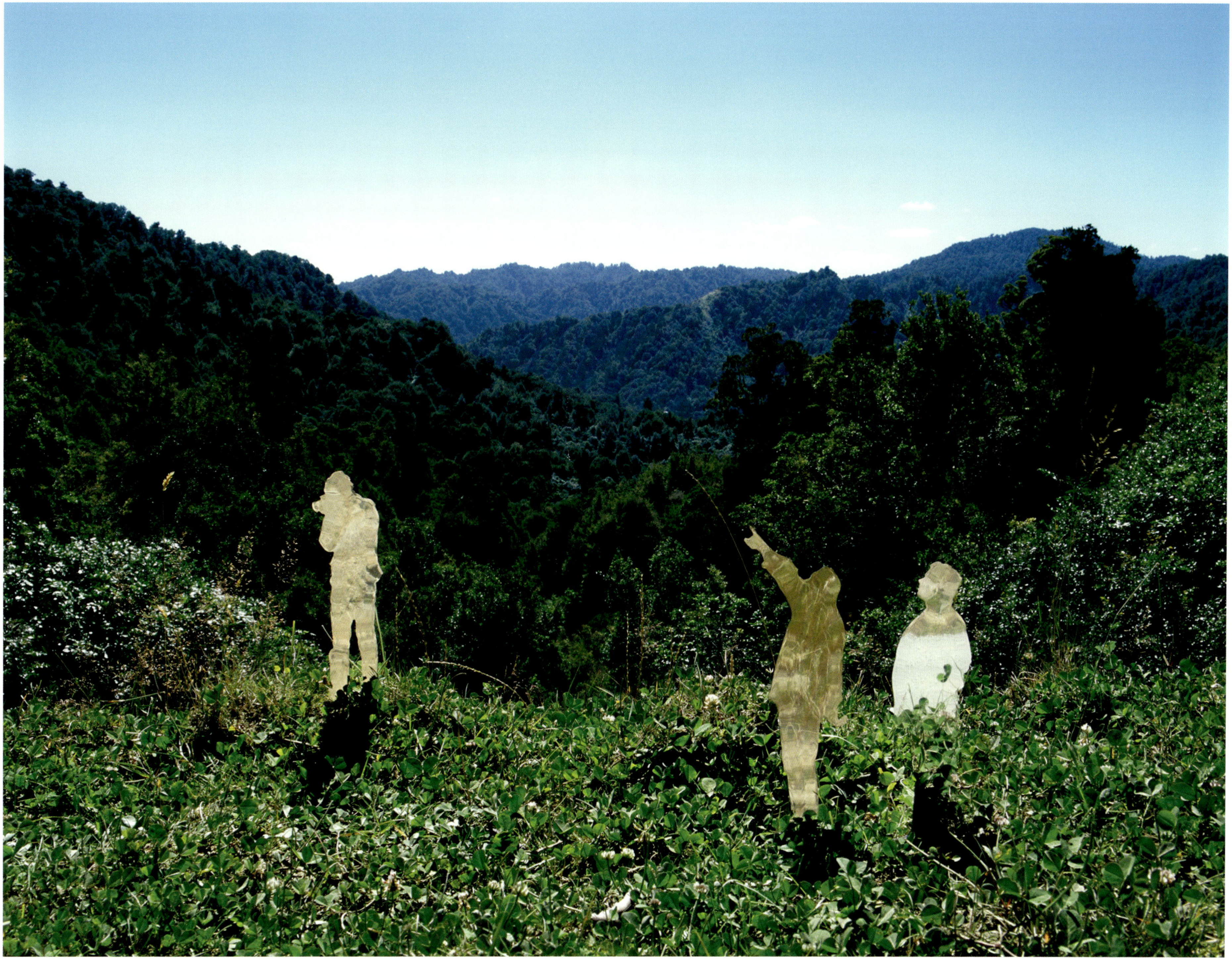

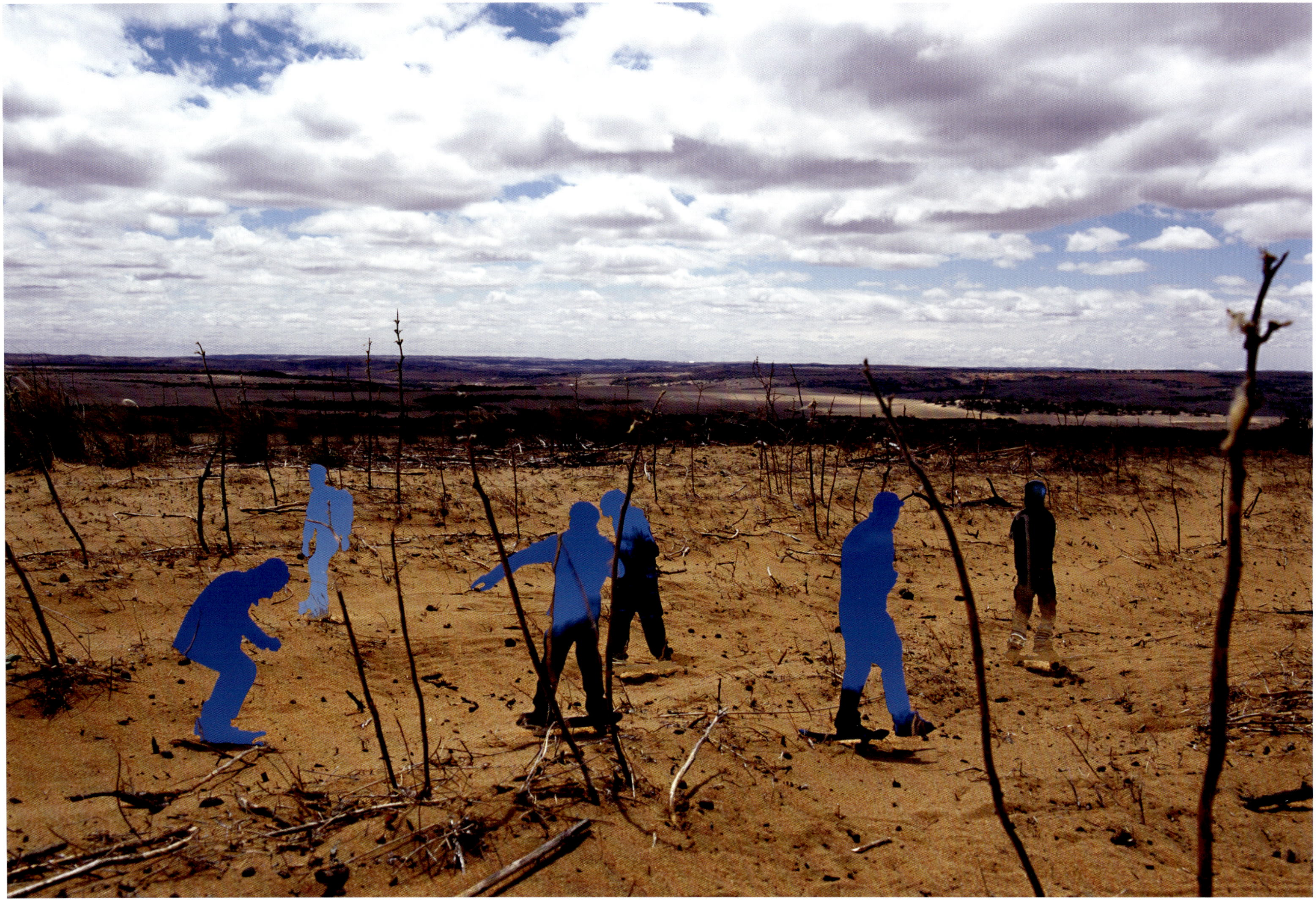

44

Horrocks Beach Rd Western Australia I

2006
Recycled advertising lightbox
广告灯箱使用再生材料制作
131x190x16см

Hot Stream Waimangu New Zealand

2006
Durst Lambda print
52x72см

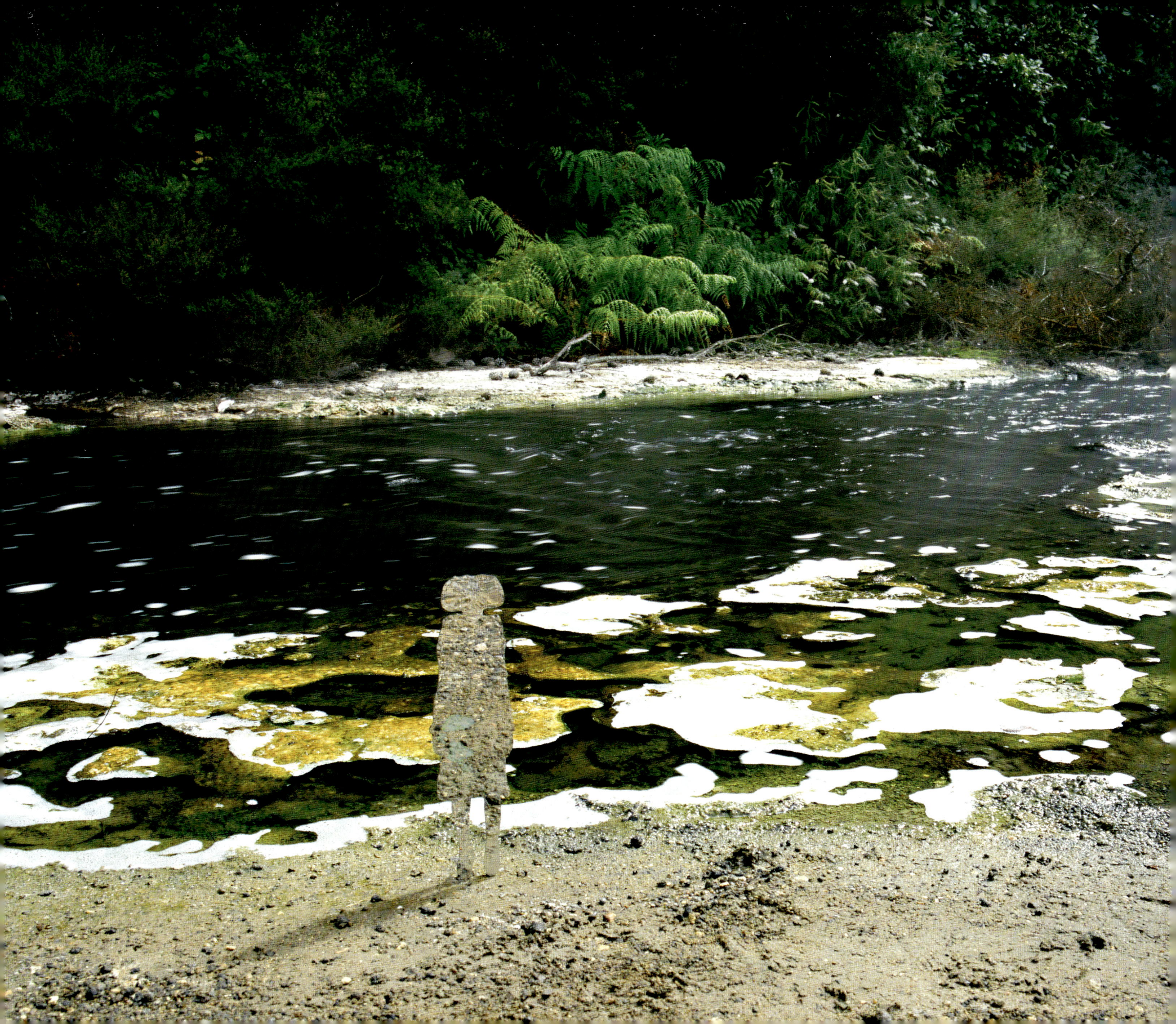

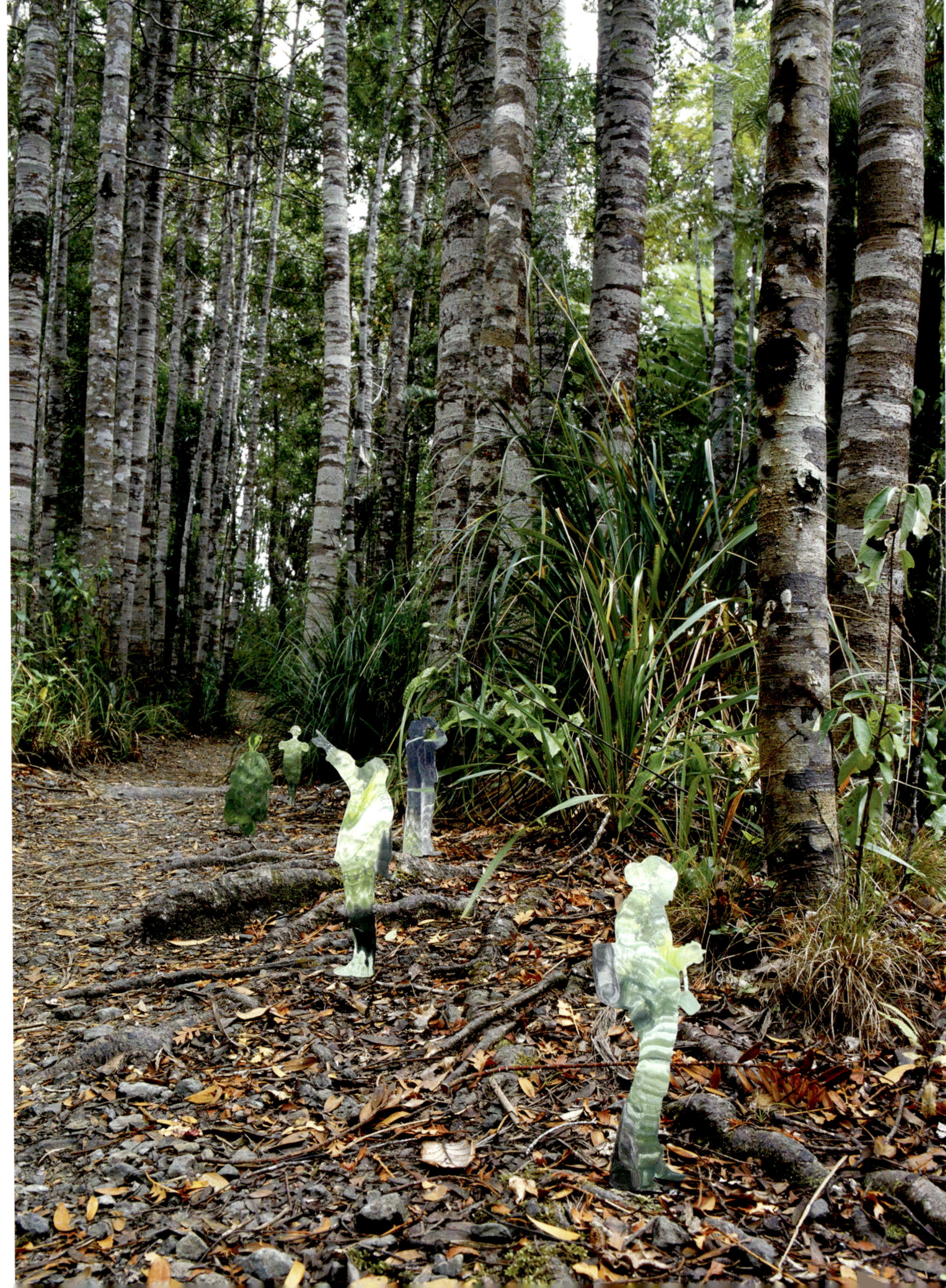

Kauri Grove Okura River New Zealand

2006
Durst Lambda print
72x52см

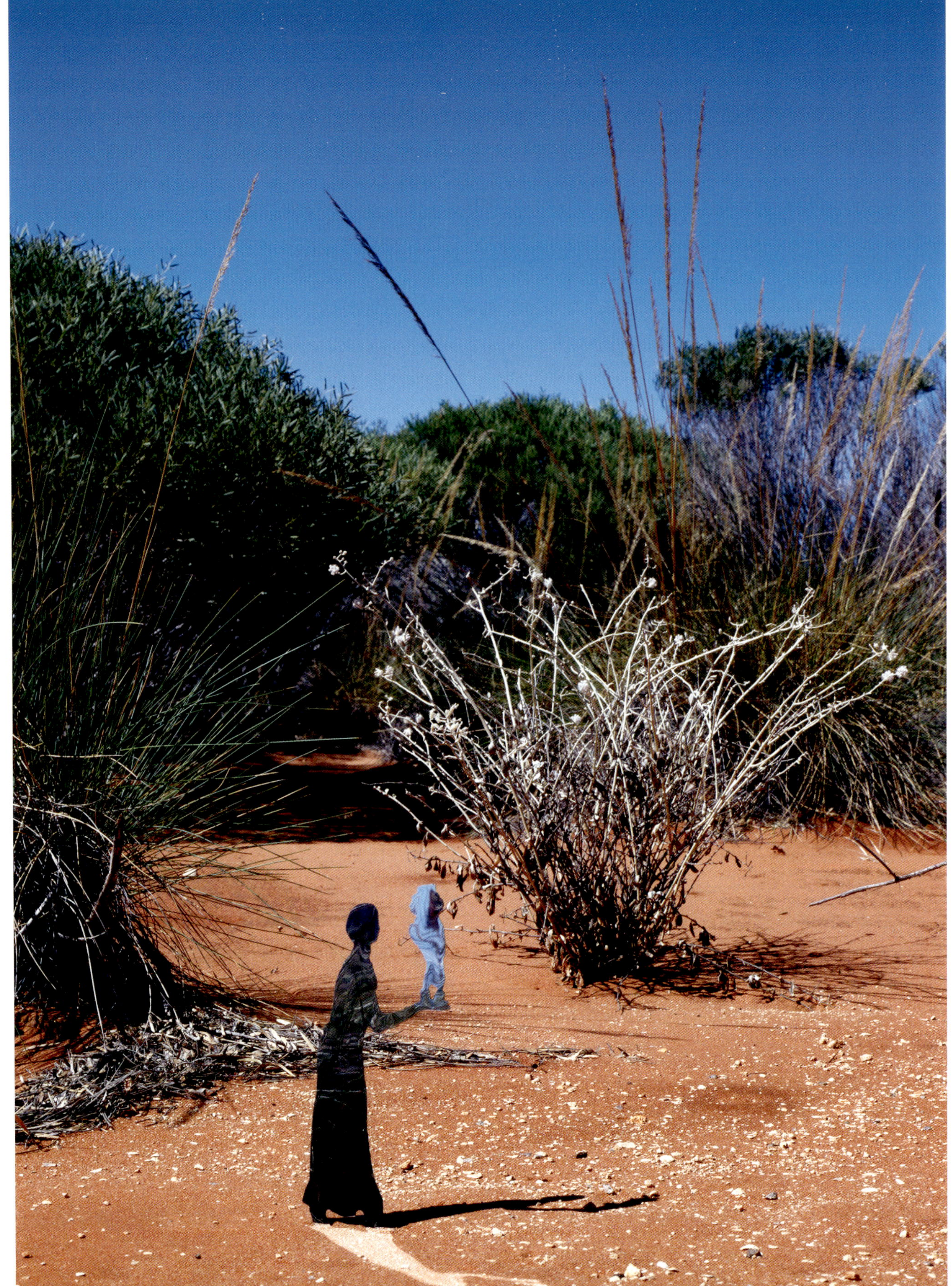

Shell Beach Shark Bay Western Australia
2006
Durst Lambda print
120x160cm

Nanga Bay Turn Off Shark Bay Western Australia I
2006
Durst Lambda print
160x120cm

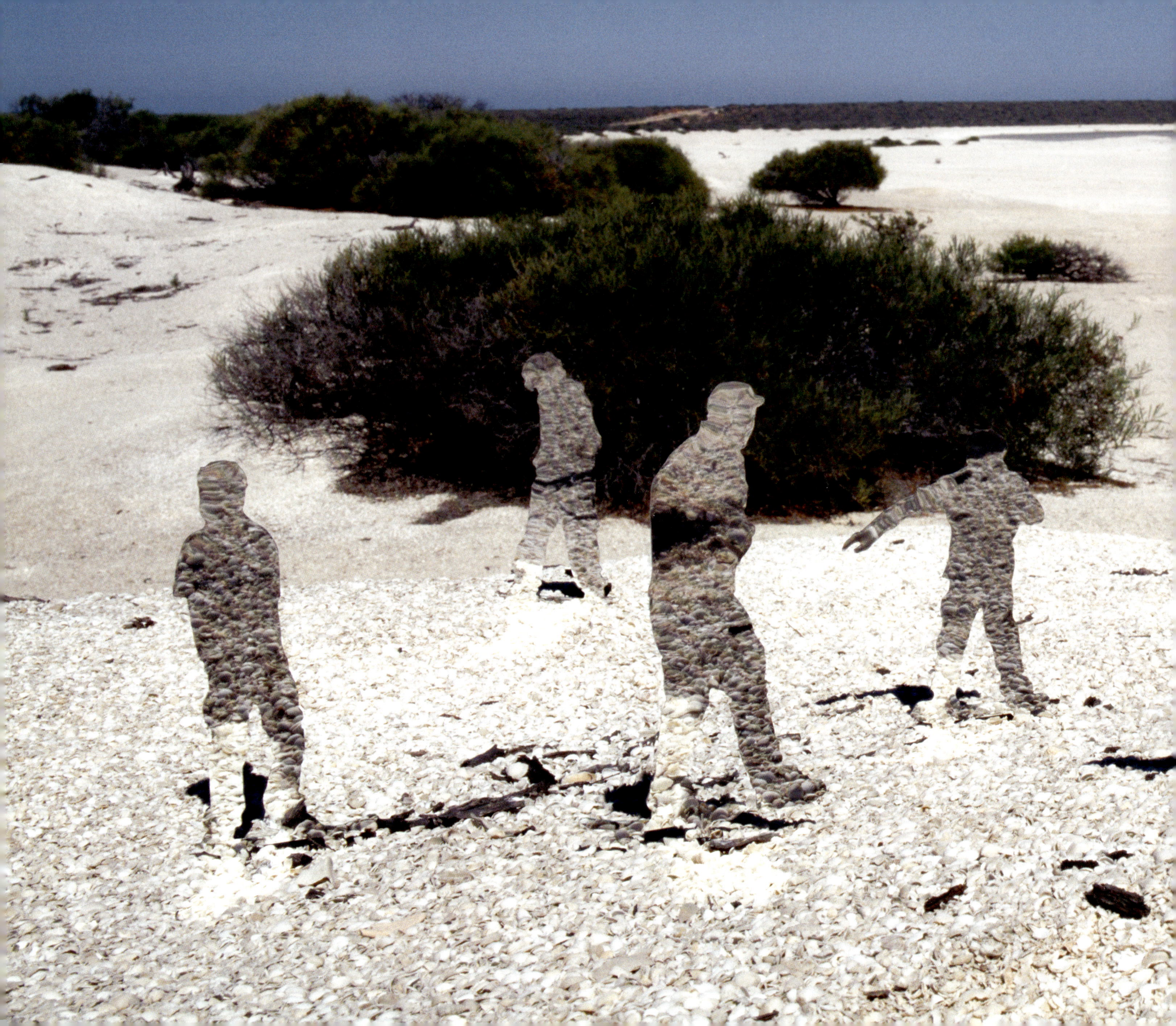

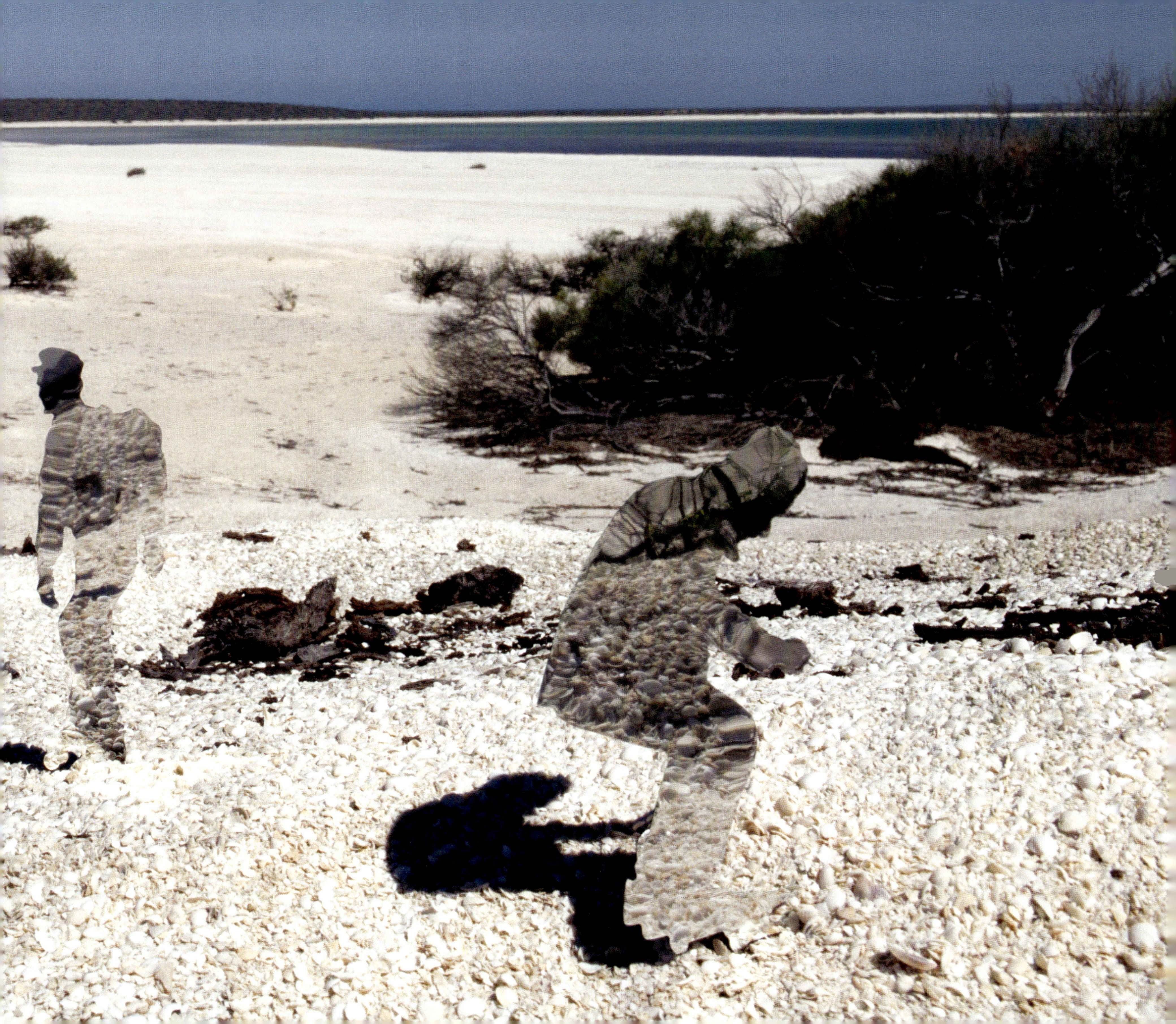

Ramsey Island II

2005
Recycled advertising lightbox
131x190x16см

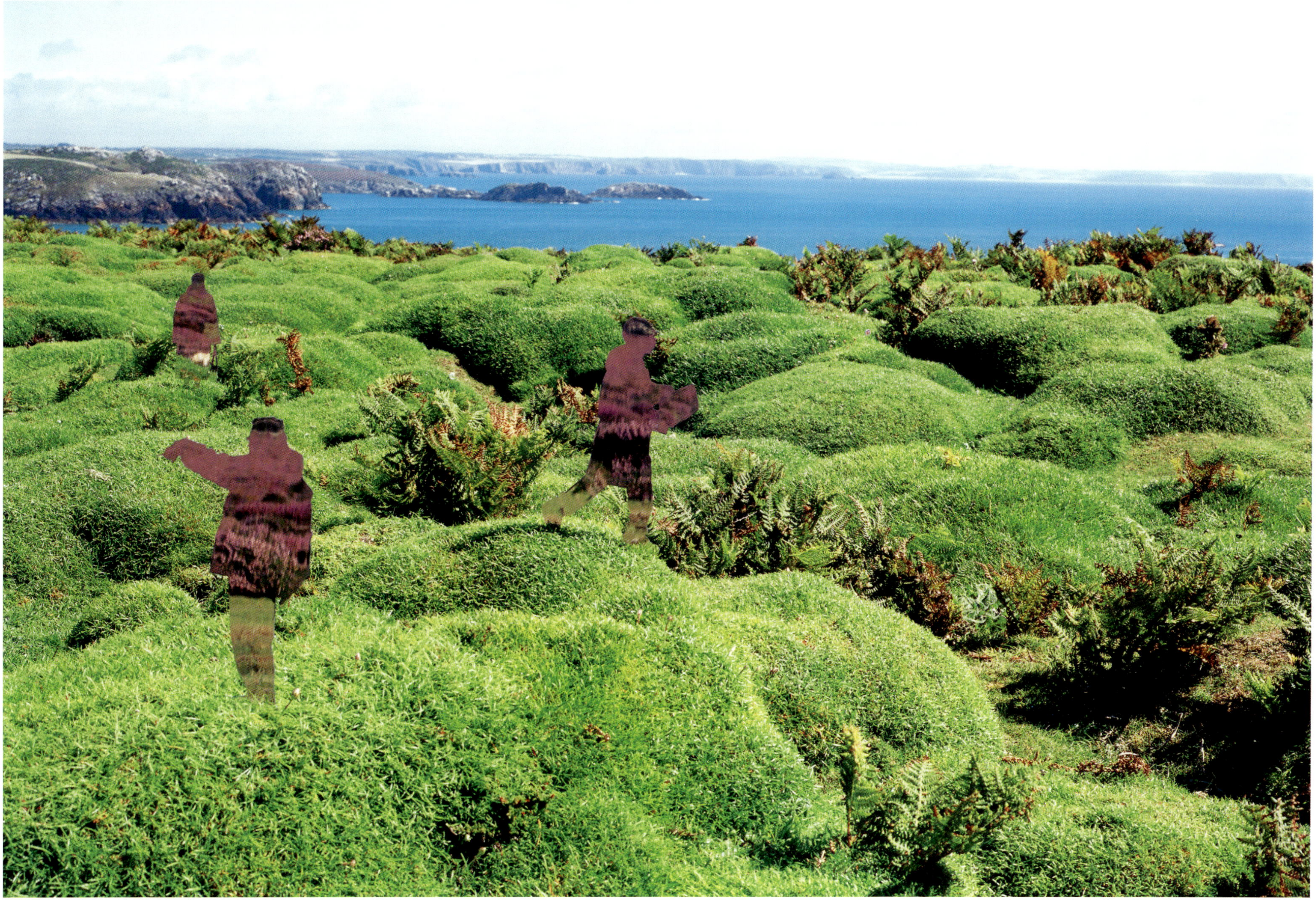

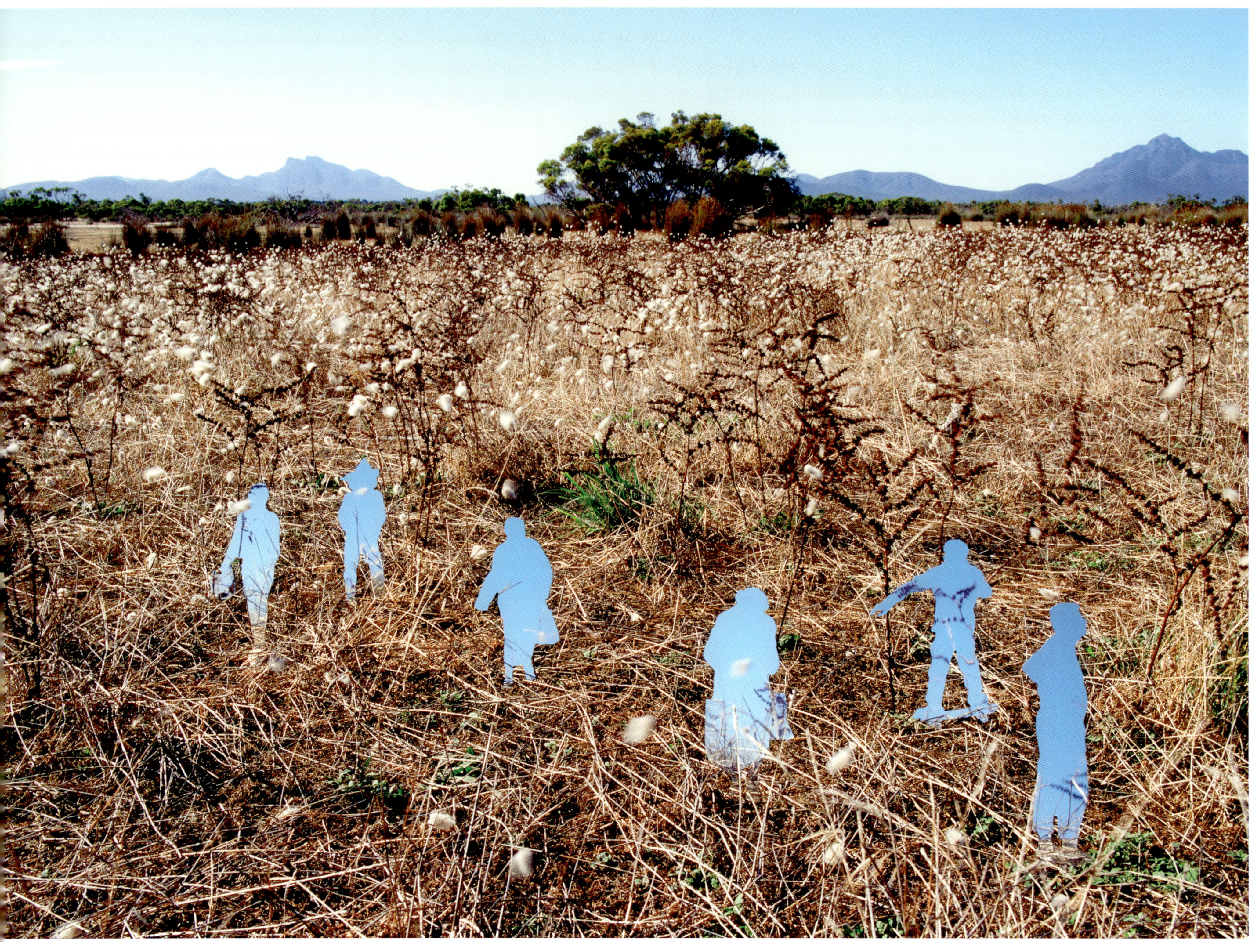

Chester Pass Rd Western Australia

2006
Durst Lambda print
52x72см

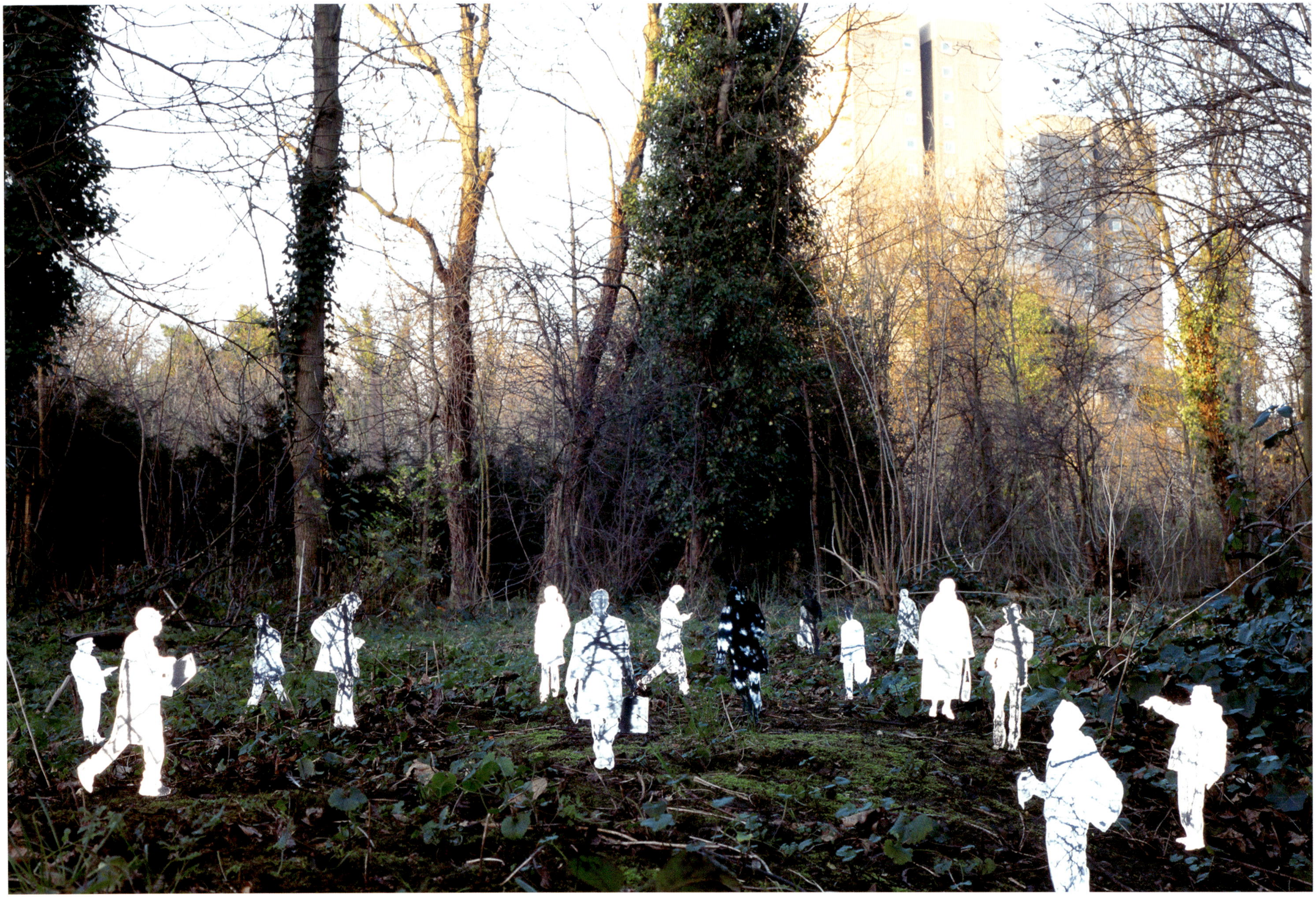

Bow Cemetery London

2005
Recycled advertising lightbox
广告灯箱使用再生材料制作
131x190x16cm

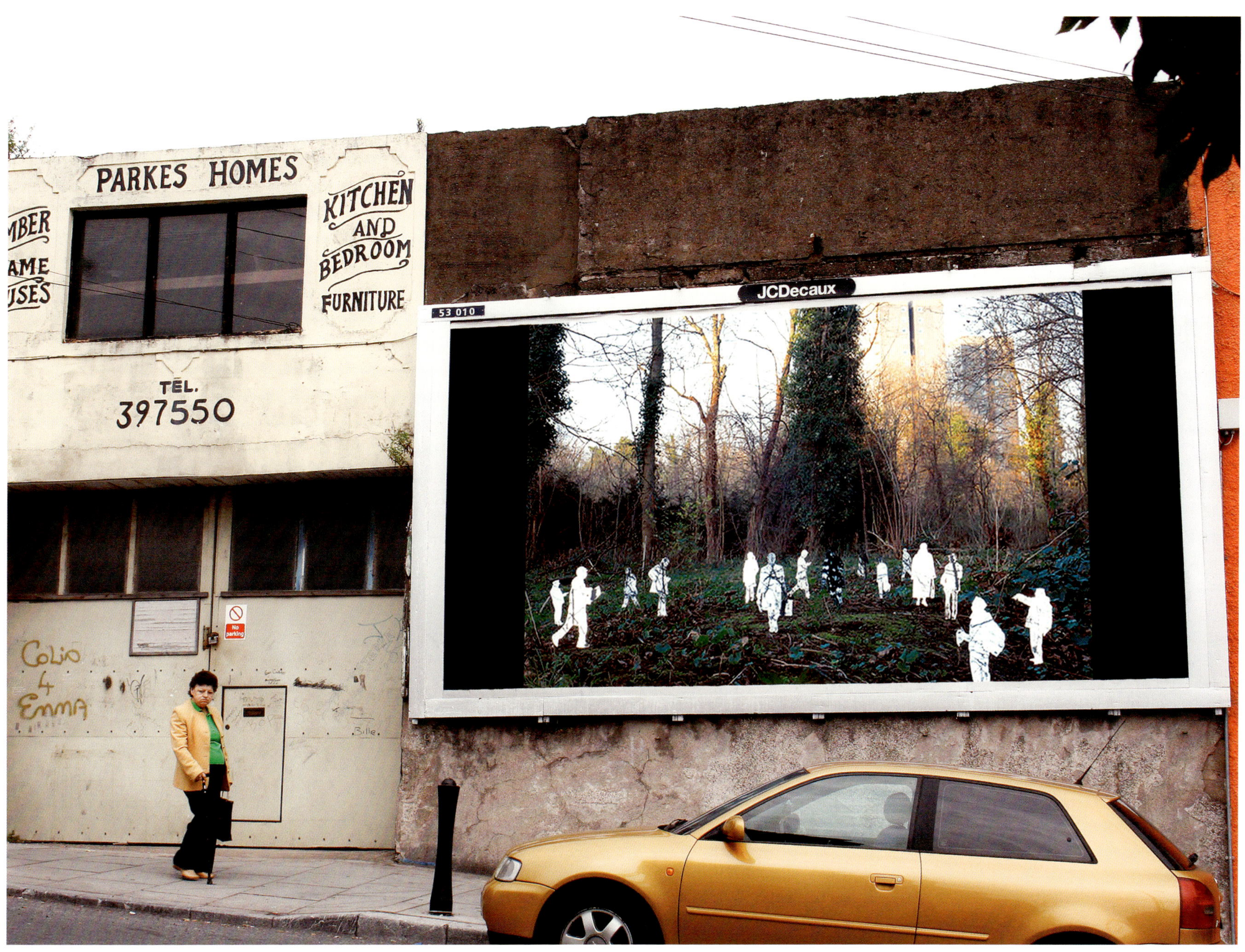

Bow Cemetery London

2007
Billboard, Arttrail Cork, Ireland
Photographer Paul White
爱尔兰科克，摄影：保罗·怀特

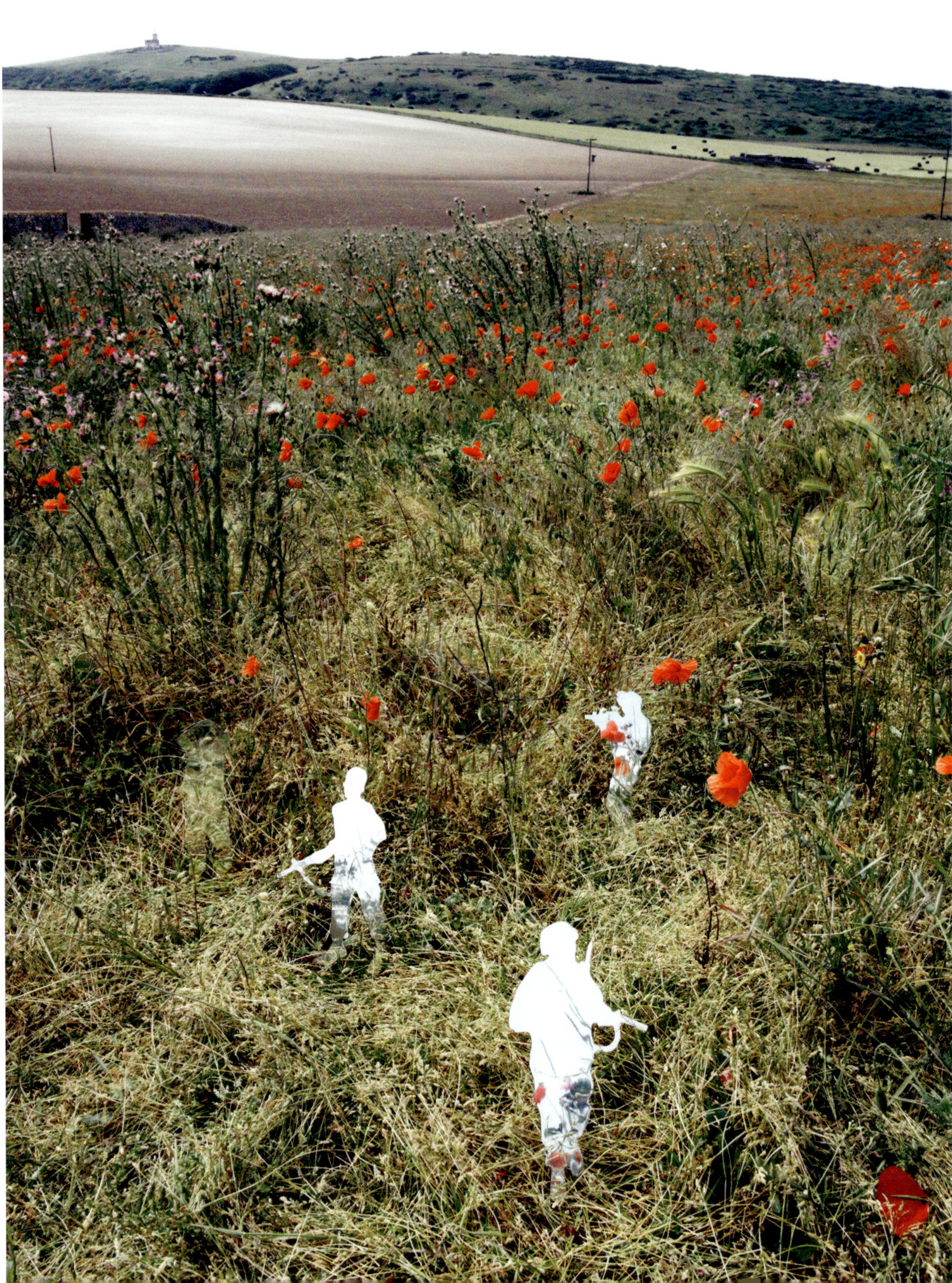

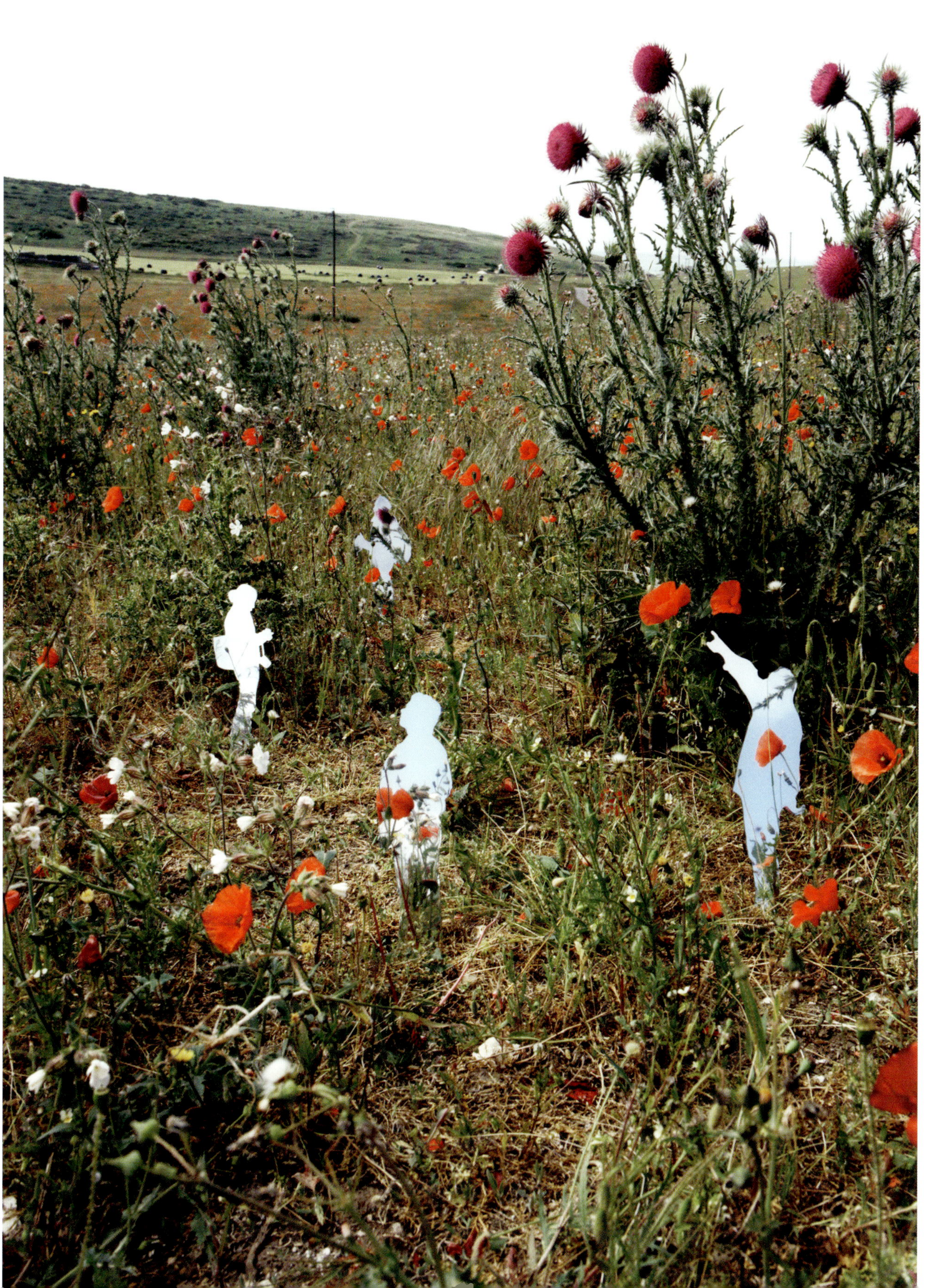

Birling Gap East Sussex I & II
2006
Durst Lambda print
72x52CM EACH

Barking London

2005
Durst Lambda print
120x160см

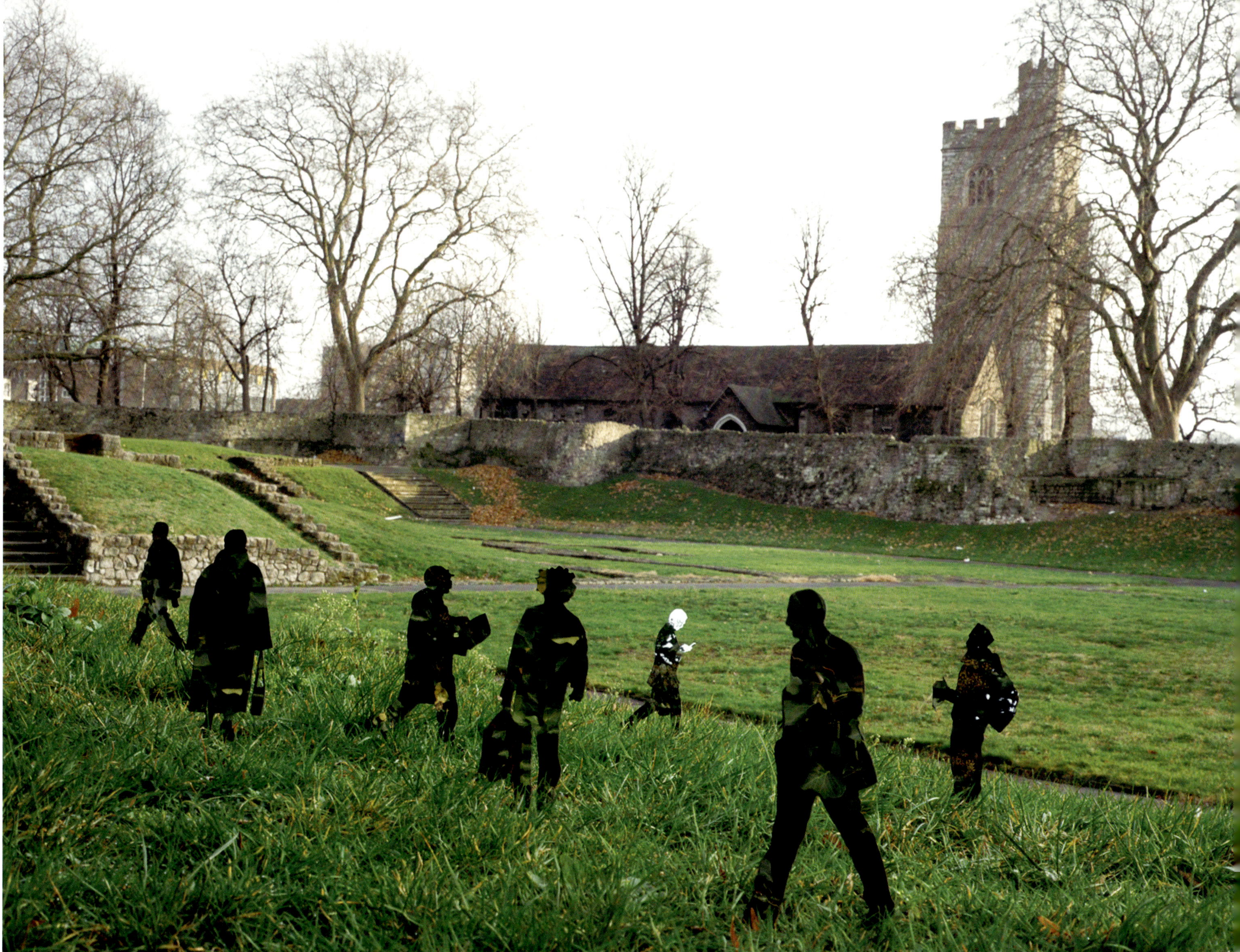

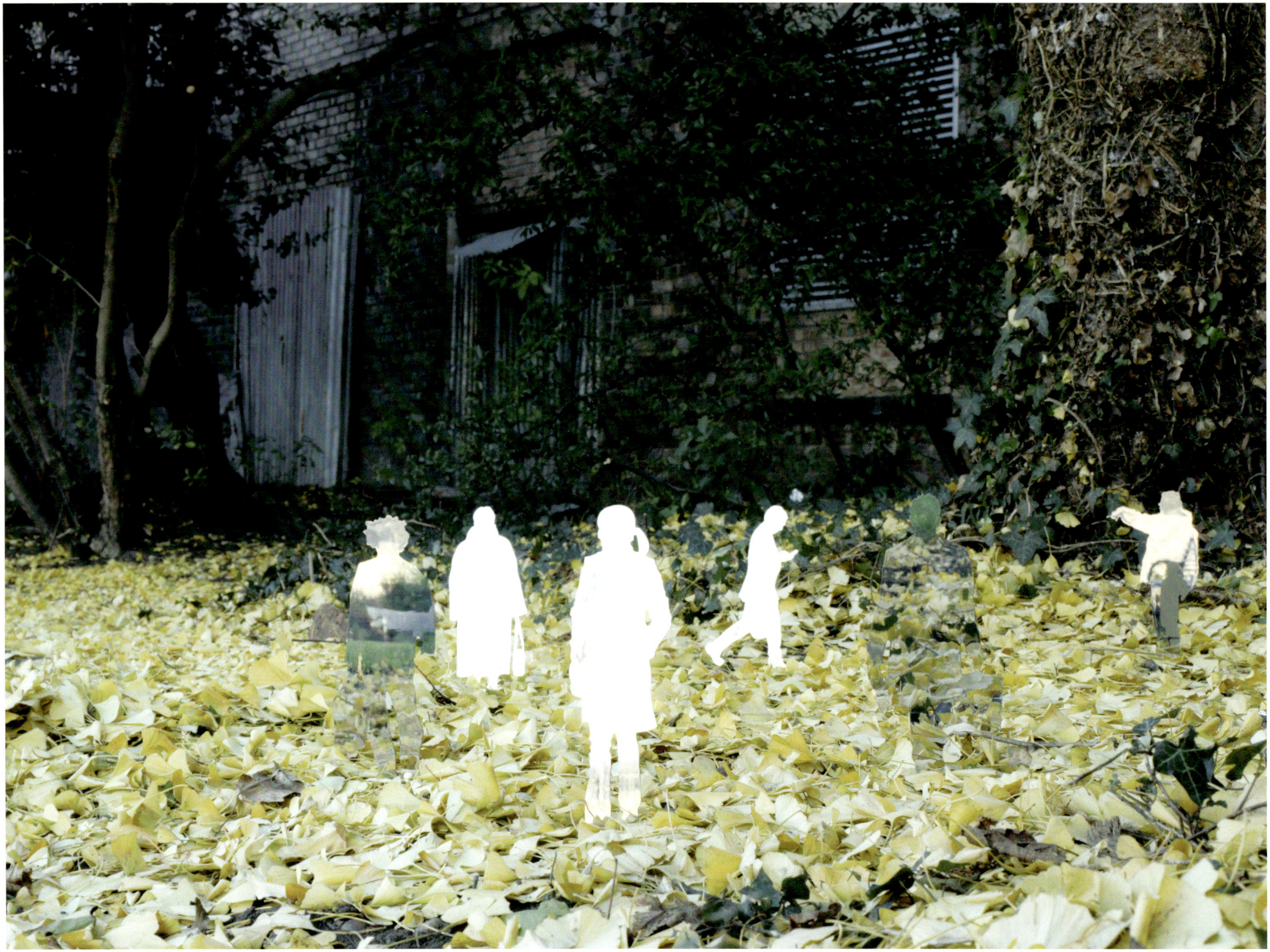

Grove Hall Park London I

2006
Durst Lambda print
52x72см

Cuckmere River East Sussex UK

2006
Durst Lambda print
52x72см

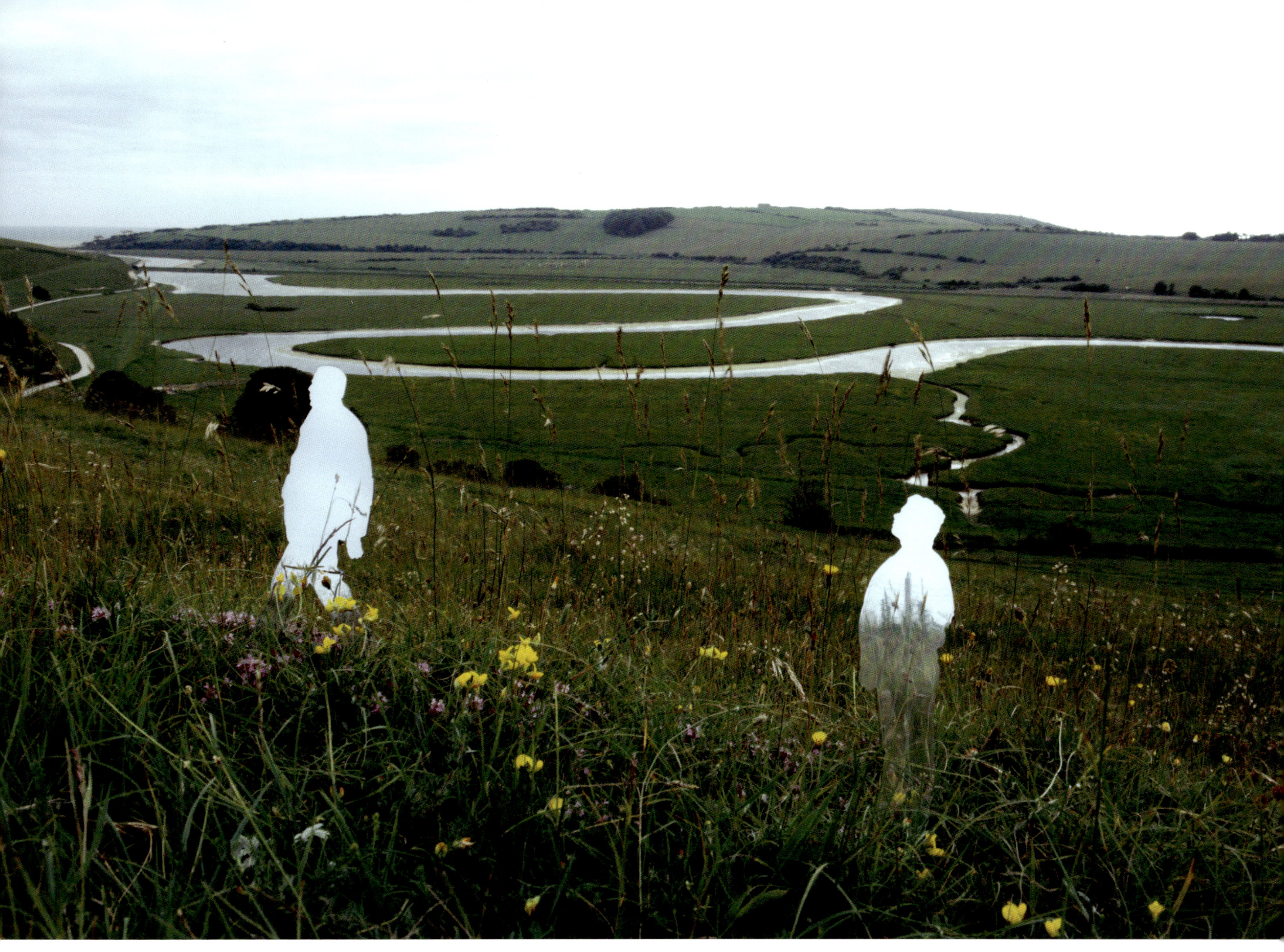

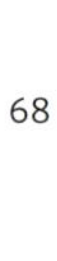

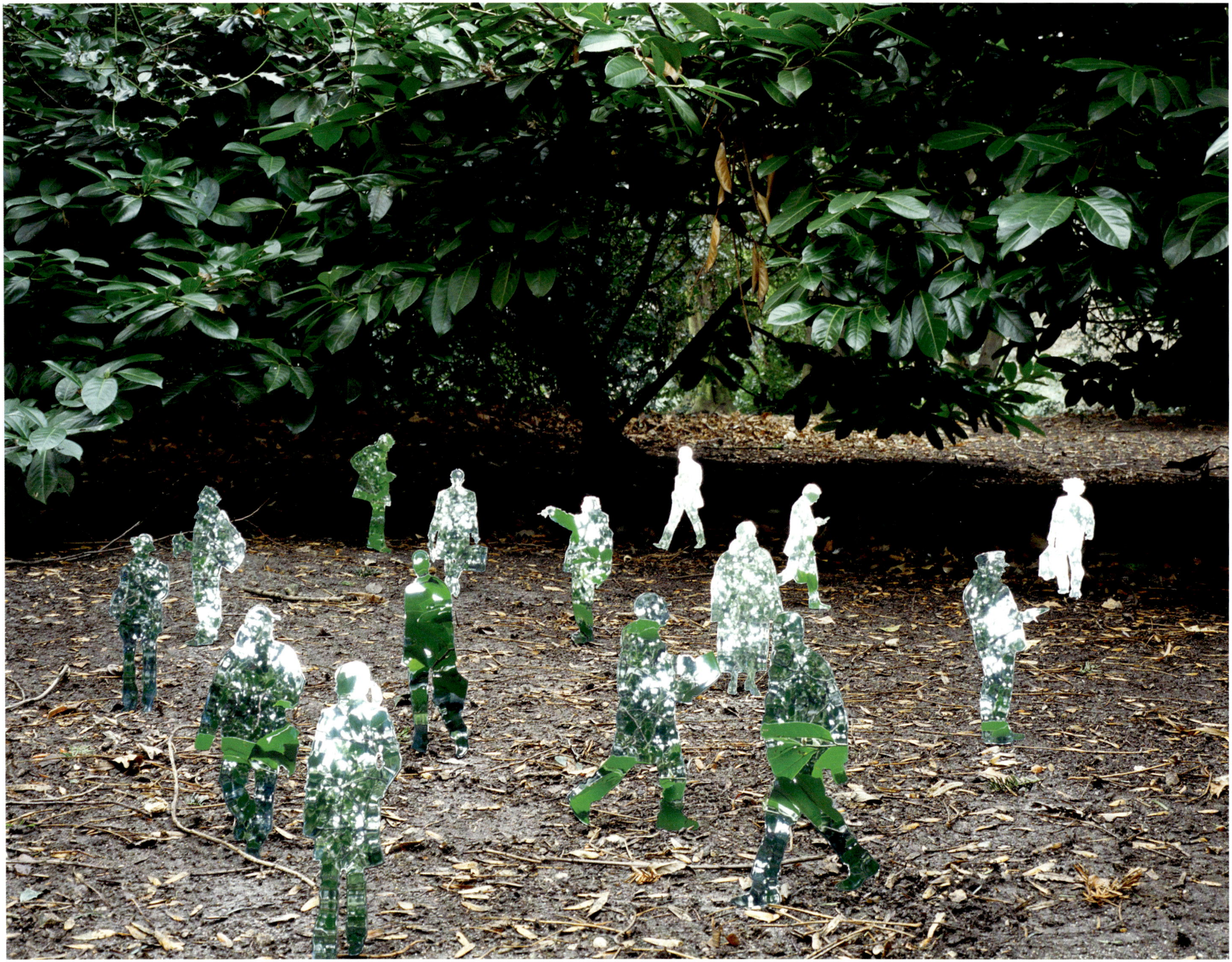

Breathing Space IV
呼吸空间 IV

2005
Durst Lambda print
120x160см

Hells Gate Death Valley
地狱之门，死亡谷

2005
Durst Lambda print
120x160cm

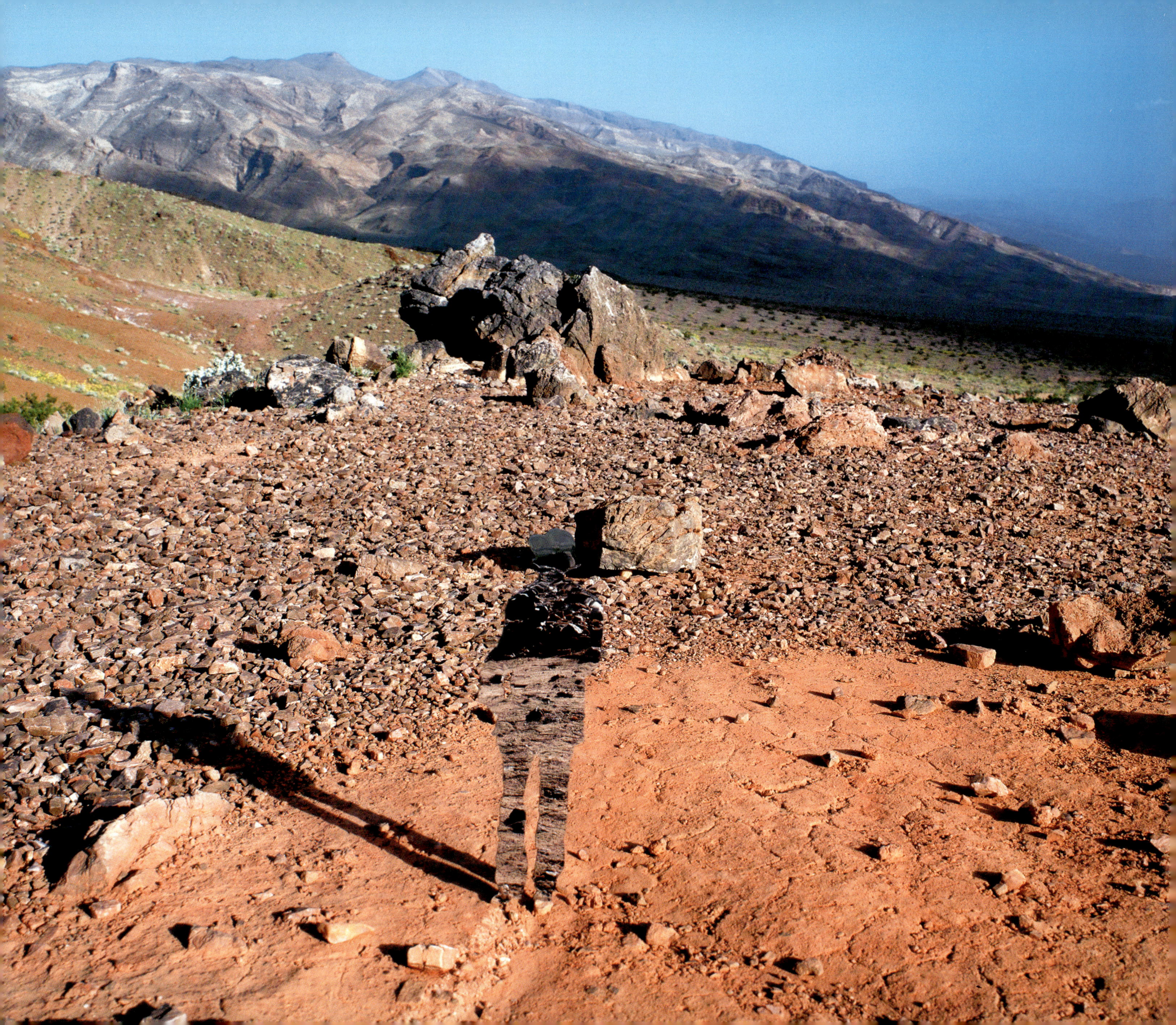

Black Canyon Rd Mojave Desert

2005
Recycled advertising lightbox
广告灯箱使用再生材料制作
131x190x16см

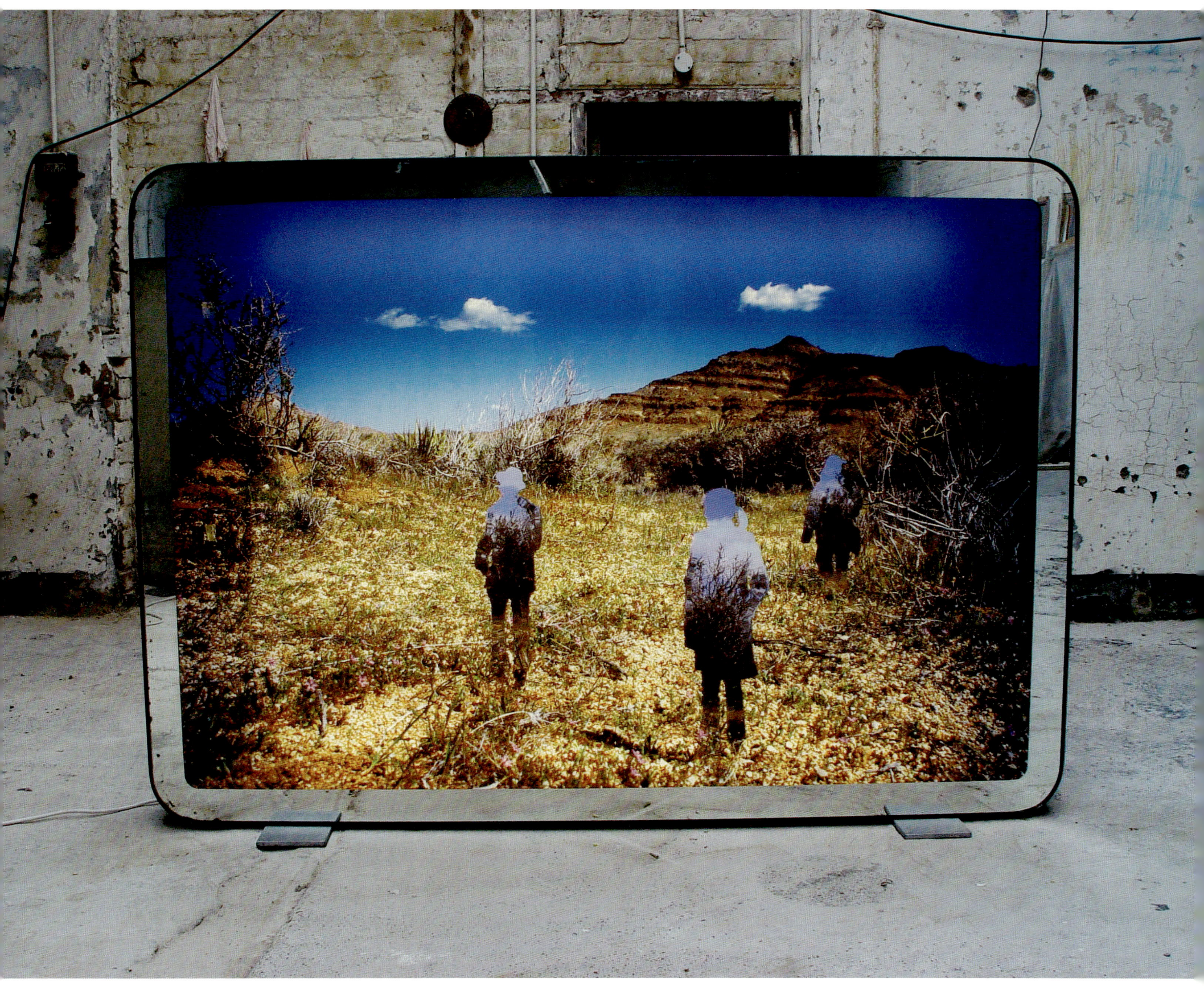

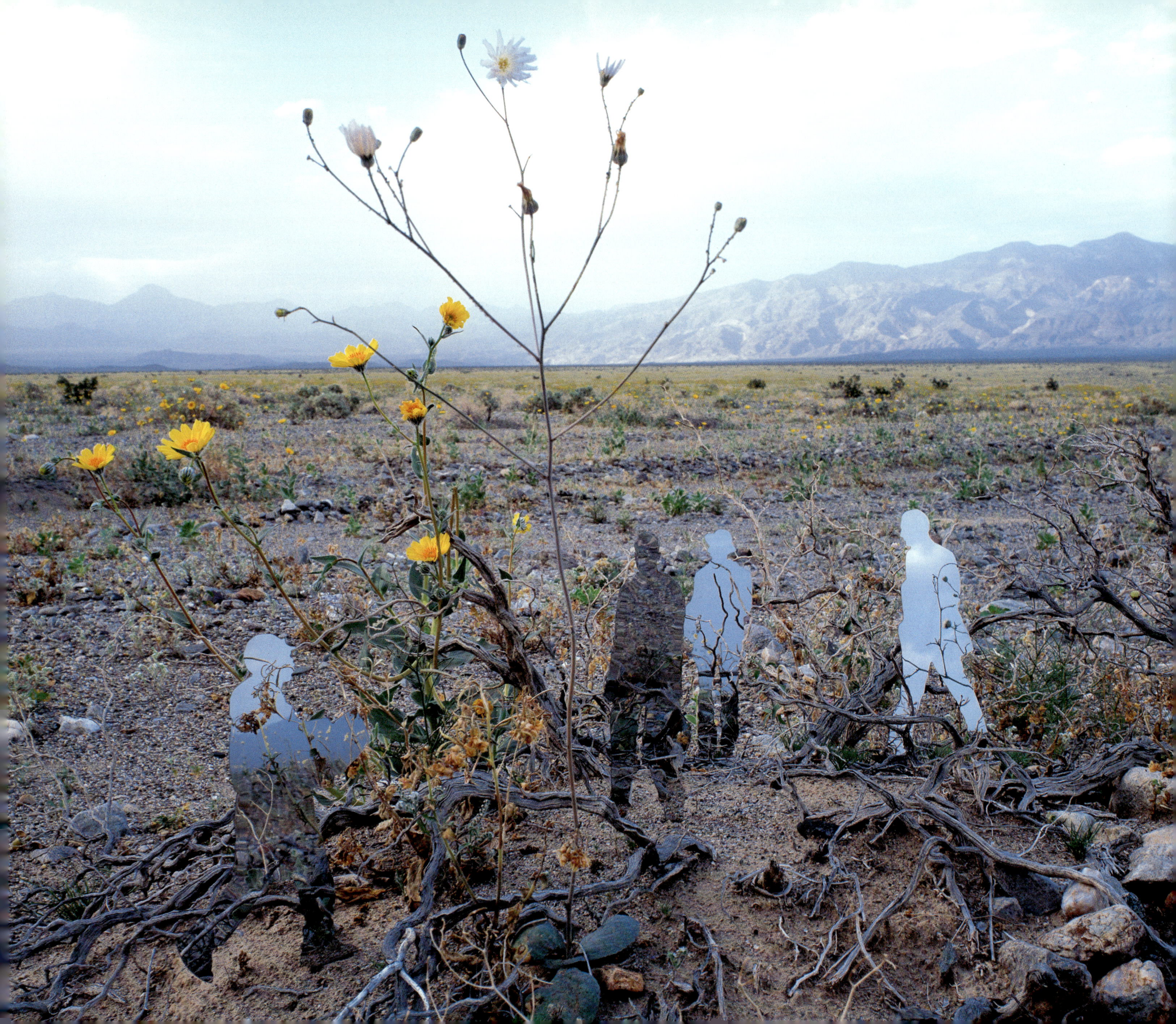

Highway 190 Death Valley
190 号高速公路，死亡谷

2005
Recycled advertising lightbox
广告灯箱使用再生材料制作
131x190x16cm

Salt Creek Death Valley
盐川，死亡谷

2005
Recycled advertising lightbox
广告灯箱使用再生材料制作
131x190x16cm

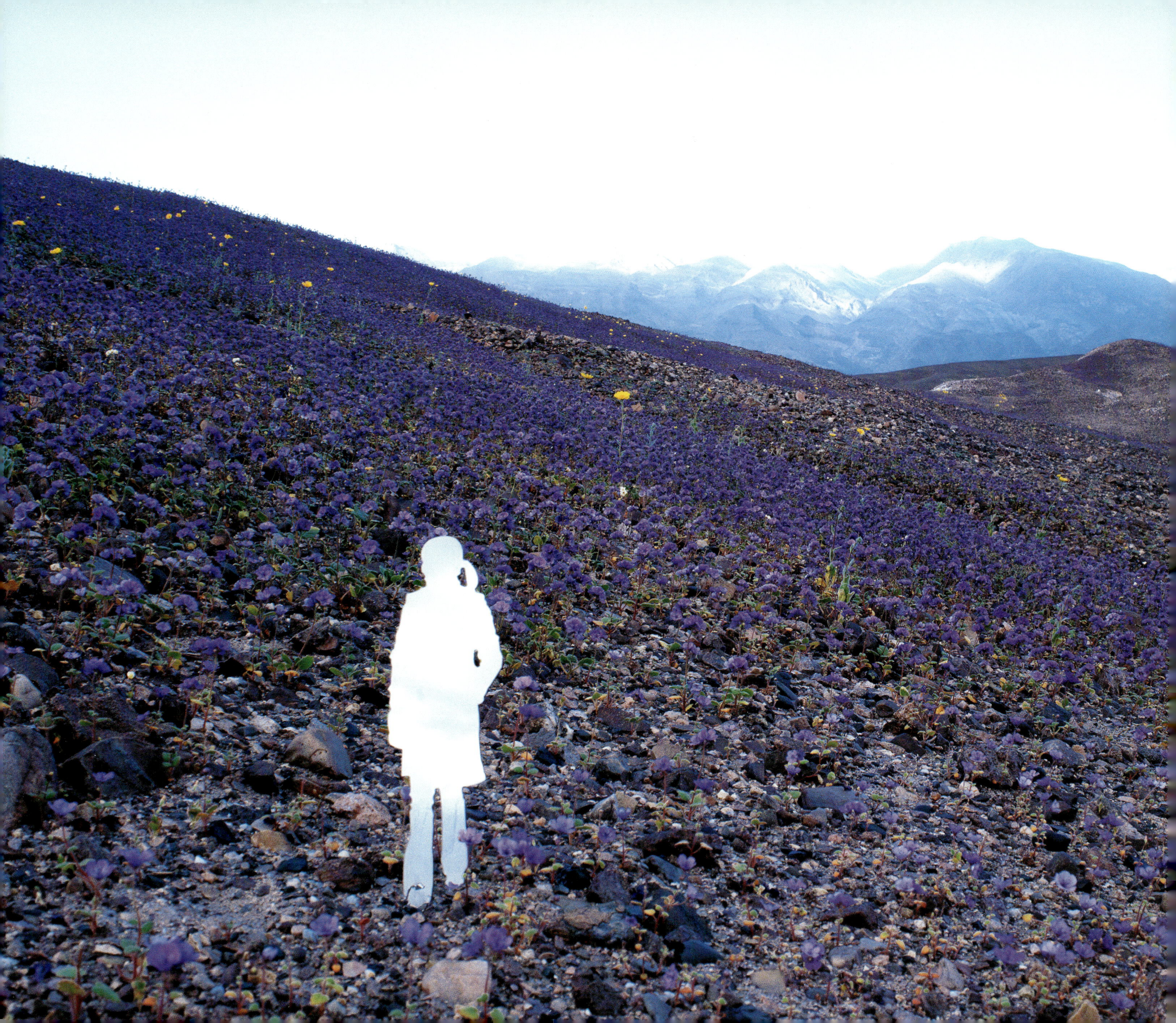

Eel River Philipsville

2005
Durst Lambda print
120x160cm

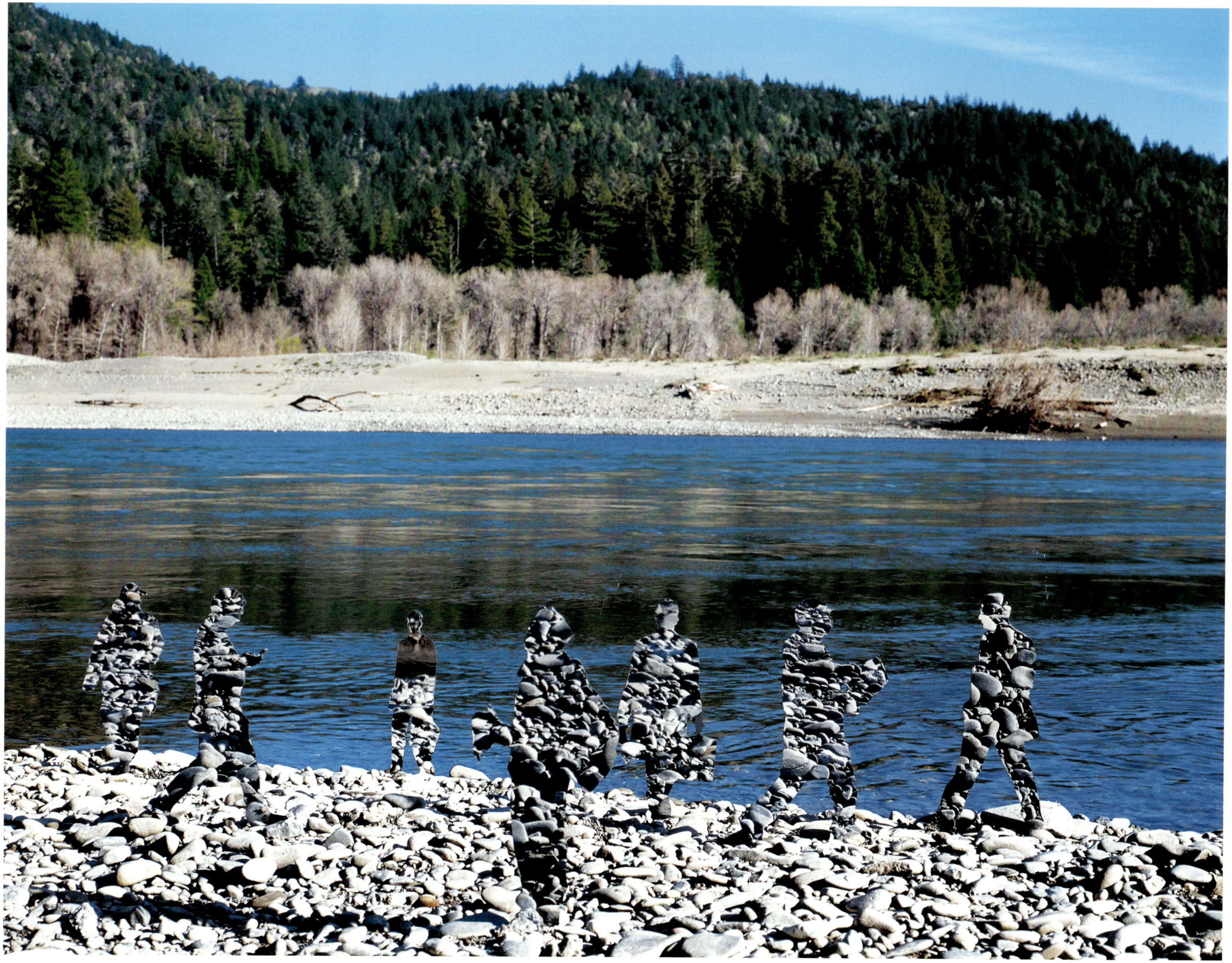

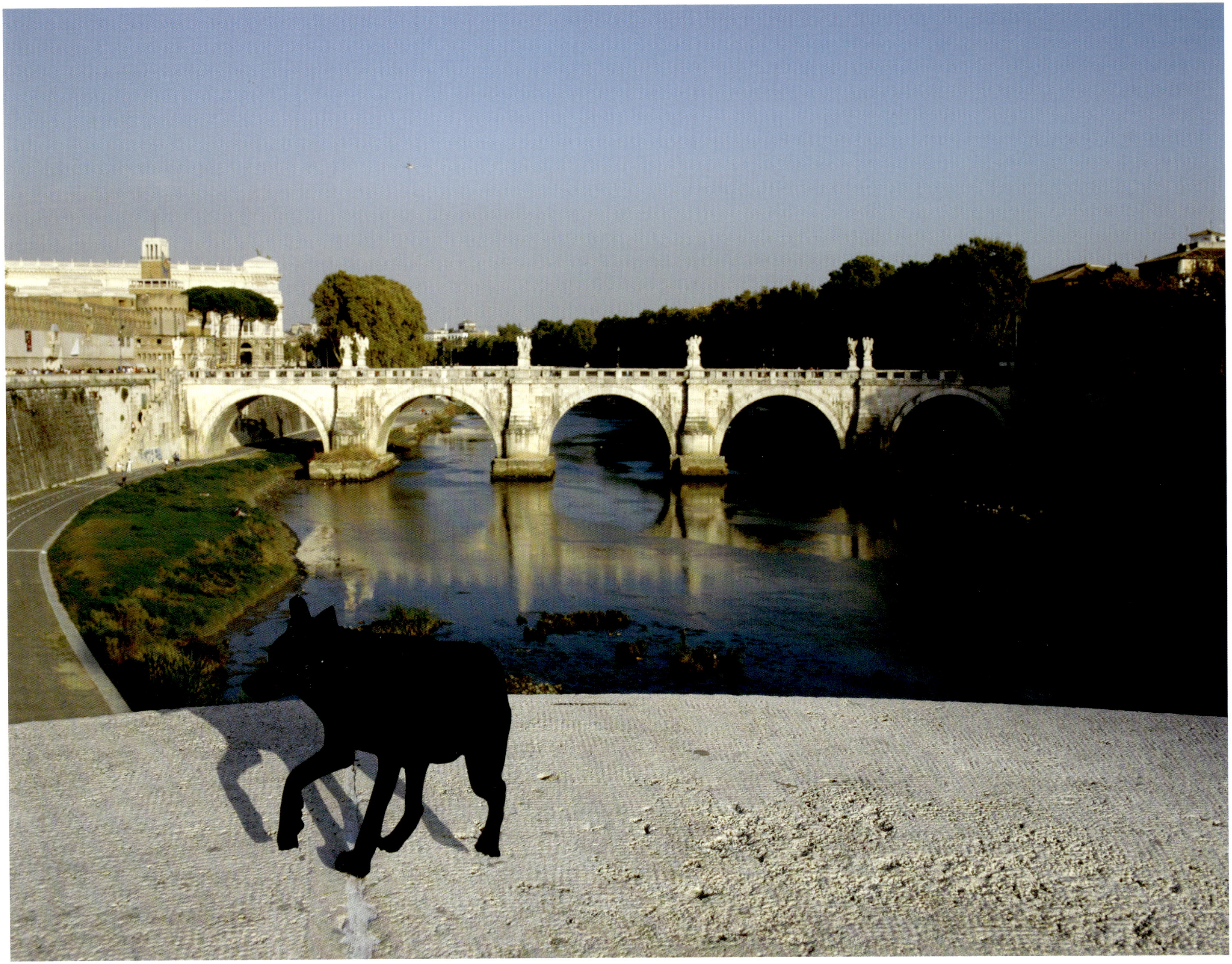

European Wolf - Ponte Sant'Angelo - Rome
欧洲狼—圣天使桥—罗马

2007
Durst Lambda print
120x160cm

EDWARD LUCIE-SMITH

爱德华·路希—史密斯的评论文章

Science Fiction is probably the most under-rated literary genre of our time. Thousands of people read it, and find in it the nourishment for their imaginations that they do not find in so-called 'quality fiction'. Maslen and Mehra, artists basing themselves in London, have invented a way of seeing that is closely related to one of the favorite tropes of the science fiction writer. What they offer, essentially, in their large-scale staged photographs, is a series of glimpses into a parallel universe. By placing reflective cut-out silhouettes in various landscape and architectural settings, and recording the result, they suggest conjunctions that might otherwise go unnoticed. The silhouettes are visitors from another world, and their reflective surfaces make them only partly visible.

A new series of these images, made in a particularly propitious environment, the city of Rome, is full of both historical and ecological echoes. One should perhaps begin with the image of the European wolf, seen against the background of the Ponte Sant'Angelo. This evokes the myth of the foundation of the city, when the abandoned twins Romulus and Remus, sons of the war god Mars and the Vestal Virgin Rhea Sylvia, were carried to safety in a wicker basket by the swollen River Tiber and were then suckled by a she-wolf. The Castel Sant'Angelo, seen in the background, was originally built as the mausoleum of the Emperor Hadrian. After many vicissitudes, it was remodeled as a papal fortress, residence and prison. In 1527 Pope Clement VII took refuge there from the ferocious sack of Rome by an army of German landsknechts.

科幻小说很可能是我们这个时代最被低估的文学体裁。成千上万的人在阅读科幻小说，吸取从所谓的"高品位小说"里找不到的营养来丰富想象力。马斯伦和梅赫拉这两位伦敦艺术家发现了一种表现手法，与科幻小说作家喜爱的比喻有着密切联系。他们的重要贡献是，大量的"摆拍摄影"展示了一系列平行宇宙的闪现。将折射的廓影置于各种自然景色或建筑物环境之中，再加上录音效果，含蓄地传达出可能会被忽略的内在联系。这些剪影人物是来自另一个世界的访客，而且镜像表面仅显现人物轮廓的局部。

近期创作的一组照片中，罗马城是最为适合的环境景象，在勾起怀旧回忆的同时重叠表现生态意识，两个事件在时空上形成呼应。也许《欧洲狼》（European wolf）是最早的一幅照片，以圣天使桥（Ponte Sant'Angelo）为背景。这让人们回想起这座城市建立的神话故事，被抛弃的孪生兄弟罗慕勒斯（Romulus）和雷摩斯（Remus）是战神玛尔斯（Mars）和女祭司瑞亚·西尔维娅的儿子，在柳条篮里被上涨的台伯河（River Tiber）河水安全地送到这里，后来由一条母狼哺乳养大。背景中可见圣天使城堡（Castel Sant'Angelo），最早是作为哈德良皇帝（Emperor Hadrian）的陵墓而建造的。之后几经变迁，先后被改建为罗马教皇的要塞、住所以及监狱。1527年，由于德国雇佣军的野蛮抢劫，教皇克莱蒙特七世（Pope Clement VII）曾经在此避难。

另一幅的内容是狼与盘羊在Via della Renella的相遇，背景的墙面上充满了乱七八糟的涂鸦和难以辨认的招贴——罗马一向不是一座干净整洁的城市，现在更是兼而有之。这些既是罗马城市环境的特征，又是这座城市的建筑丰碑，如圣天使城堡。作品让狼和盘羊这样的生物实现同处栖息，其寓意是要在城市的野蛮和真正的荒野形成强烈的反差。盘羊是所有家羊的野生祖先，这就名副其实地体现了野生与驯养之间的永恒差异。作品多次出现盘羊的形象，这里是单独表现的。在马斯伦和梅赫拉的另一作品《本土》罗马组照中，盘羊歇栖在Villa Borghese花园的护墙上。盘羊身下的矮墙上是用哥特体大写字母写下的"创世纪"——在一些维多利亚时代大而厚的圣经里，《旧约》圣经

Mountain Lion - Subway - New York
美洲狮—地铁—纽约
2008
Durst Lambda print
160x120cm

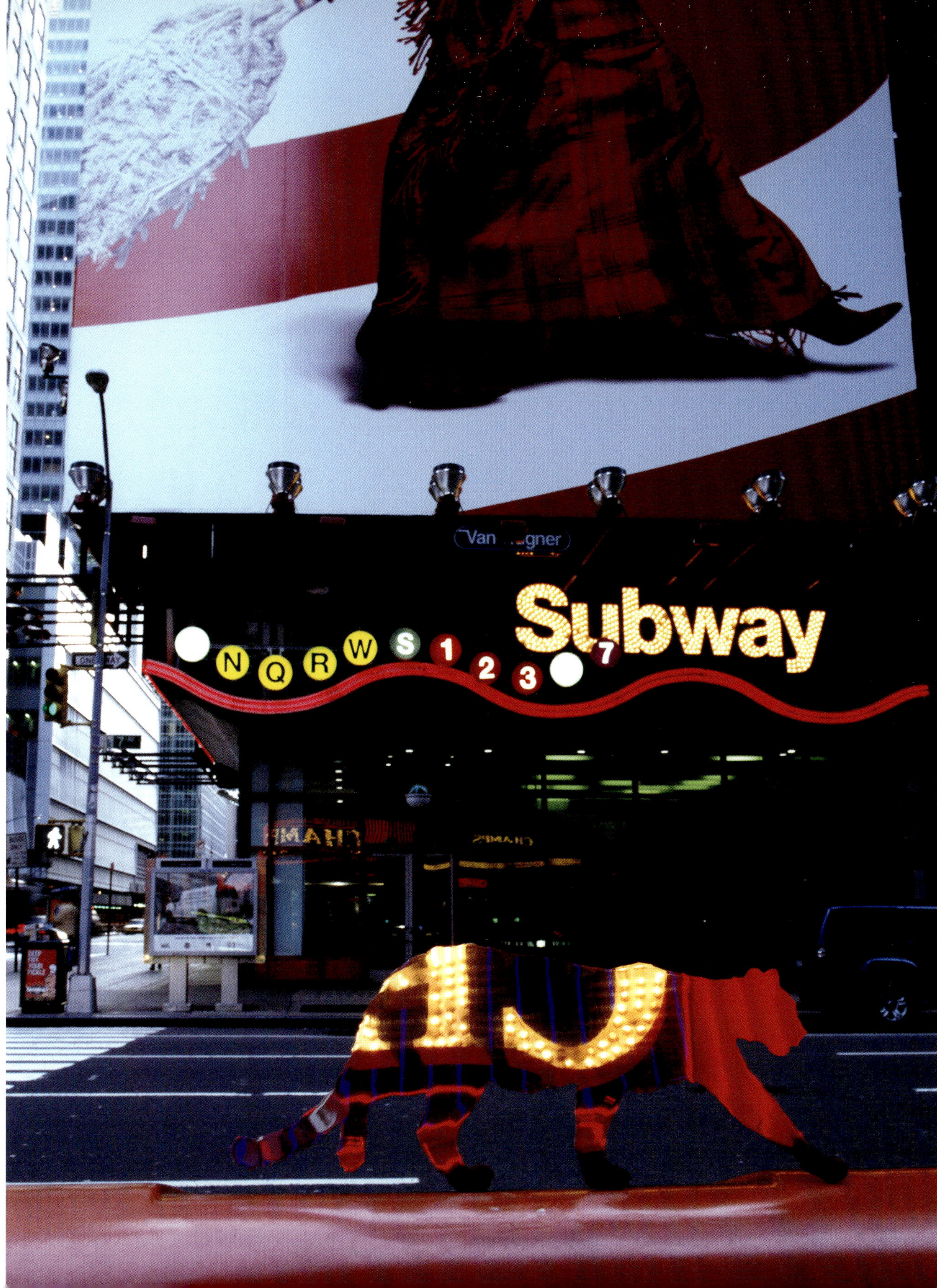

Van gner
Subway
N Q R W S 1 2 3 7

Another image shows a wolf confronted by a mouflon in the via della Renella. In the background are aggressive graffiti and defaced posters – Rome, which has never been a tidy city, now abounds in both. They are as characteristic of the Roman urban environment as the city's great architectural monuments, such as the Castel Sant'Angelo. The significance here seems to be the contrast between the urban wilderness and the true wilderness that creatures like the wolf and the mouflon inhabit in reality. Mouflons are the wild ancestors of all domestic breeds of sheep, and as such represent the eternal contrast between the wild and the tamed. The mouflon image reappears, this time in isolation, in another work from Maslen and Mehra's Native Rome series – this time perched on a parapet in the gardens of the Villa Borghese. On the retaining wall below the creature the word 'Genesis' appears in large Gothic letters – the kind of typeface that might head an Old Testament text in some massive Victorian bible. Reflected in the creature's metallic body is the tower of one of Rome's innumerable churches.

The images just described come from a much larger series, or series of series, photographed in different parts of the world. All the images show creatures that might once have existed, in another epoch, in the location shown. Very often, like the wolf that makes its presence felt in Rome, they have a specific symbolic value. They are intended to remind us of the continuing, if often ghostly, presence of what is wild within what is at least nominally civilised. In this sense they are an updated version of a favourite student slogan from the Paris

文句的标题才可能会用这种字体。折射在动物金属般身体上的是罗马到处林立的教堂楼塔。

前面评述的照片选自更大的一组照片，或者可以称为组照中的组照，拍摄于世界各地。照片中的 所有生物都曾在世间生存，在某个纪元也许就生存在拍摄这张照片的地点。 常见的主题是狼，让人们感觉到狼存在于罗马，具有特别的象征价值。作品的主旨是要提醒人们，在这个文 明的社会里，至少是名义上的，倘若常常是梦幻般的，也还继续存在着原生态。从这 个意义上来看，这正是1968年巴黎"事件"中学生流行的口号的升级版本，"马路下面就是沙滩。"(Sous le pave, le plage) 照片中经常掺杂的都市涂鸦也被用来强调现代城市环境的野蛮特性——一次又一次地概括了危险感。其它作品几乎都是反映当今世界各大城市的这一基本特征。美 洲狮踱步于纽约地铁入口附近的街头，在其身上闪烁的霓虹灯光象征着城市的危险。 再者，我们看到康加犬——类似狮子的小亚细亚中部本地犬，用来保护羊群免受狼的袭击——出现在伊斯坦布 尔圣索非亚大教堂的画面上。 保护神室女座映射在康加犬的身体侧面。

另一组照片《镜像》对这一方程式的左右作了颠倒。镜像雕塑的人物剪影是典型的都市居住者，从 商人到滑板者，意想不到地被搬入旷野之中。一方面，这些人影作为失去了伊甸园的居住者，现在只能生存在自己的想象之中。另一方面，他们是突然间回归自然的生物，令人可悲地缺乏生活设施和没有足够的心理准备。

《本土》和《镜像》两组组照都是直接拍摄的——也就是说，将镜像雕塑放置到选定的环境中进行拍摄。而其它相关主题的组照则是拼贴而成的。例如，《施工中》提出的挑战是，将肆无忌惮地蔓 延的建筑物粘贴在自然景色之中，这在以前被认为是不可逾越的雷池。《濒危的 美国人》将美国汽车大喝汽油的梦魇照片与用车身涂料来表现的美国濒危植物的画作形成对比。

'evenements' of 1968: "Sous le pave, le plage." ["Beneath the pavement, the beach."] The frequent inclusion of urban graffiti in these images also serves to stress the often feral quality of the modern urban environment – the sense of danger that it all too frequently encapsulates. Other images reflect – often very literally – the essential character of some of the other great cities of the world. A mountain lion paces the street near one of the entrances to the New York subway, neon signs flashing on its body as an emblem of urban danger. And a Kangal dog – a lion-like breed native to central Anatolia, where they are used to guard the flocks against wolves – is seen in Istanbul's great church of Aya Sofya, with an image of a protective Virgin shining on its flank.

Another large series, Mirrored, reverses the equation. Here the mirror sculptures are silhouettes of typical city dwellers, ranging in type from businessmen to skateboarders, who have been miraculously transported to wild locations. The figures can be seen, on the one hand, as the inhabitants of a lost Eden that now exists only inside their own heads, or on the other hand as beings who are pathetically ill-equipped and ill-prepared for this sudden return to nature.

The Native and Mirrored series are directly photographic – that is to say, the mirror sculptures are placed in the chosen setting, and photographed in situ. Other, related series, make use of collage. Under Construction, for example, asks questions about the relentless spread of building into landscapes that were

最终，若环境允许的话，镜像雕塑也会被用作物件出现在"真实"场景中，而不用相机去拍摄。但显而易见的是，所有的系列照片，包括装置艺术在内，构成了与主题紧密相关的各个组成部分，同时，也形成了一种出奇不意、灵活多变的绘画语言。

近些年来，我常常想到，当代艺术越来越大的弱点是表达方式——风格，或用一个难听的字眼。噱头——日趋显得比这里说到的更为突出。这便是为什么艺术创作取自于奇异的地点。例如，中国在艺术领域中的作用日益突出。与中国工业化的成功和随之的快速崛起相关，中国艺术的一系列题材已经趋于全球化。同样，近些年女权运动艺术声势浩大，发展迅猛，以纽约布鲁克林博物馆创建的专业女权运动艺术展馆为代表，现在又扩建并且专门设计用来收藏芝加哥的人像装置艺术作品《晚餐聚会》(Dinner Party)。简而言之，中国的艺术家和女权运动艺术家先锋已经拟定了自己的探索领域，创造了一种视觉语言，或可以称之为群体语言，使得他们能够与非专业观众直接交流。这不是其它艺术形式所能够依赖的。艺术家表现出来的东西往往与原本想要传达的意象衔接不上。现代主义画家经历了长时期对纯粹"形式至上"的探索之后——以二十世纪六十年代末期和七十年代初的极简主义得出了合乎逻辑的结论，艺术潮流倾向于回归寓意和叙事。在现代主义运动兴起之前，这一领域就有众多的探索者。而在今天，原本的寓意缺乏应有的内涵，叙事结结巴巴，无内容可言。

显然，这里的情形不同。评论马斯伦和梅赫拉作品的难点之一在于，似非而是，没有必要使用那些看似是批评家拿手的华丽辞藻。想要传达的寓意让你通过视觉就很容易理解。另一方面，他们的作品并没有给人平庸乏味的感觉。有趣的是，两组运用"二重唱"镜射的照片以不同的手法相互呼应。这种纯粹按照自然规律的呼应，各种各样物体表面的镜射取自于这些物体周围的景象。有时，镜射造成物体本身的渐渐消失，融入到周围的自然景色或城市景观之中。例如，米尔顿·凯恩斯的绘画作品，以及城市在总体规划中使用反射玻璃，均是这种手法的极好运用。雕塑也可产生寓意上

formerly considered to be sacrosanct. Endangered Americans contrasts ghostly images of gas-guzzling American automobiles with drawings of endangered American plant species rendered in autobody paint.

Finally, the mirror sculptures are sometimes used, when occasion offers, as items displayed in 'real' settings, without photographic intervention. It is clear, however, that all the series, including the installations, form part of what is an absolutely coherent, and at the same time, a surprisingly flexible graphic language.

It has often struck me, in recent, years, that an increasing weakness of contemporary art is that the manner of saying something – the style, or worse still, the gimmick – increasingly takes primacy over what is actually being said. This is one reason why art from formerly exotic locations, China for example, has played an increasingly prominent role in the artistic cosmos. Art from China tends to have a readily identifiable range of subject matter, which is connected to the country's industrial success and consequent sudden rise in status. Similarly, recent years have seen a steep rise in prestige for feminist art, symbolised by the creation of a specialist feminist art department at the Brooklyn Museum in New York, which now has an extension especially designed to house Chicago's iconic installation, The Dinner Party. To put matters succinctly, both leading Chinese artists and leading feminist artists have marked out a territory for themselves and have created a visual language or group of languages that enable them to communicate directly with an non-specialist audience.

的呼应，创造出一种情景，让人感觉到这些物体若隐若现。隐匿从另一面产生异样的感觉，这正是作品的情感核心所在。

"异样"不仅通过新鲜感和人们的幻觉魔力——我在文章开头提到，与科幻小说中平行宇宙的对比——而且通过人类共同的知觉，带来巨大的视觉冲击。毫无疑问，这些作品都是高科技艺术作品。艺术家，或确切地说，其他任何人不久前都还无法得以运用这些技术。一旦意识到这个问题，就必然会引起我们内心的深切关注。高科技艺术作品只会产生于对脆弱的生态平衡构成威胁的社会里。

然而，这不是简单的说教。尤其是《本土》组照，始终吸引着观众对历史背景、对人类漫长的进化过程以及我们今天生存之地的关注。虽然我们在理论上崇拜纯洁的大自然，但是，这种崇拜源于一种矫揉造作的城市情调。这不是什么新的情感，在十七世纪克劳德·洛兰 (Claude Lorraine) 的绘画中就能找到这种感情的表露。具有象征意义的是，克劳德最坚定的赞助人都是路易十四身边埋头苦干的官僚人物。他的作品旨在提醒他们为了效忠君主而放弃了种种乐趣。

在《本土》和《镜像》组照背后的是一个反义词，是对事实上或许从未存在的伊甸园的热望。我认为这正是这些作品的部分魅力所在，既宣扬了某种道德，一种尊重大自然的道德，同时也提出了质疑。你可以栖息在这些地方，却只不过是一个幽灵而已。他们提出的是完全解决不了的问题——这里无法找到恰当的解决办法。

This is not something one can rely on elsewhere. Too often there is a disconnection between the imagery the artist has chosen and what that imagery is supposed to mean. After the long Modernist excursion into an exploration of purely 'formal' values – an excursion that came to a logical conclusion with the Minimal Art of the late 1960s and early 1970s, art has tended to return to the allegorical and the narrative, which are territories that it fully inhabited before the rise of the Modern Movement. Too often, today, the supposed allegories lack inevitable meaning, and the narratives stutter into nothing.

That is clearly not the case here. One of the difficulties of writing about the work of Maslen and Mehra is, paradoxically, that it doesn't need the elaborate explanations that now seem to be chief business of the critic. The intended message is not at all difficult to disentangle from what you see. On the other hand, it isn't obvious in the sense of being banal. A fascinating thing about the duo's use of mirrors is the way in which this usage resonates in different ways. They resonate purely physically, through the ways in which the various mirrored surfaces pick up their surroundings. Sometimes this involves a near-disappearance of the sculpture itself, which melts into the surrounding landscape or townscape. The image of Milton Keynes and the cities use of reflective glass in its master-plan, for example, presents this aspect particularly well. The sculptures also resonate metaphorically, creating a situation where we perceive them as being simultaneously present and absent. This absence, in turn, creates the sense of otherness that is the emotional core of the work.

EDWARD LUCIE-SMITH - 爱德华·路希—史密斯是艺术史学家、艺术评论家、策展人、诗人和摄影家，他的当代艺术著作以多种语言出版。最为著名的有《自1945年以来的艺术运动》《二十世纪的视觉艺术》和《今日艺术》。他曾策划在维罗纳Palazzo Forti画廊举办的研究性展览《新古典主义艺术》。在他众多的著作中，有关于美国女权运动艺术家朱迪·芝加哥的专著[2000年5月出版]、《未来艺术》[2002年10月出版]，以及对当代艺术的最新发展趋势的研究，其中包括对马斯伦和梅赫拉作品的研究。

The otherness makes its impact not only through our sense of the strange and the magical – at the beginning of this essay I suggested a comparison with the parallel worlds of Science Fiction – but also through its impact on the collective conscience. These are undoubtedly high-tech artworks, made using means that, only a short time, ago, would not have been available to artists, or, indeed, to anyone else. This aspect, as soon as we recognize it, inevitably draws our attention to the underlying moral. High-tech artworks can only be produced by societies that threaten a fragile ecological balance.

Yet this is not simple preaching. The Native series, in particular, continually draws the spectator's attention to the historical context, and to the long process of evolution that has brought us, as human beings, to the place where we stand now. Though we worship, at any rate in theory, virginal nature, this worship springs from a sophisticated urban sensibility. This sensibility is not new. It was already finding expression in the 17th century, in the paintings of Claude Lorraine. Typically, Claude's most faithful patrons came from the leading figures in the hard-working bureaucracy that surrounded Louis XIV. His paintings reminded them of all the pleasures they had given up in order to serve the monarch.

Lying behind both the Native images, and the images of the Mirrored series that are their antonym, lies a longing for an Edenic world that perhaps never truly existed in fact. I think it is part of the fascination of these works that they both preach a certain kind of morality, a morality of respect for nature, and at the same

time question it. You can inhabit these scenes, but only as a ghost.
The problems they pose are ultimately insoluble – there are no slick solutions
to be found here.

Essay from the exhibition Native at Milton Keynes Contemporary - WHITEWALL.
Sponsored by thecentre:mk 2008

EDWARD LUCIE-SMITH is an art historian, art critic, curator, poet and
photographer who has written books on contemporary art published in many
languages. Among his best-known titles are 'Movements in Art since 1945',
'The Visual Arts of the 20th Century' and 'Art Today'. He curated the survey
exhibition 'New Classicism in Art', at Palazzo Forti in Verona. Among his
many books is a monograph on the American feminist artist Judy Chicago
[published in May 2000], and 'Art Tomorrow' [published in October 2002],
a survey of the most recent developments in contemporary art, which
includes work by Maslen & Mehra.

《本土》组照

NATIVE

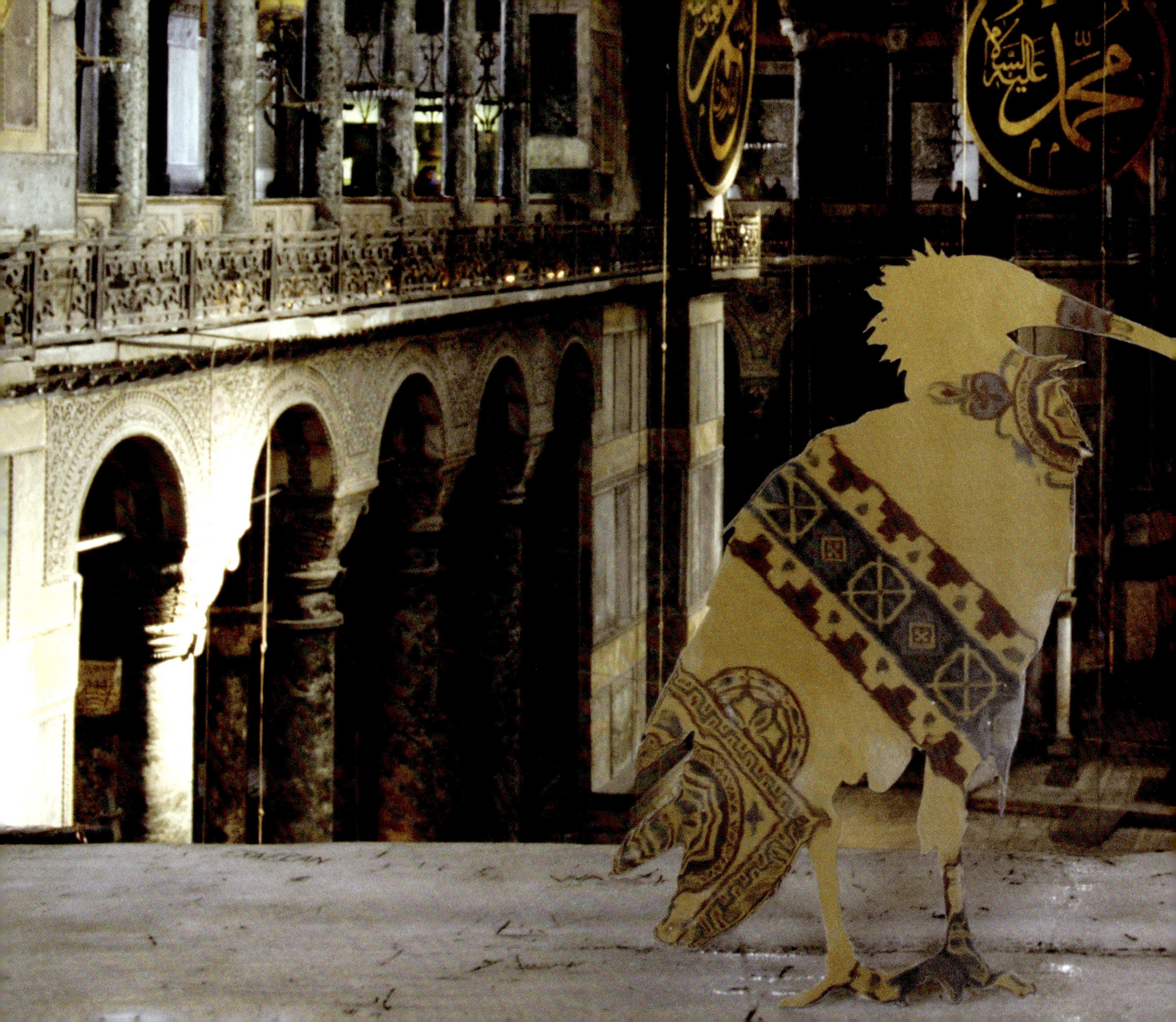

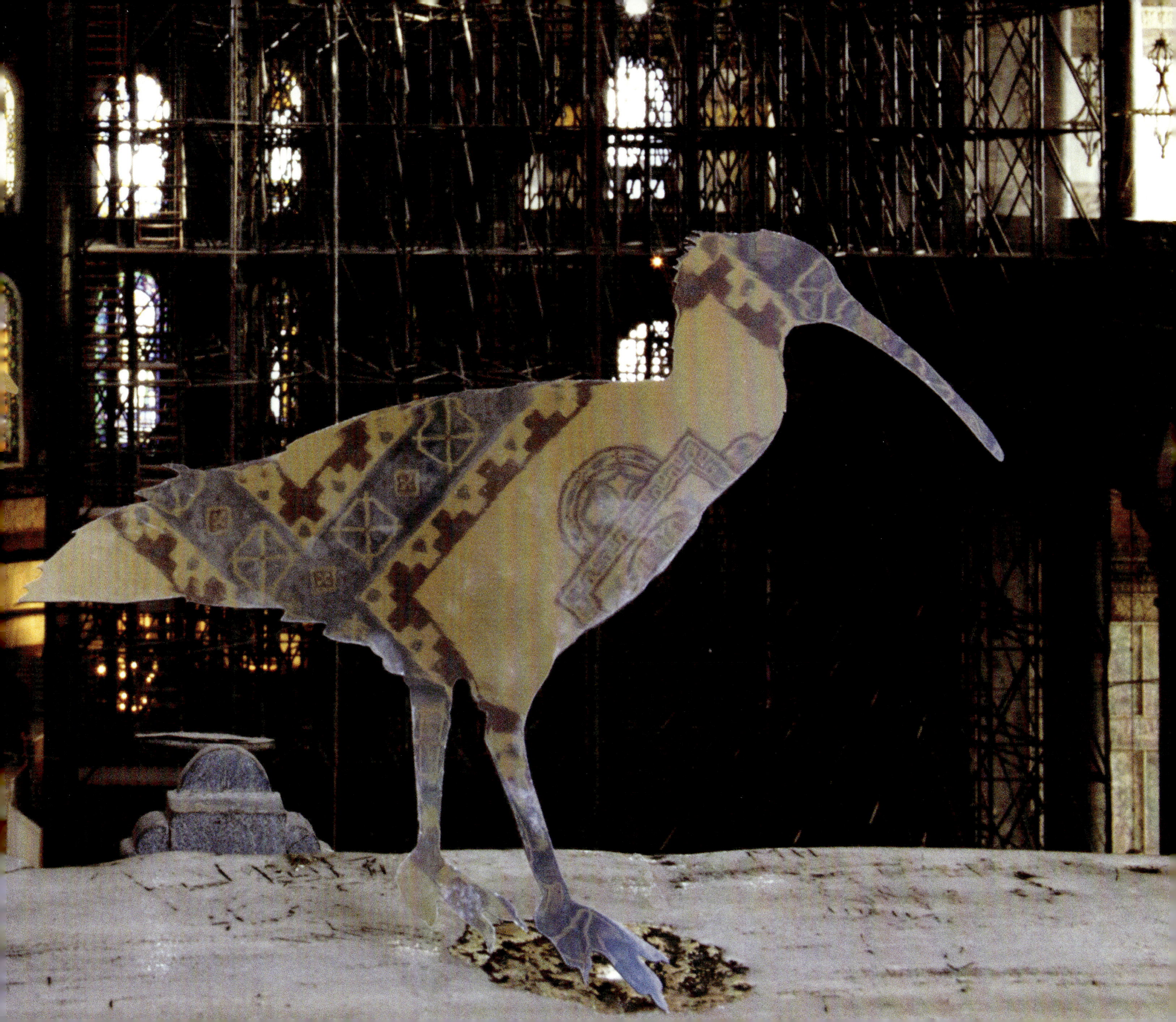

DETAIL ON PREVIOUS PAGE:
详细介绍见上页:

Bald Headed Ibis - Aya Sofya - Istanbul II
秃鹮—圣索非亚大教堂—伊斯坦布尔II

2008
Durst Lambda print
120x160cm

94

Kangal Dog - Aya Sofya - Istanbul I
康加犬—圣索非亚大教堂—伊斯坦布尔I

2008
Durst Lambda print
160x120cm

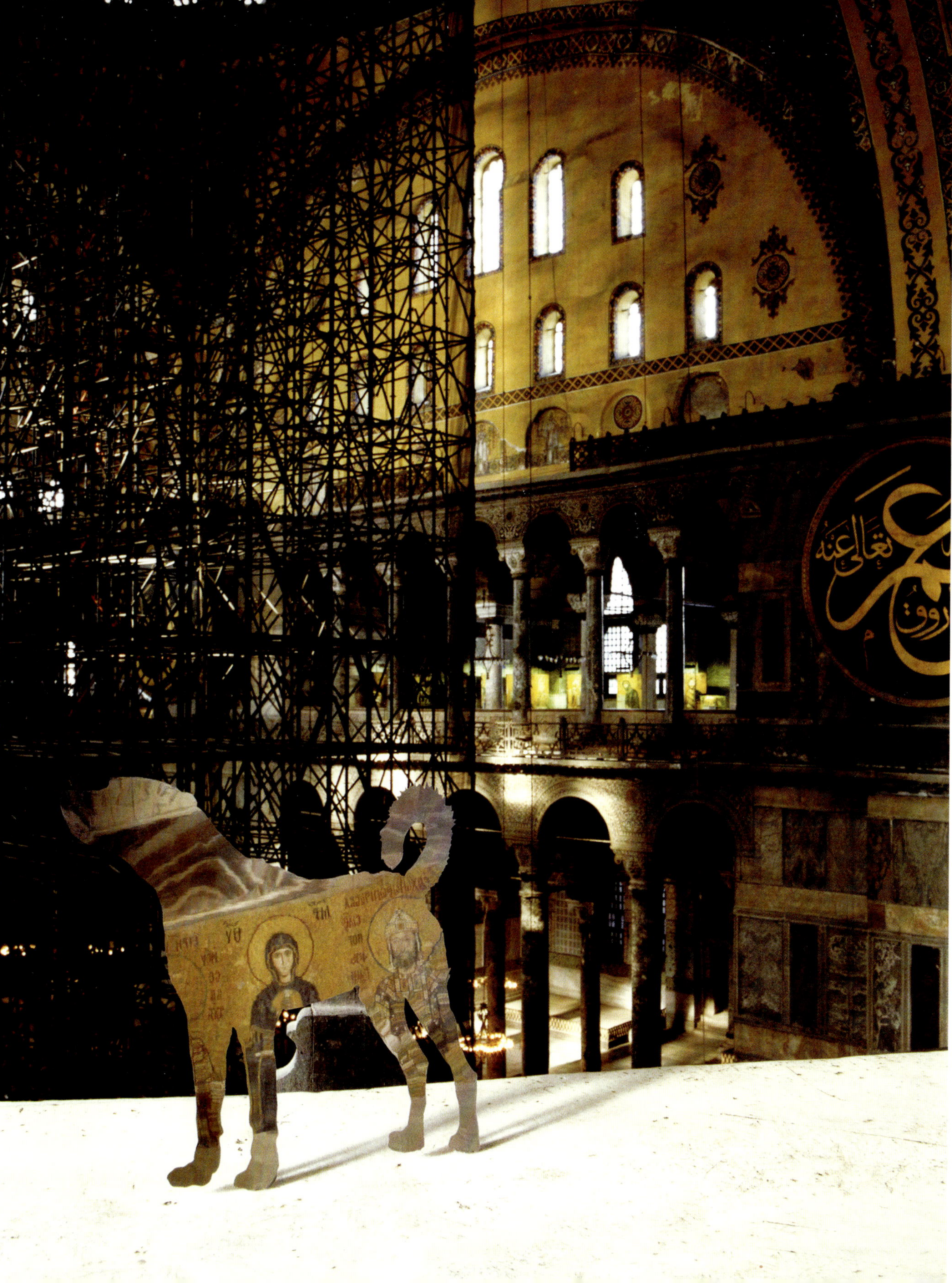

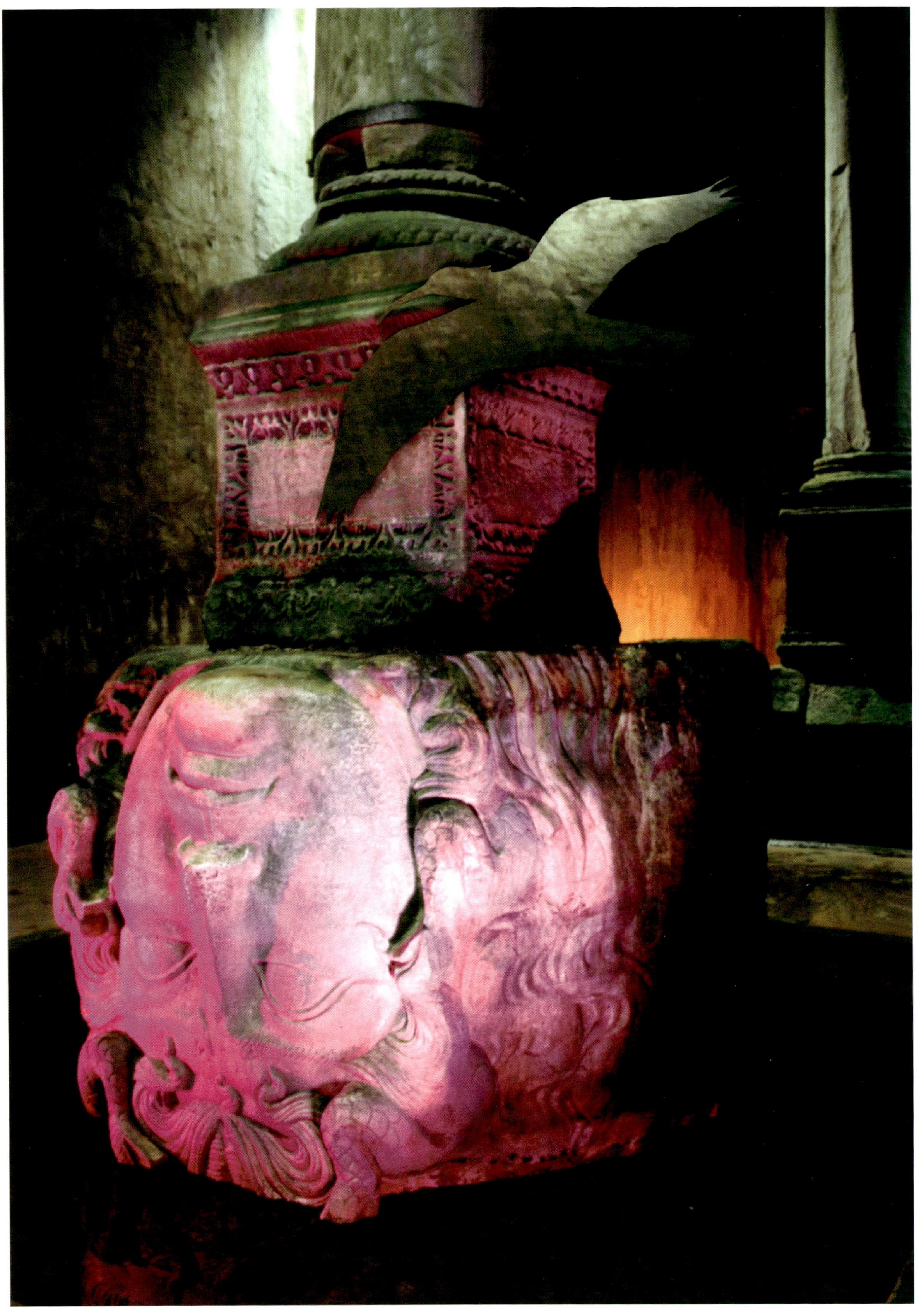

Bald Headed Ibis - Basilica Cistern - Istanbul
秃加—地下宫殿—伊斯坦布尔
2008
Durst Lambda print
72x52cm

Bald Headed Ibis - Aya Sofya - Istanbul I
秃加—圣索非亚大教堂—伊斯坦布尔 I

2008
Durst Lambda print
52x72cm

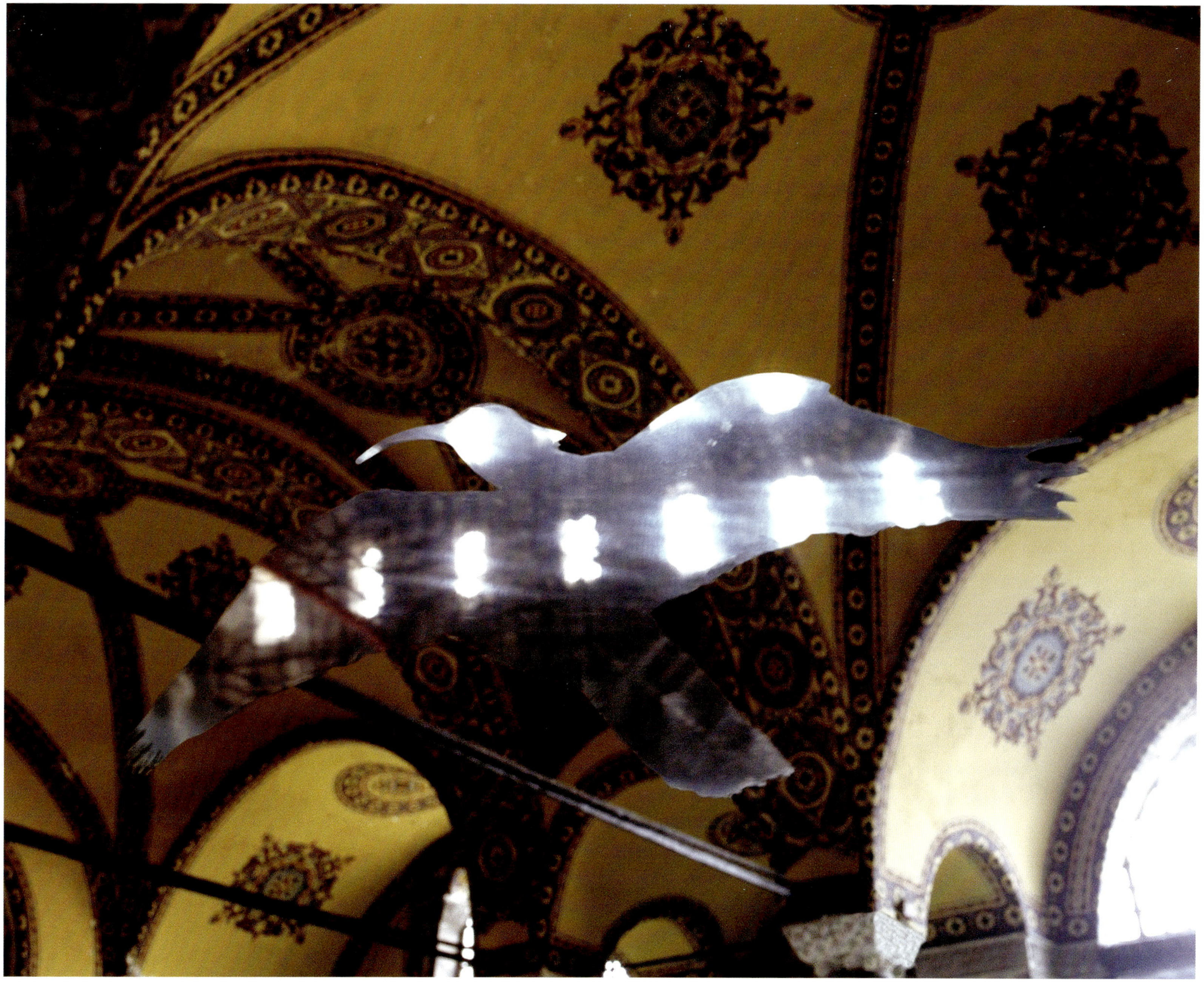

American Eagle - Times Square - New York series I image I
美国鹰—时代广场—纽约组照I照片I

2007
Durst Lambda print
120x160cm

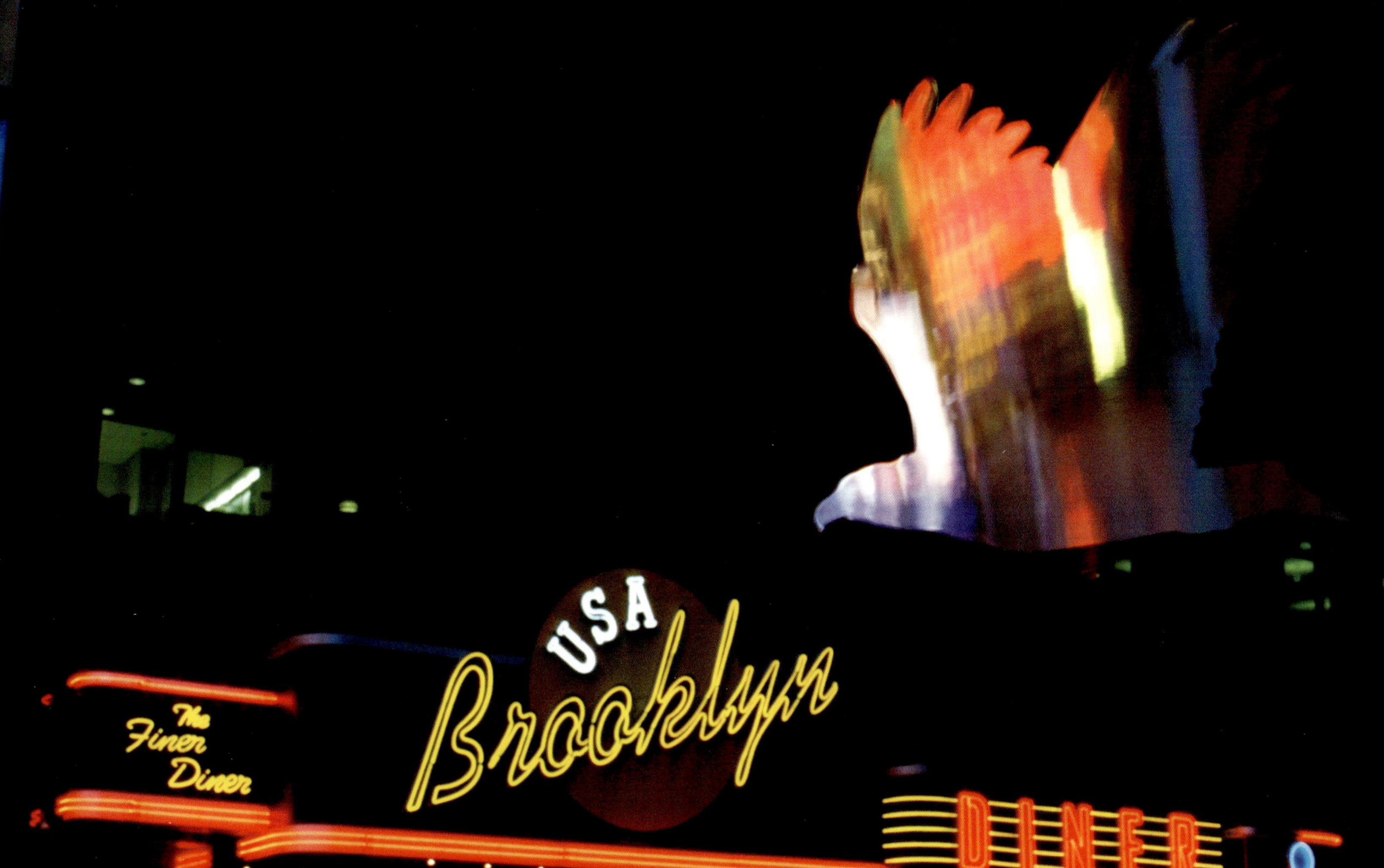
RESTAURANT
USA
Brooklyn
The Finer Diner
DINER

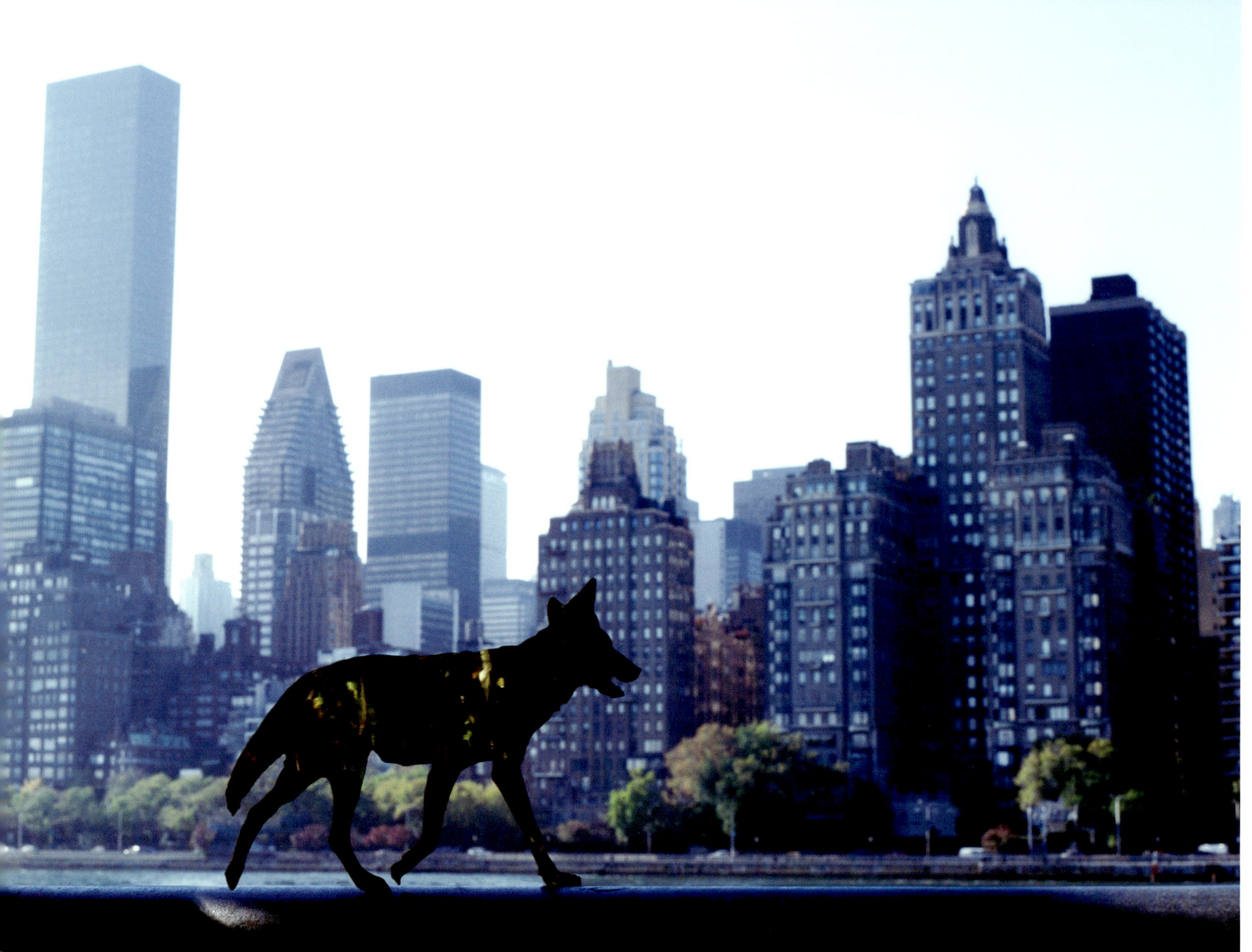

Coyote - Roosevelt Island - New York I
草原狼—罗斯福岛—纽约I

2007
Durst Lambda print
120x160cm

American Eagle - Times Square - New York series IV image II
美国鹰—时代广场—纽约组照IV照片II

2007
Durst Lambda print
52x72см

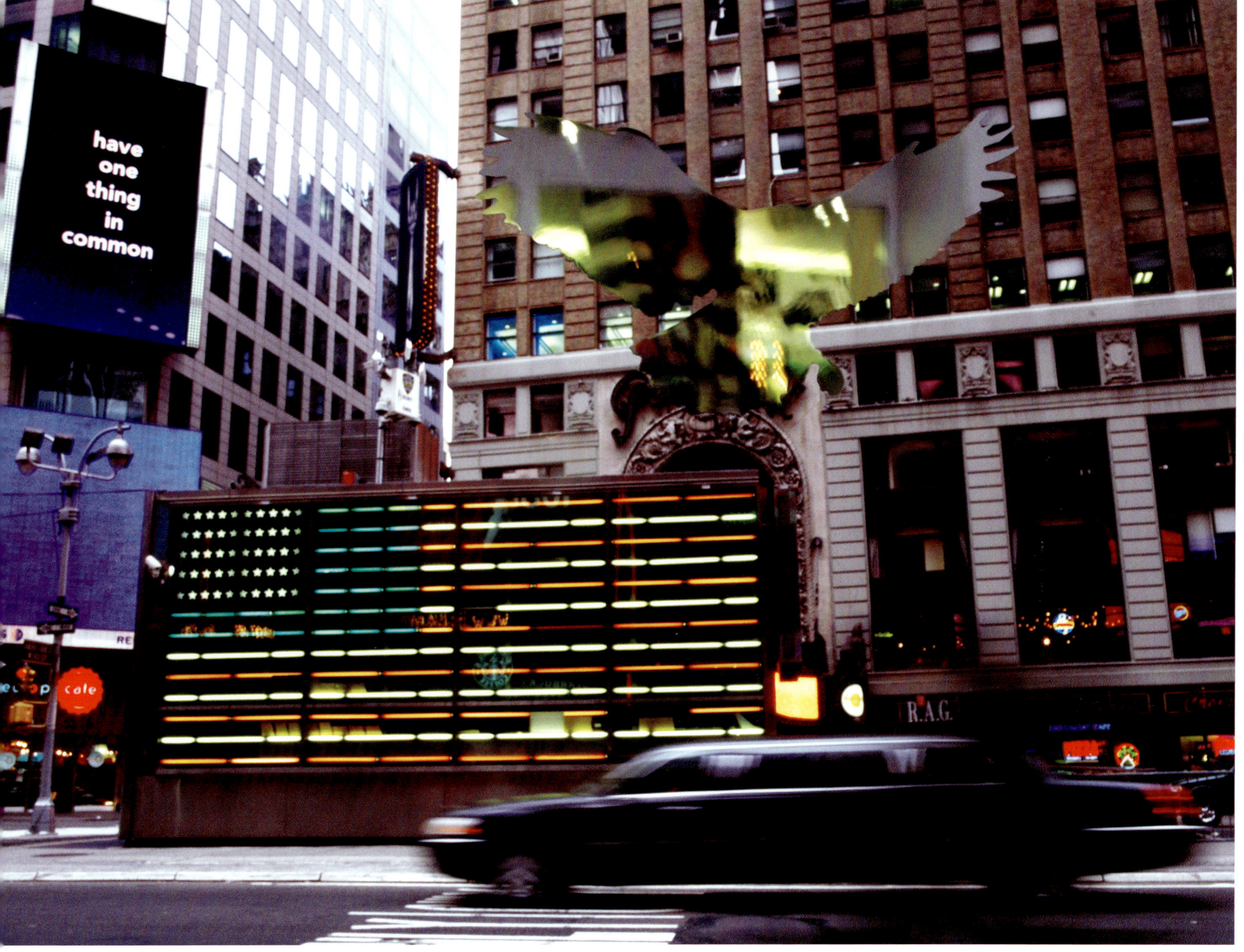
have
one
thing
in
common

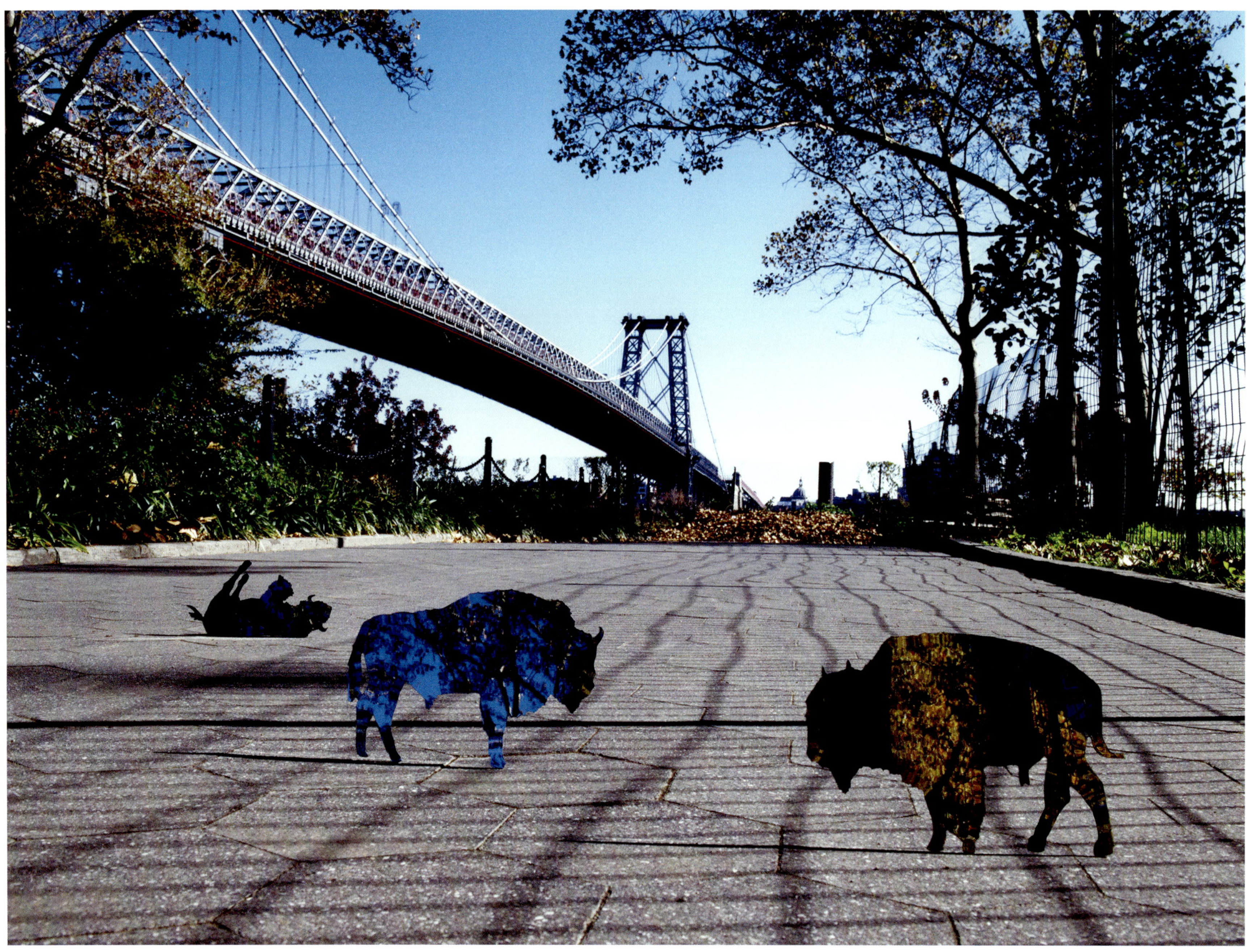

American Buffalo - Williamsburg Bridge - New York
美国野牛—威廉斯堡桥—纽约

2007
Durst Lambda print
120x160cm

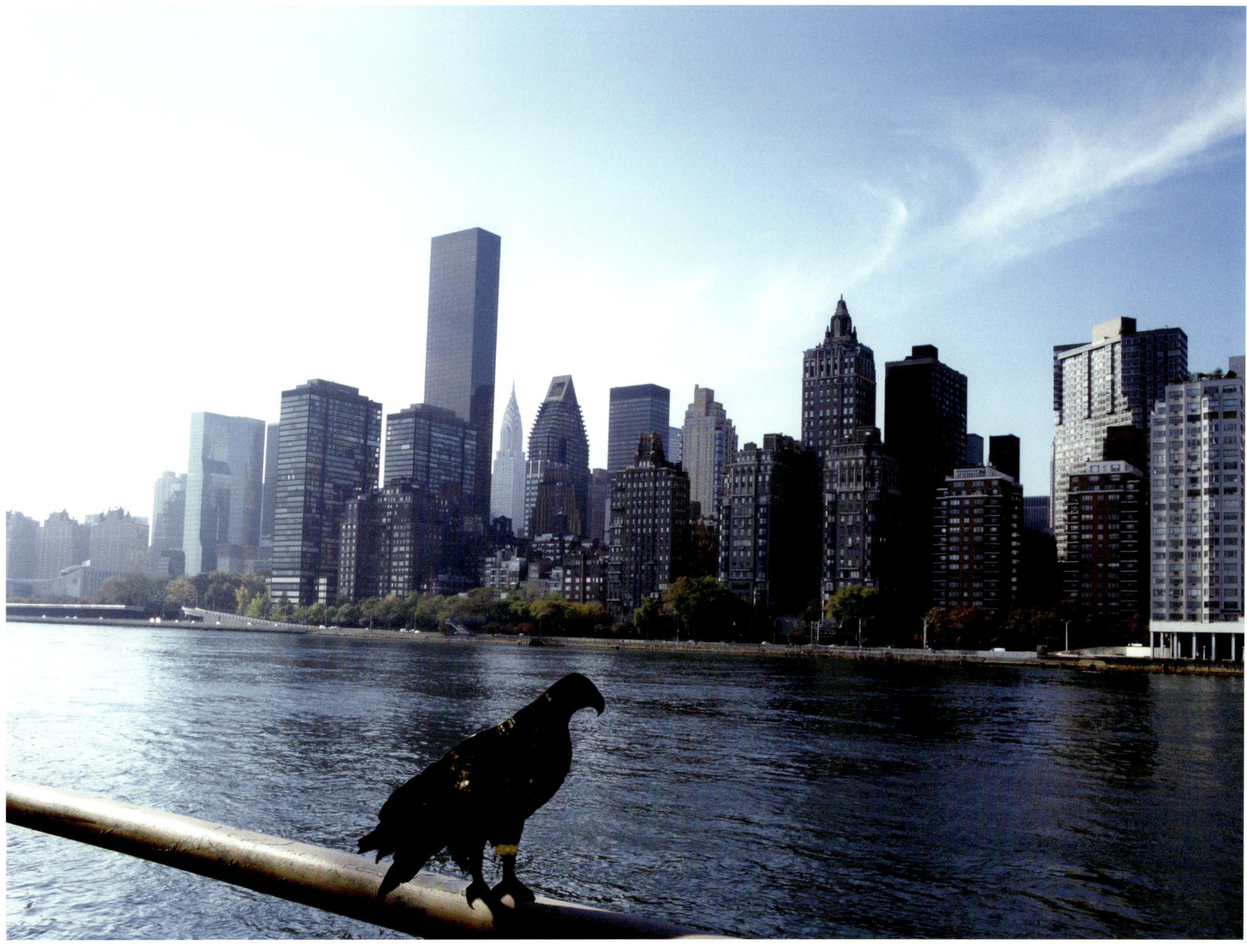

American Eagle - Roosevelt Island - New York III
美国鹰—罗斯福岛—纽约组照III

2007
Durst Lambda print
52x72cm

American Eagle - Empire City - New York
美国鹰—帝国城—纽约

2008
Durst Lambda print
120x160см

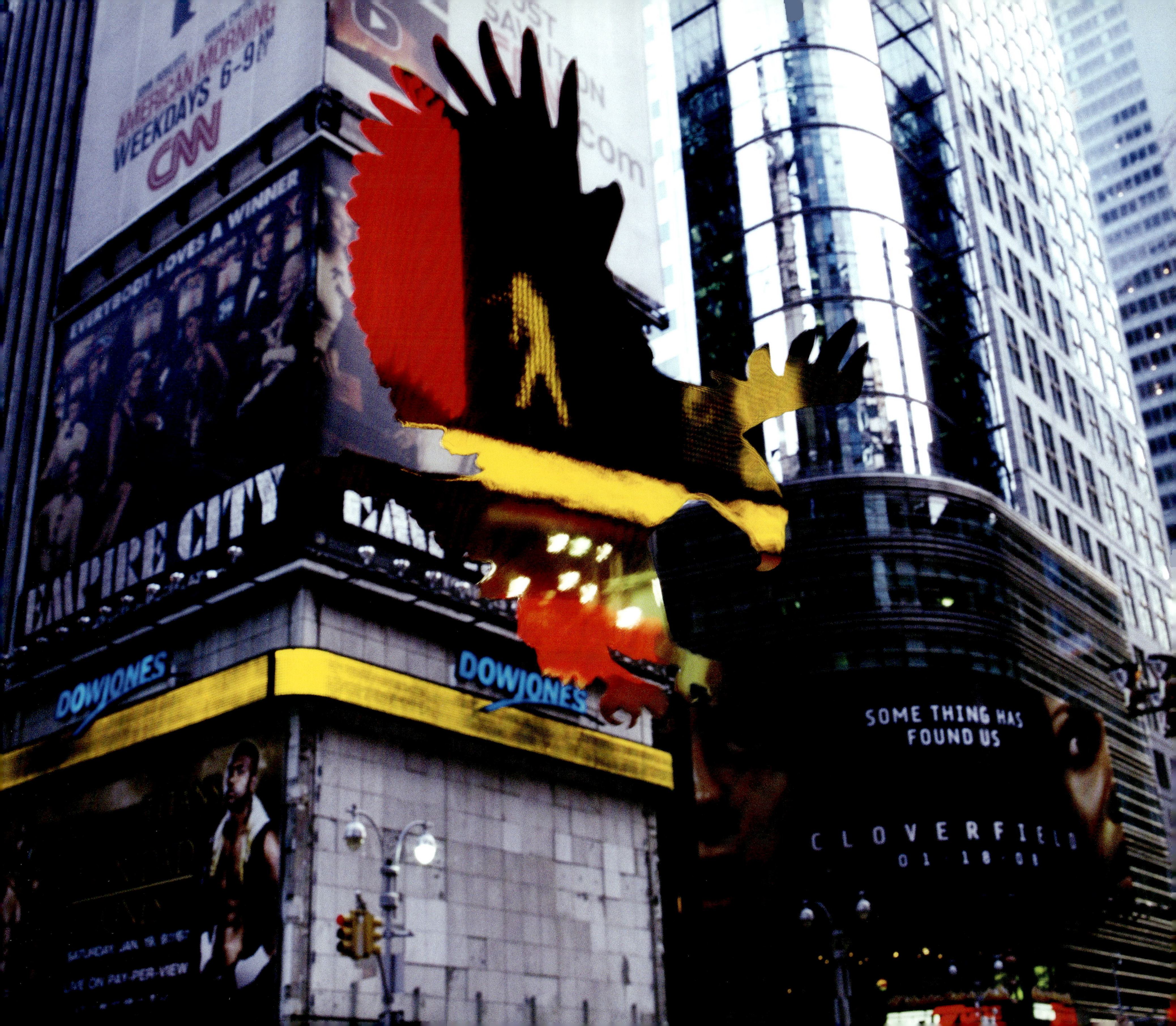

AMERICAN MORNING
WEEKDAYS 6-9
CNN
EMPIRE CITY
EVERYBODY LOVES A WINNER
DOWJONES
DOWJONES
SOME THING HAS
FOUND US
CLOVERFIELD
01·18·08
SATURDAY JAN 19 8/7
LIVE ON PAY-PER-VIEW

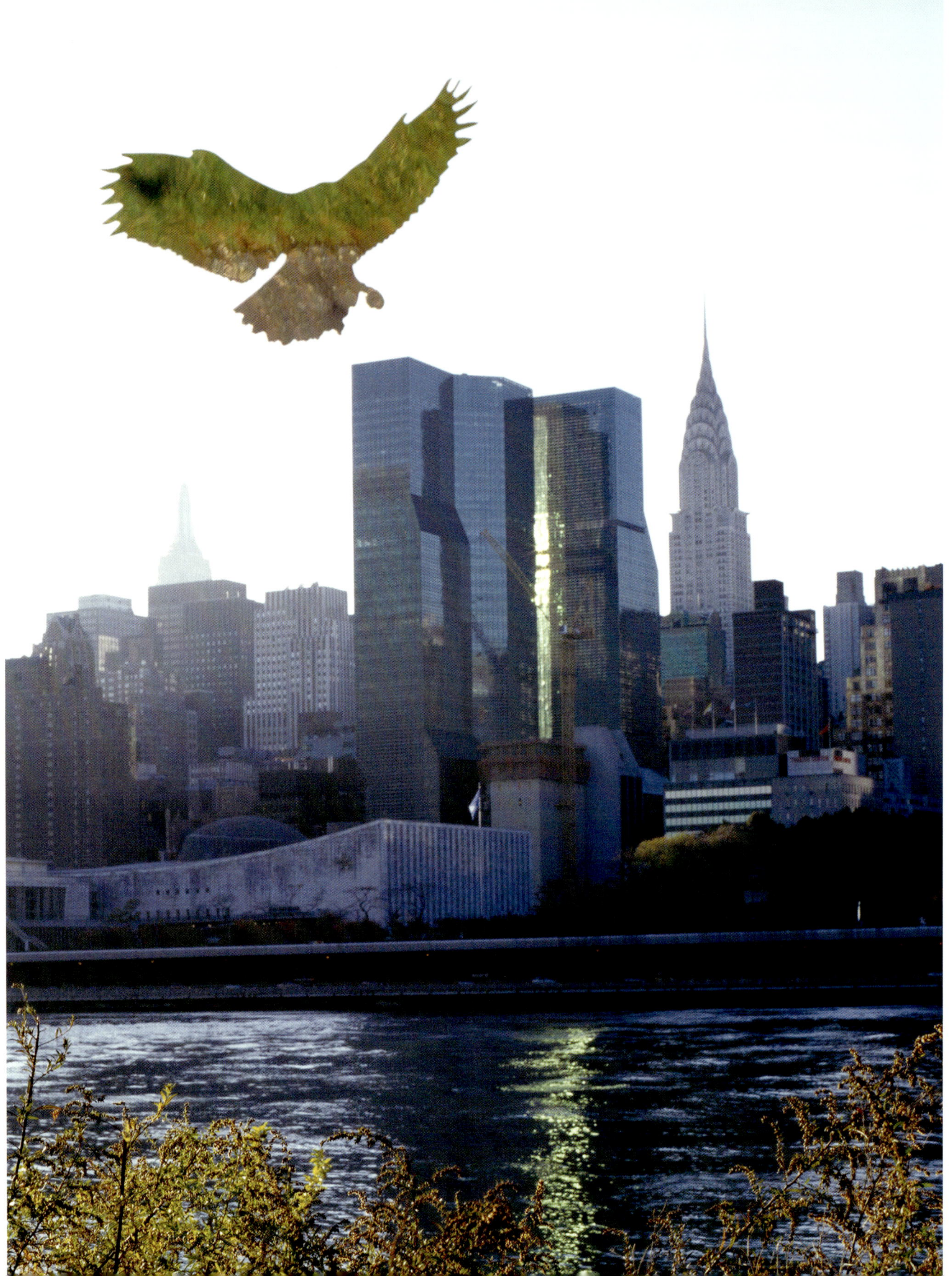

American Eagle - Roosevelt Island - New York II
美国鹰—罗斯福岛—纽约II

2007
Durst Lambda print
72x52см

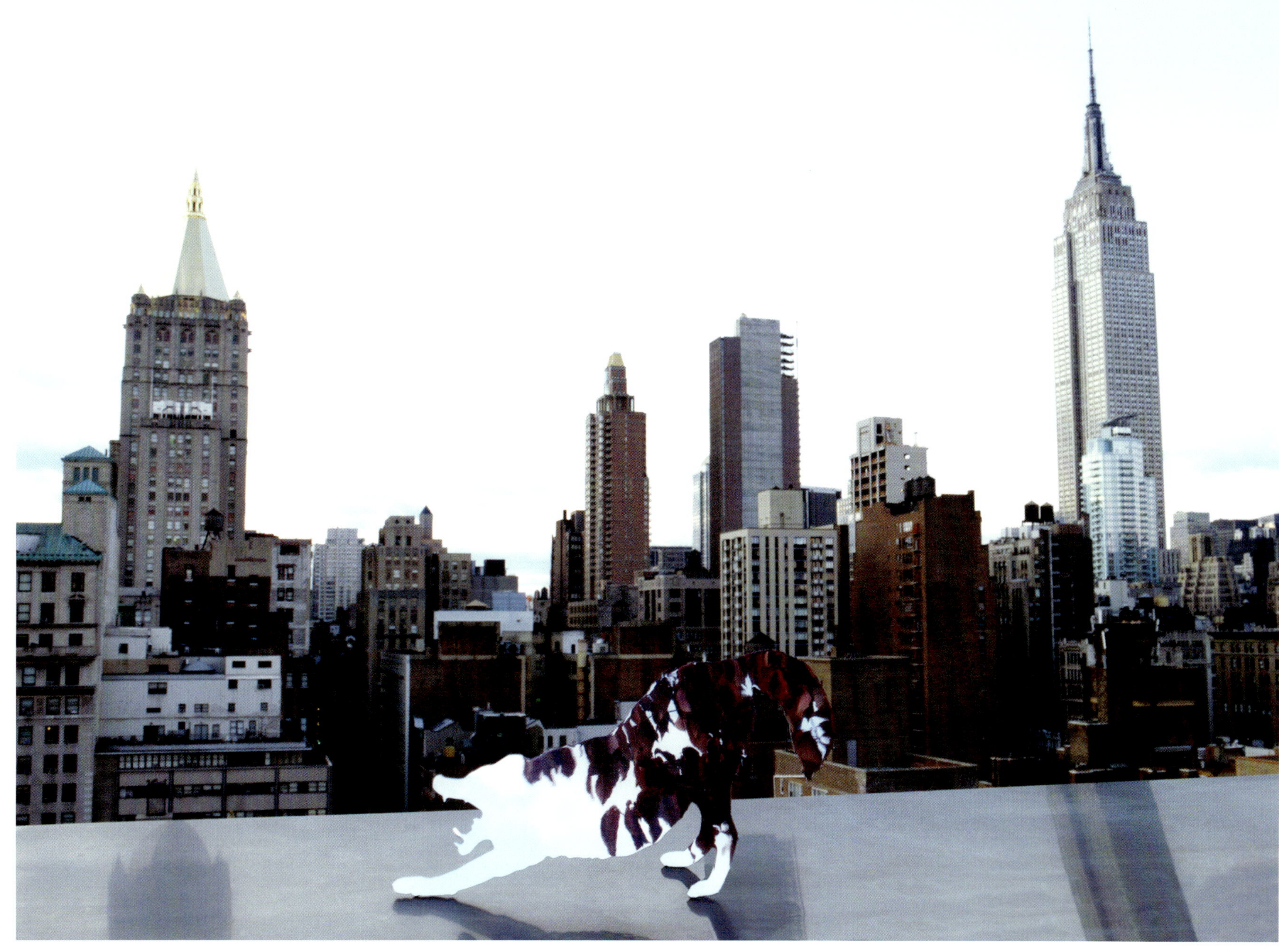

Coyote - Manhattan - New York II
草原狼—曼哈顿—纽约II

2007
Durst Lambda print
52x72cm

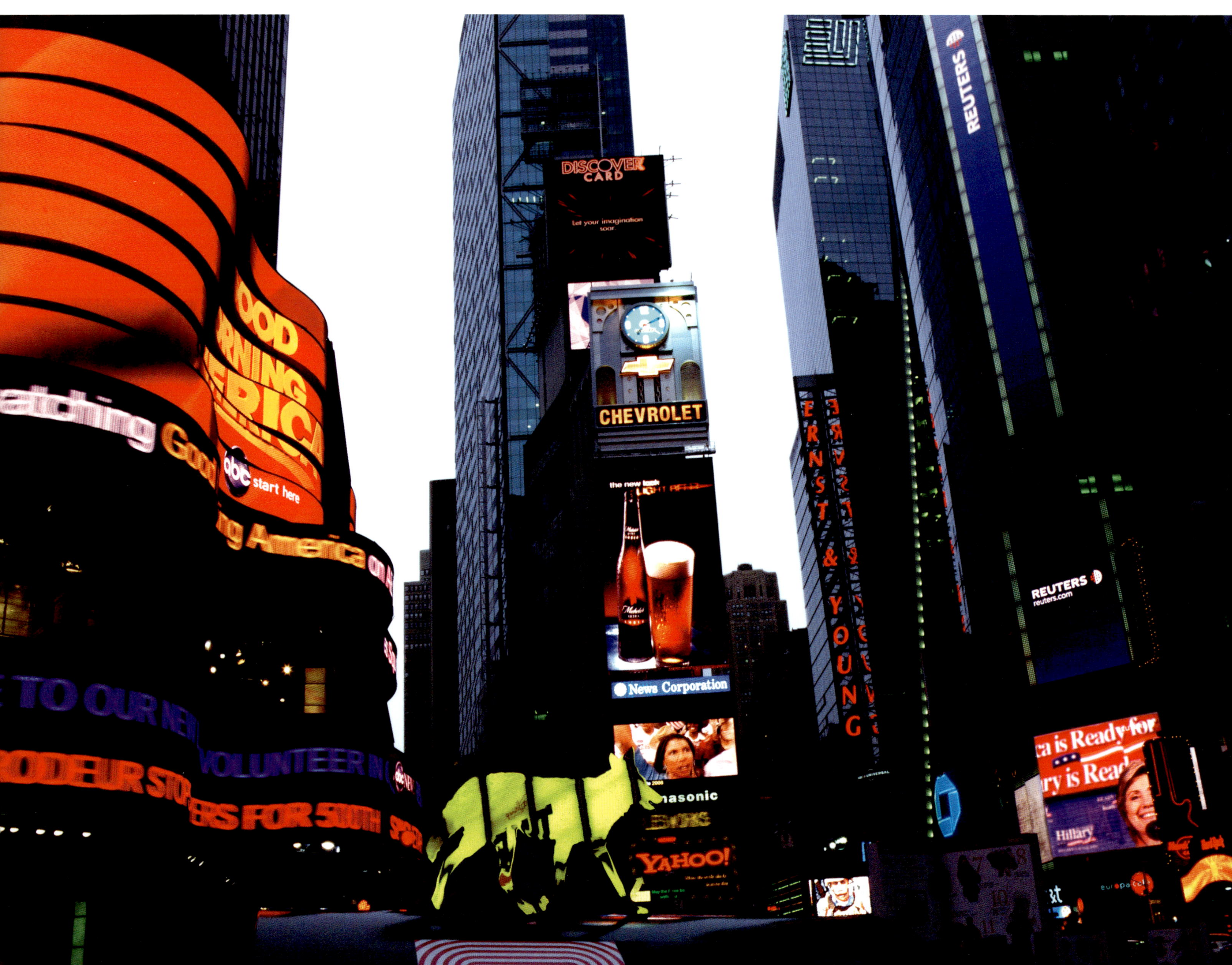
GOOD MORNING AMERICA
atching Good
abc start here
g America
DISCOVER CARD
Let your imagination soar
CHEVROLET
REUTERS
REUTERS
reuters.com
the new look
E TO OUR NE
VOLUNTEER IN
ODEUR STO
RS FOR 50th
News Corporation
Panasonic
YAHOO!
ERNST & YOUNG
ca is Ready for
ry is Read
Hillary
europa

Coyote - Times Square - New York
草原狼—时代广场—纽约

2007
Durst Lambda print
120x160см

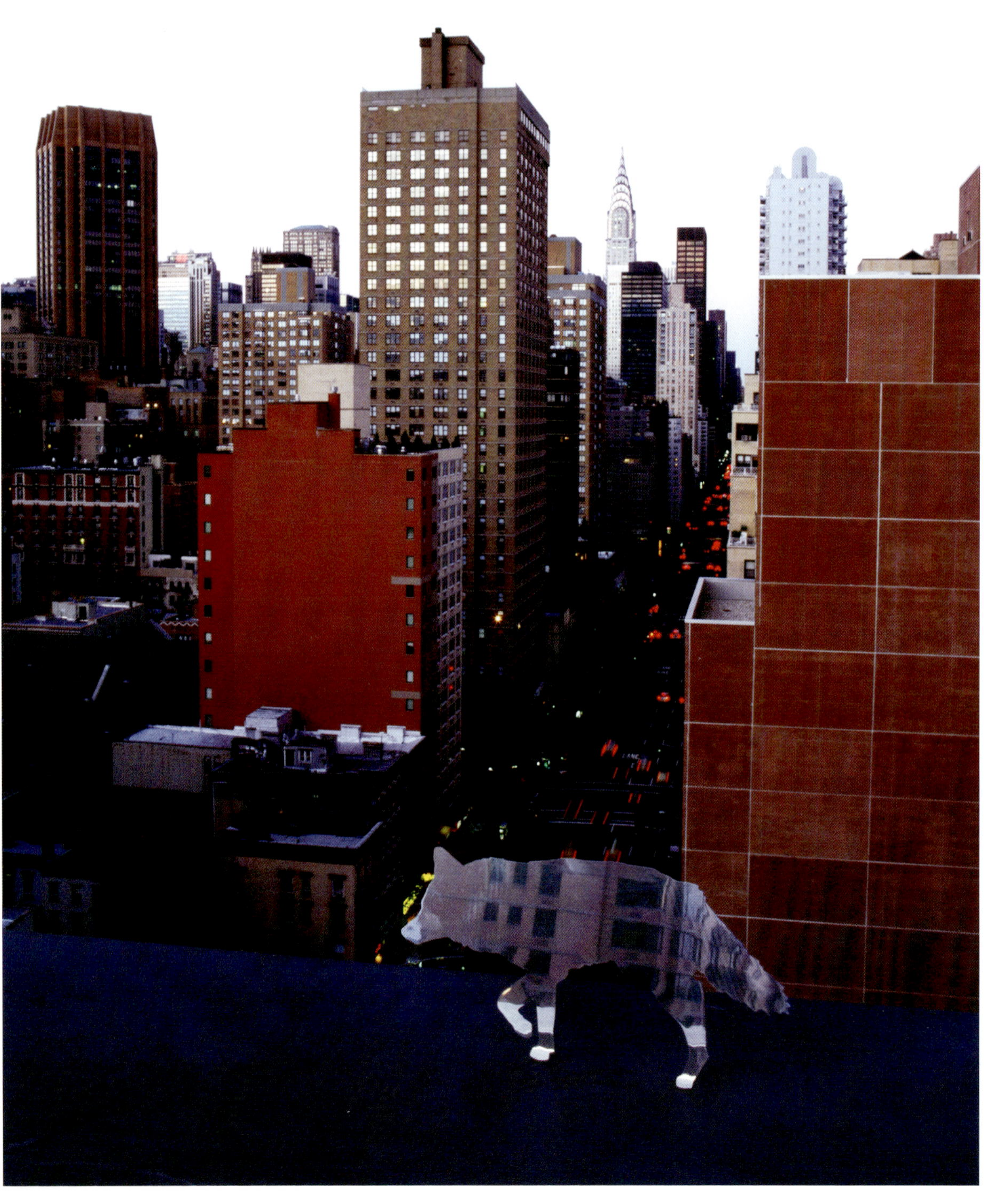

Coyote - Manhattan - New York I
草原狼—曼哈顿—纽约I

2007
Durst Lambda print
72x52см

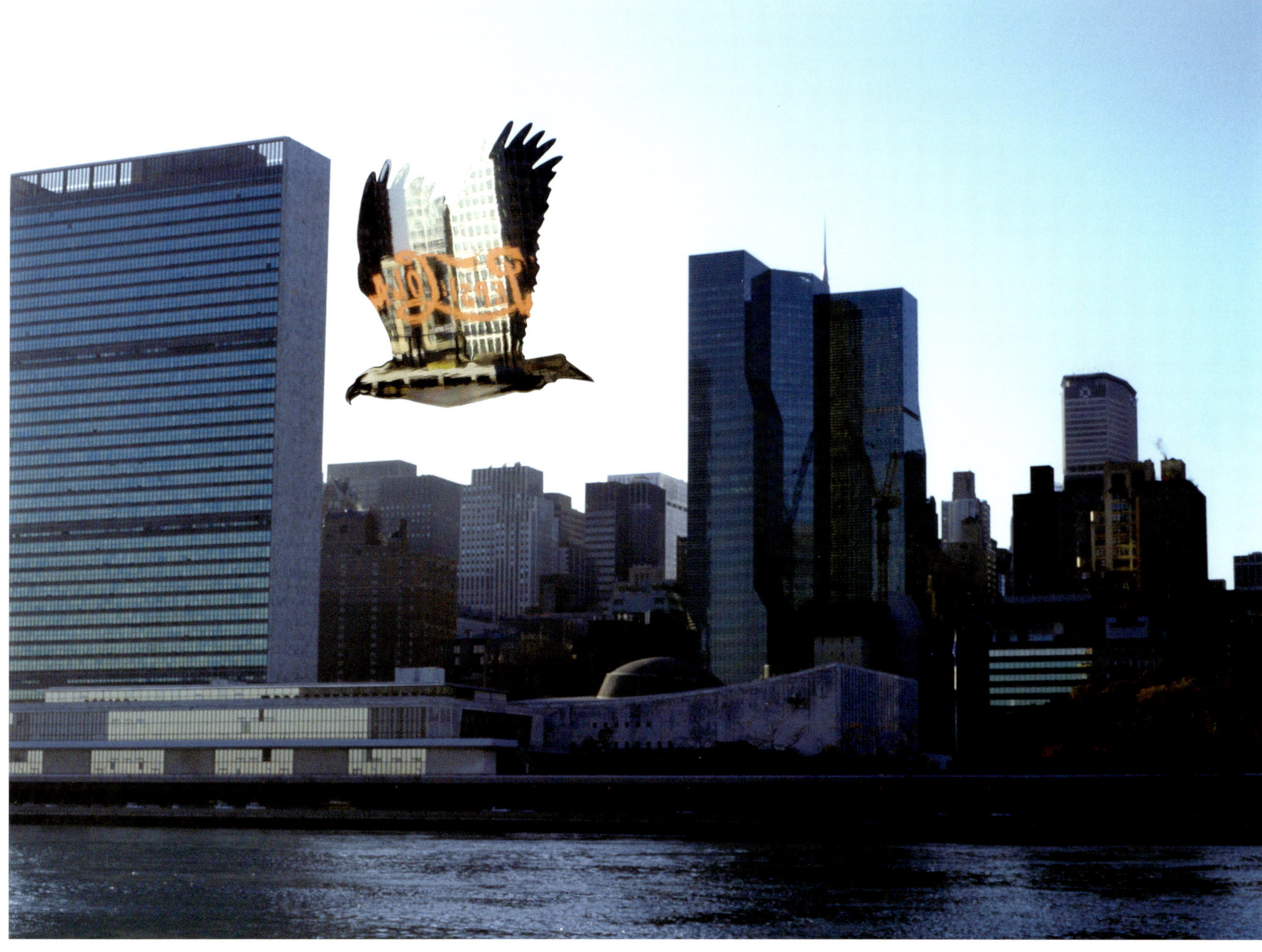

American Eagle - Roosevelt Island - New York I
美国鹰—罗斯福岛—纽约I

2007
Durst Lambda print
52x72см

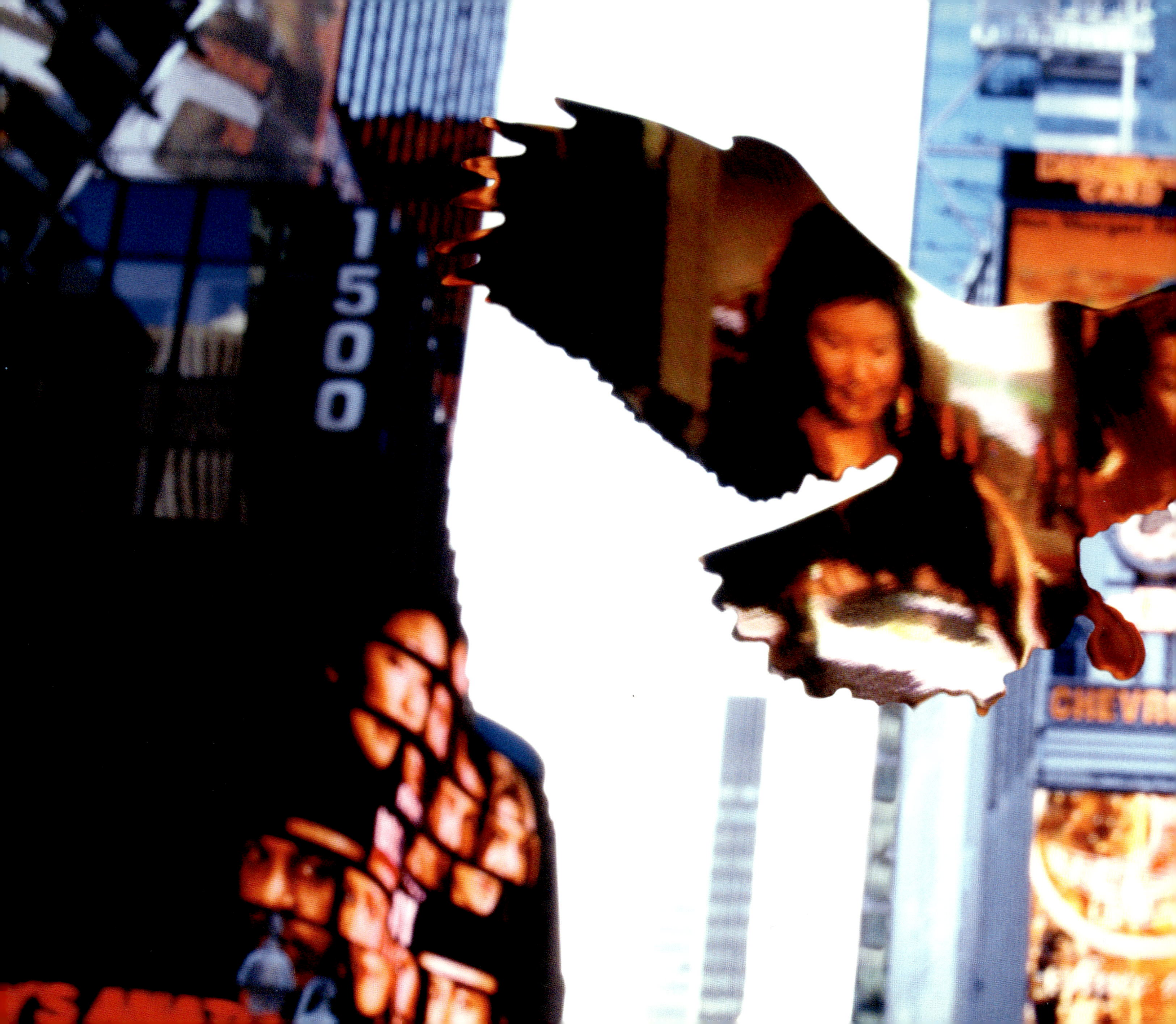

1500
CHEVR

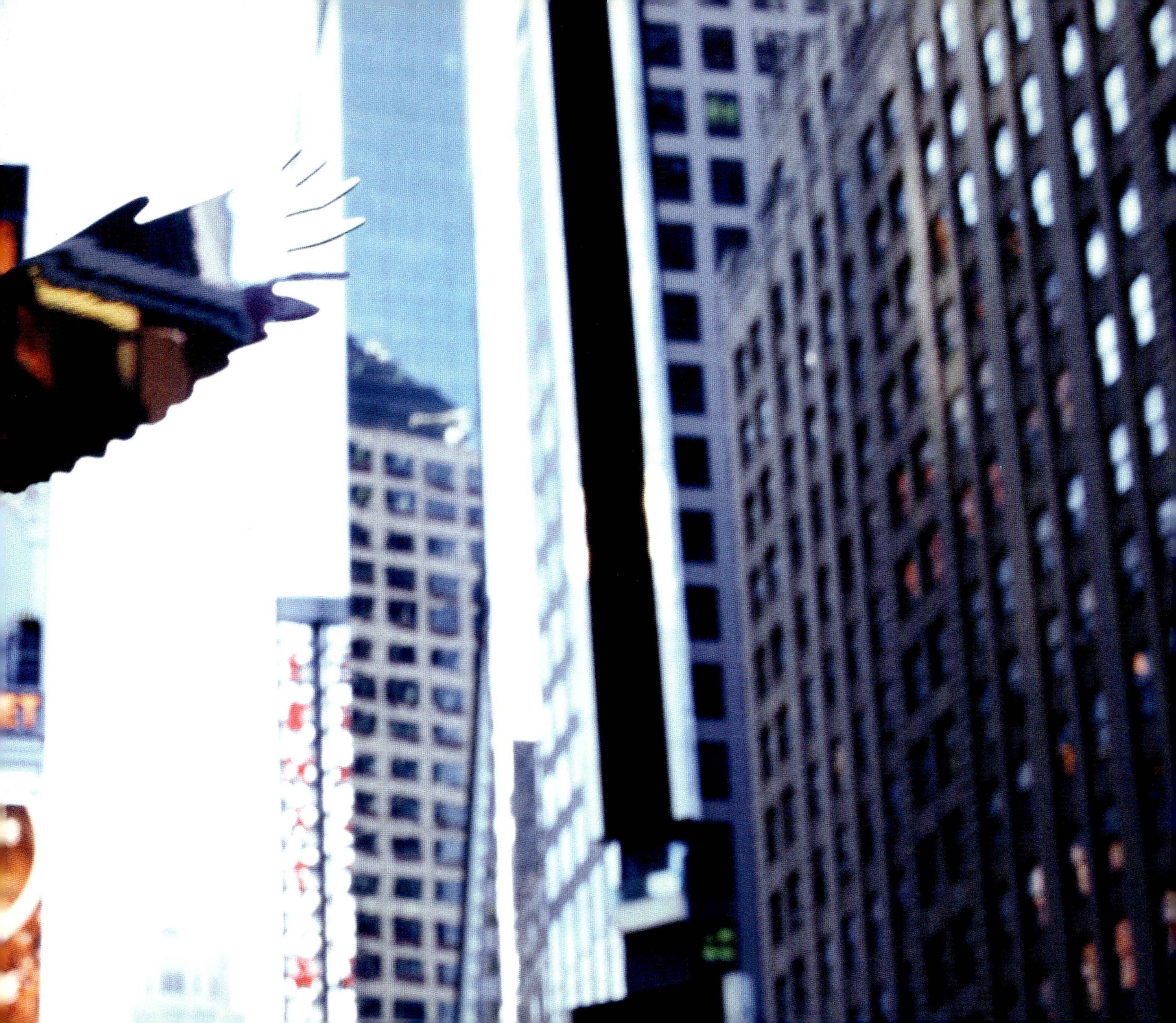

DETAIL ON PREVIOUS PAGE:
详细介绍见上页:

American Eagle - Times Square - New York series III image I
美国鹰—时代广场—纽约组照III照片I

2007
Durst Lambda print
52x72см

American Eagle - Times Square - New York series II image I
美国鹰—时代广场—纽约组照II照片I

2007
Durst Lambda print
160x120см

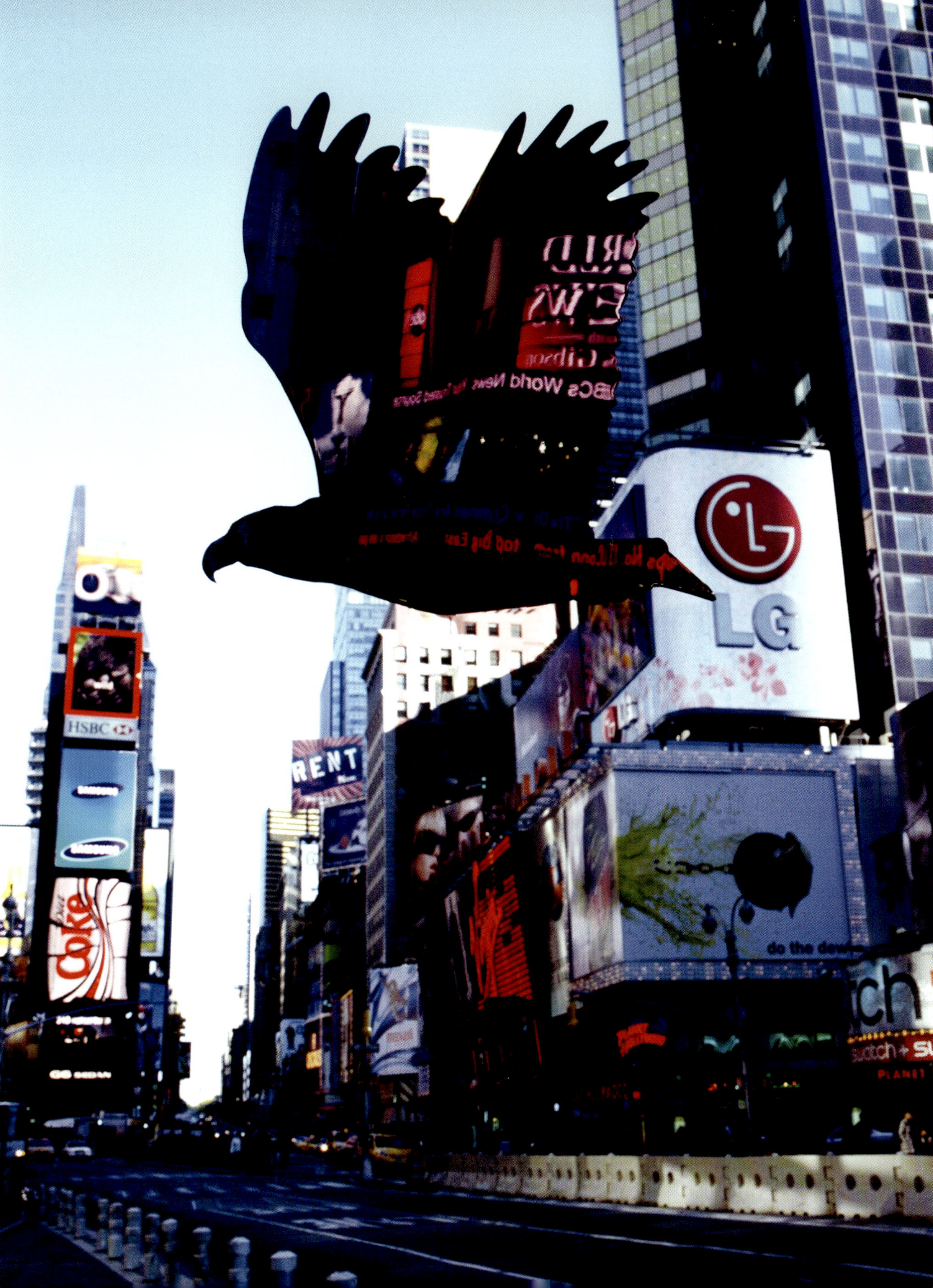
LG
HSBC
Coke
RENT
do the dew
swatch swa
PLANET

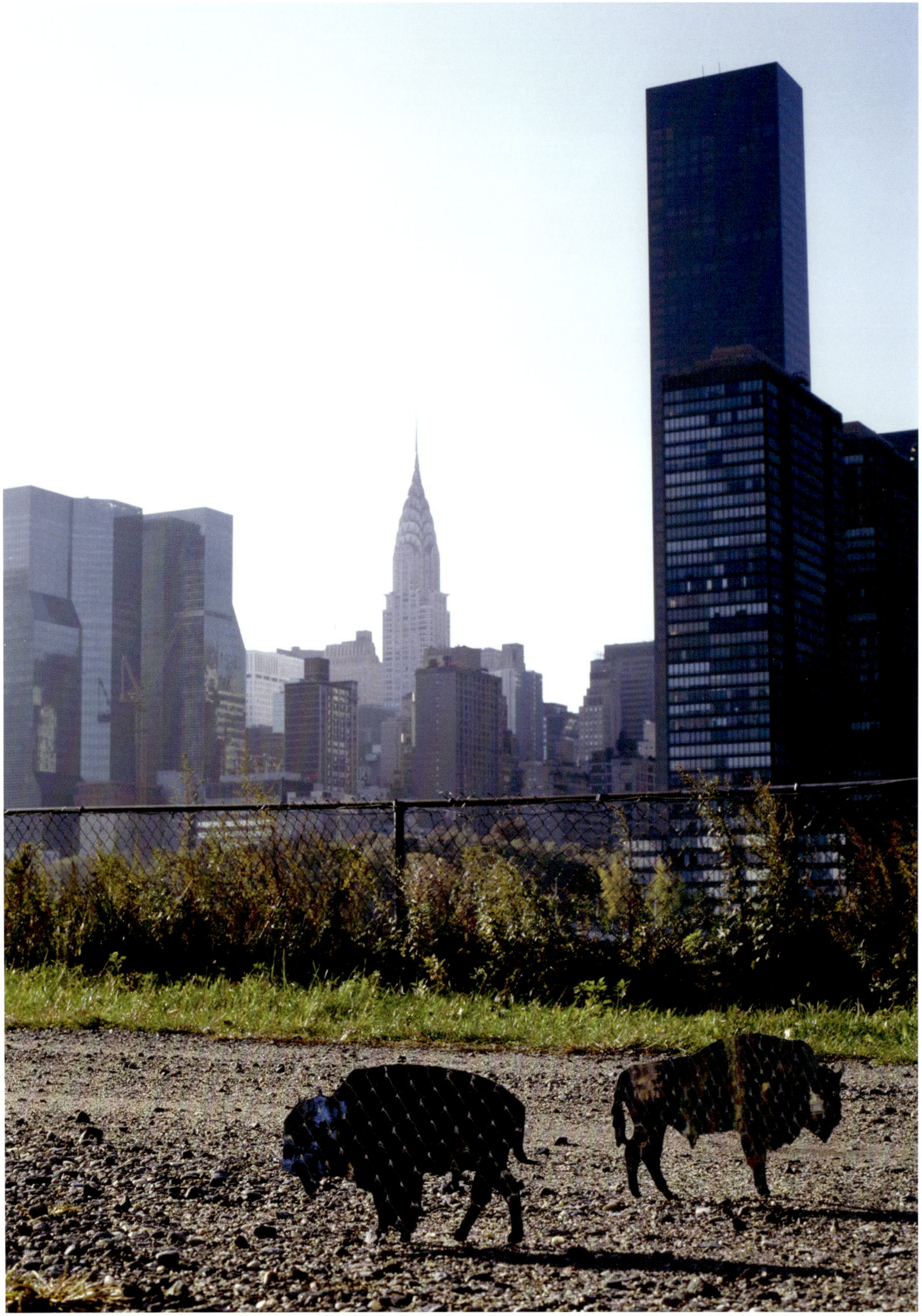

American Buffalo - Roosevelt Island - New York
美国野牛—罗斯福岛—纽约

2007
Durst Lambda print
72x52cm

European Wolf Mouflon - Via Della Renella - Rome
欧洲狼 · 盘羊一Via Della Renella一罗马

2007
Durst Lambda print
160x120cm

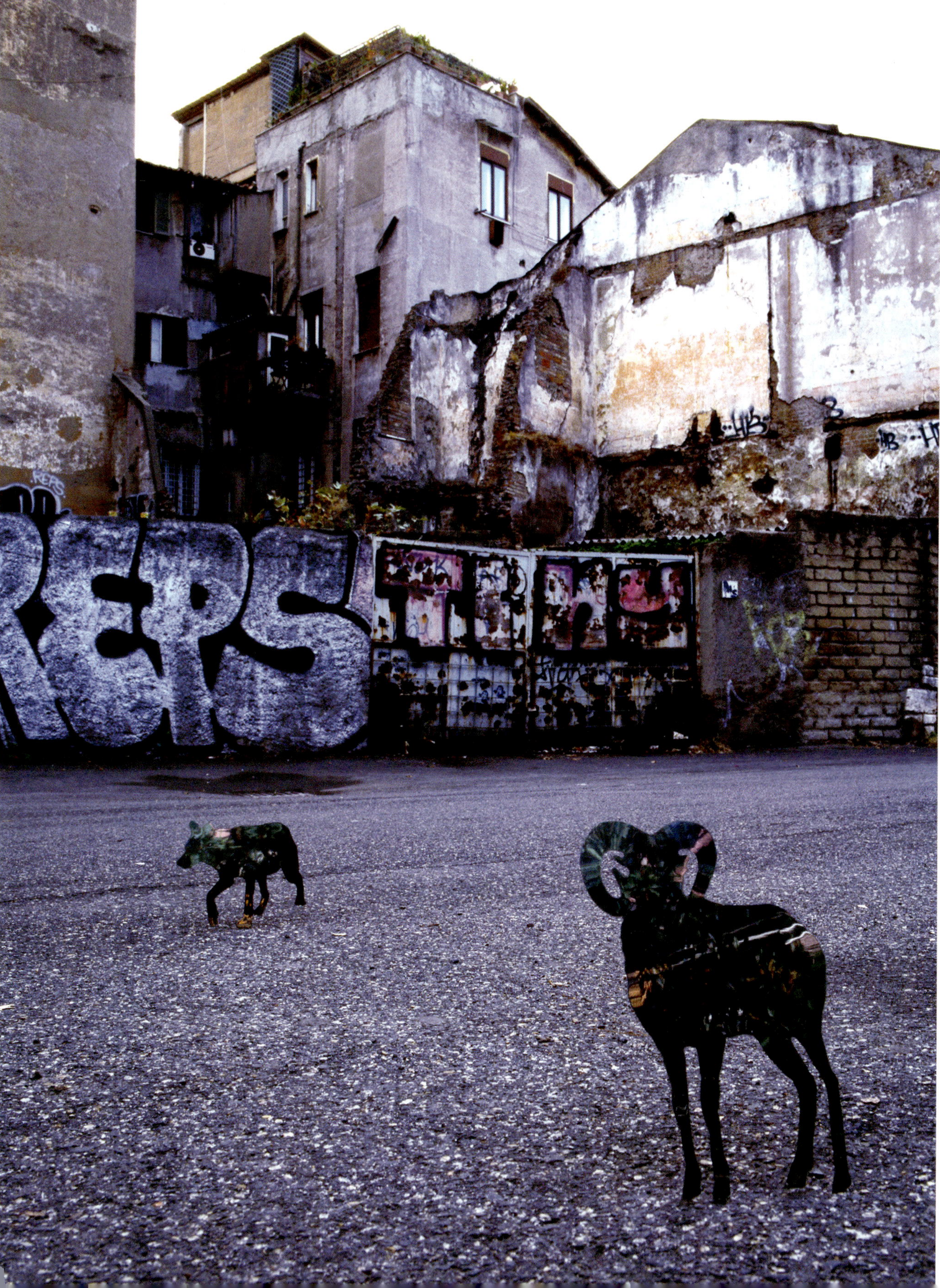

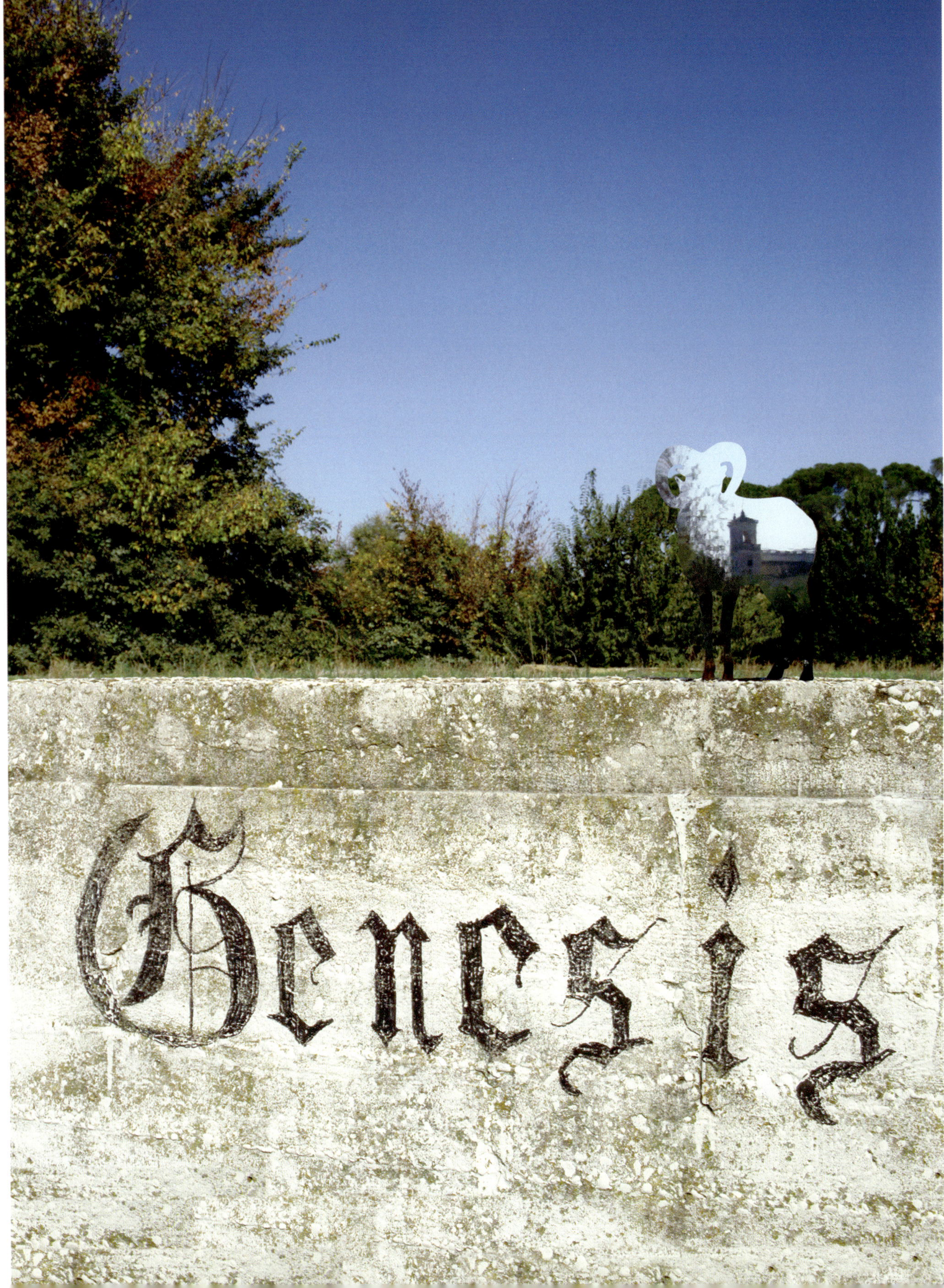

124

Mouflon - Villa Borghese - Rome
盘羊—Villa Borghese—罗马

2007
Durst Lambda print
160x120см

Ibex - Louvre - Paris III
野山羊—卢浮宫—巴黎III

2006
Durst Lambda print
160x120см

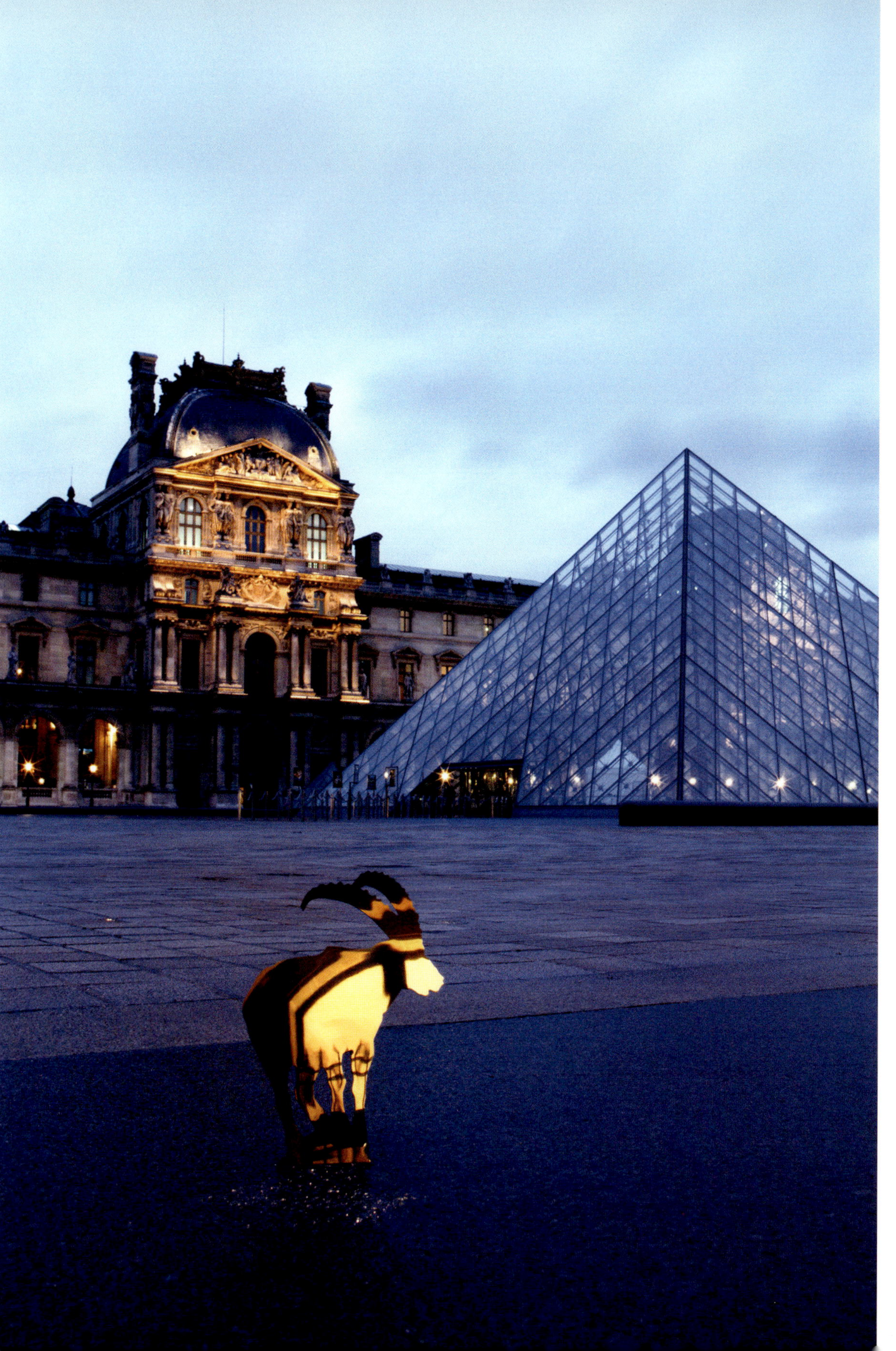

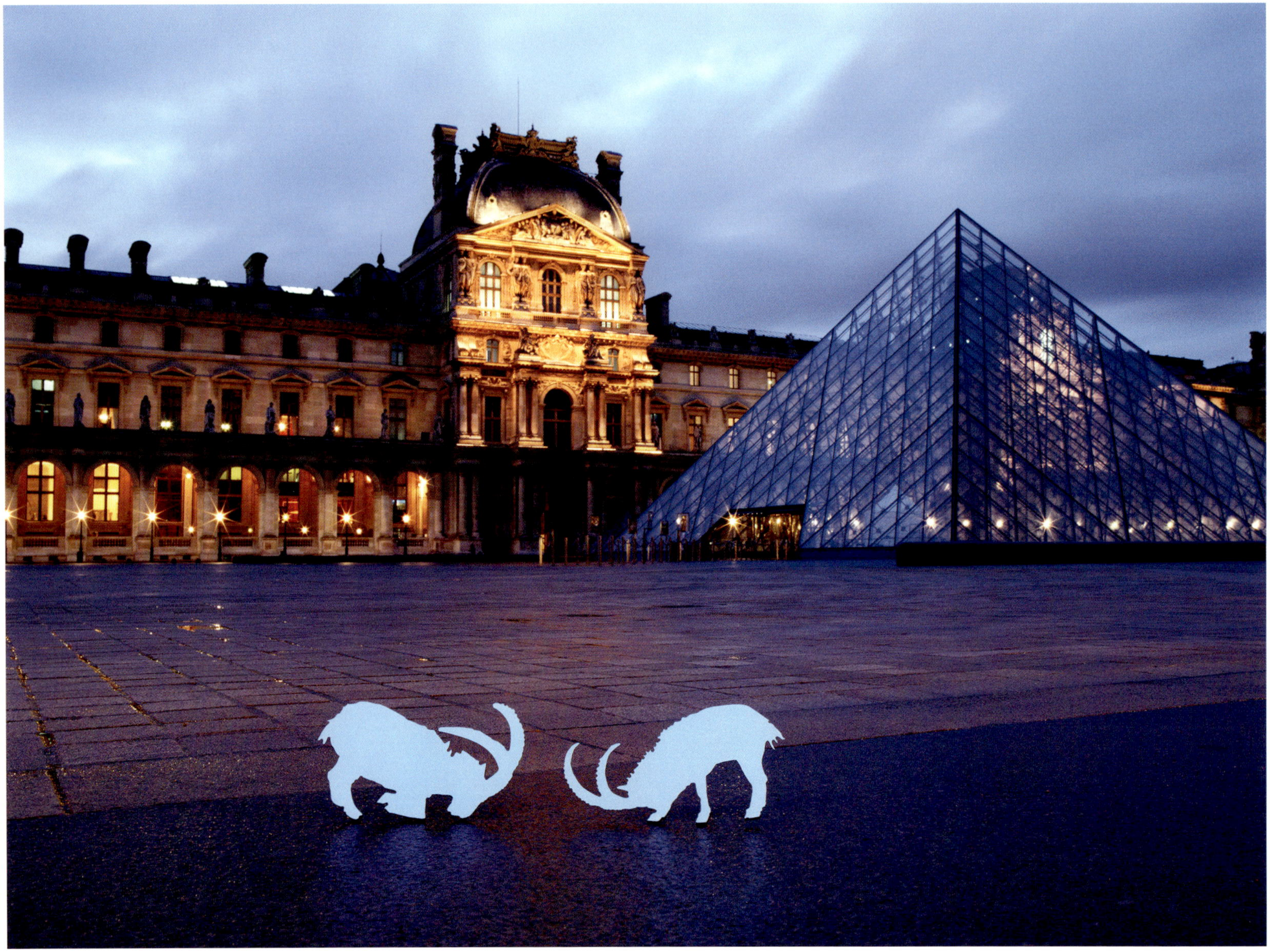

Ibex - Louvre - Paris I
野山羊—卢浮宫—巴黎I

2006
Durst Lambda print
52x72cm

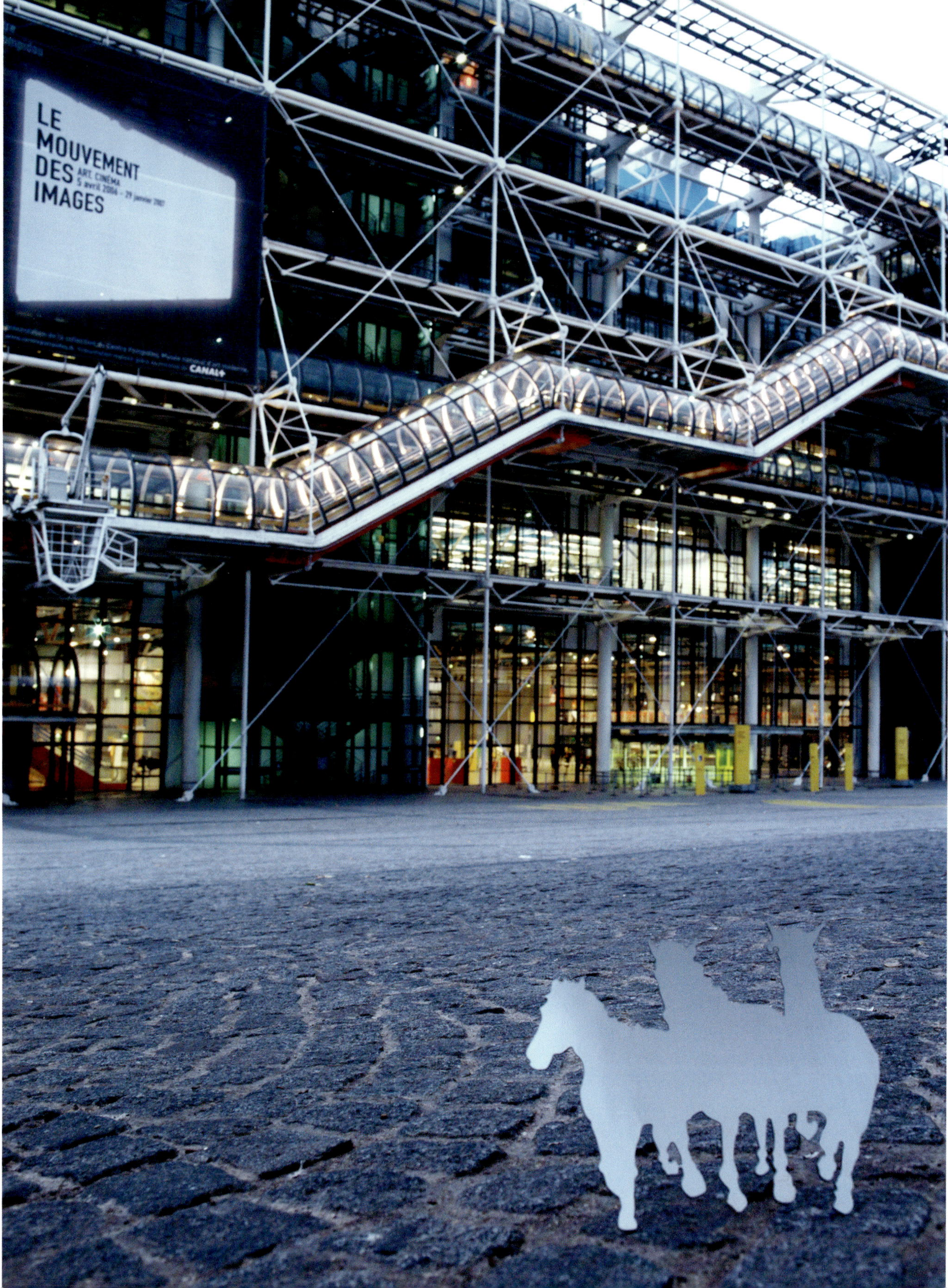

Camargue Horses - Pompidou - Paris
卡马格马—蓬皮杜艺术中心—巴

2006
Durst Lambda print
72x52см

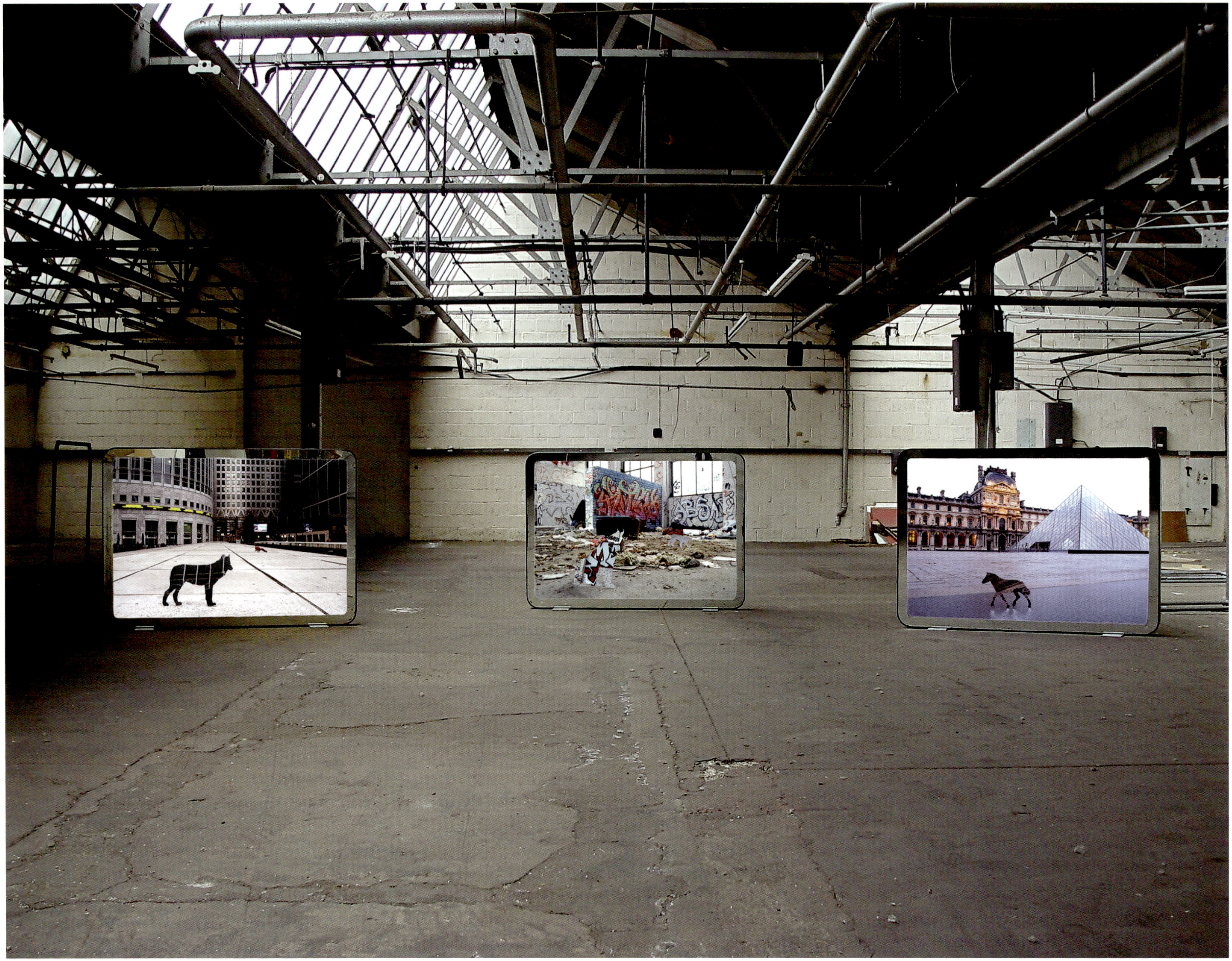

Lynx - Lehderstrasse 32 - Berlin I
灯箱装置 + 山猫—Lehderstrasse 32—柏林I
2007
Recycled advertising lightbox
广告灯箱使用再生材料制作
131x190x16cm

Lightbox Installation, London
灯箱装置 伦敦
2007
131x190x16cm EACH
Recycled advertising lightboxes
广告灯箱使用再生材料制作

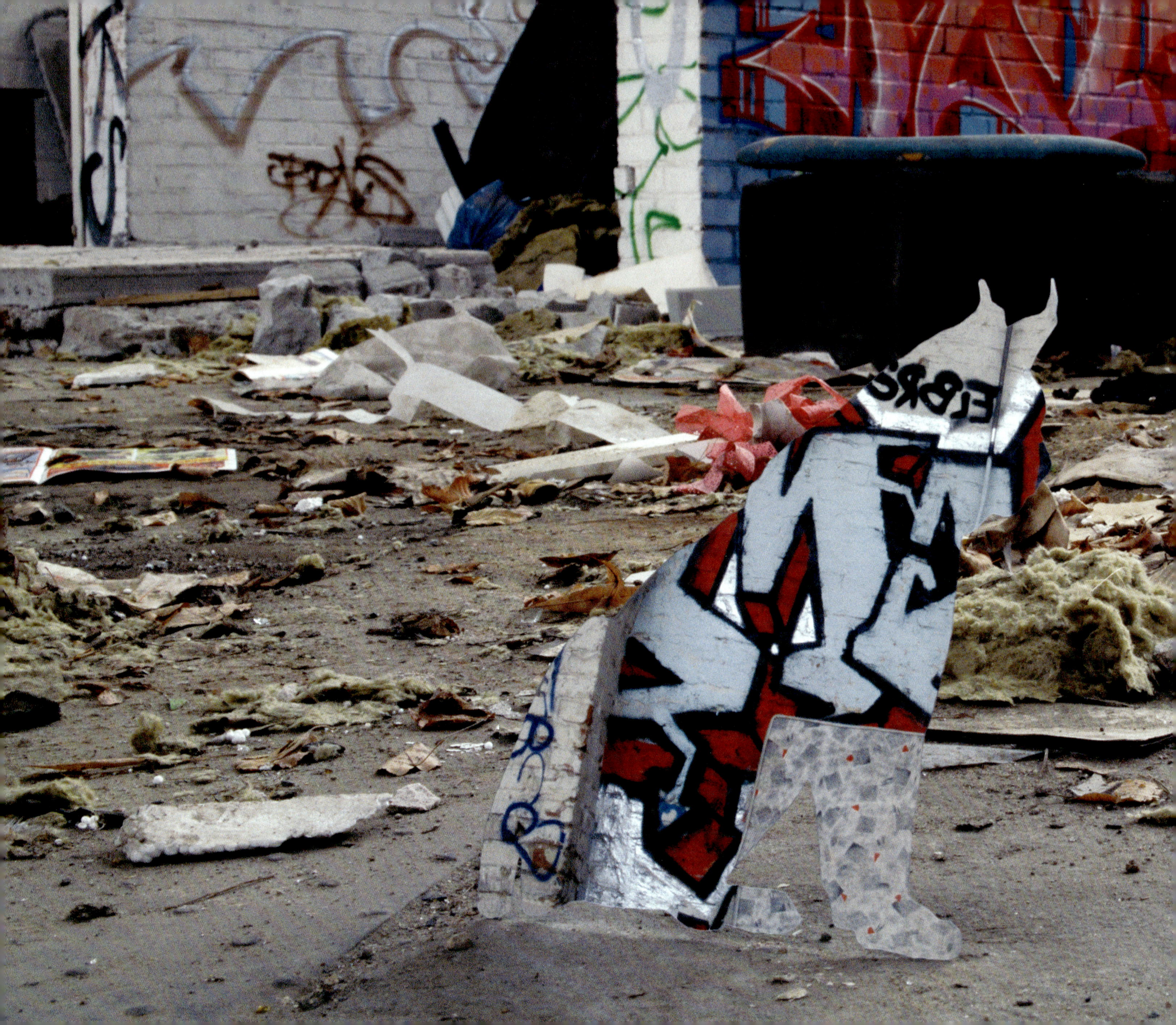

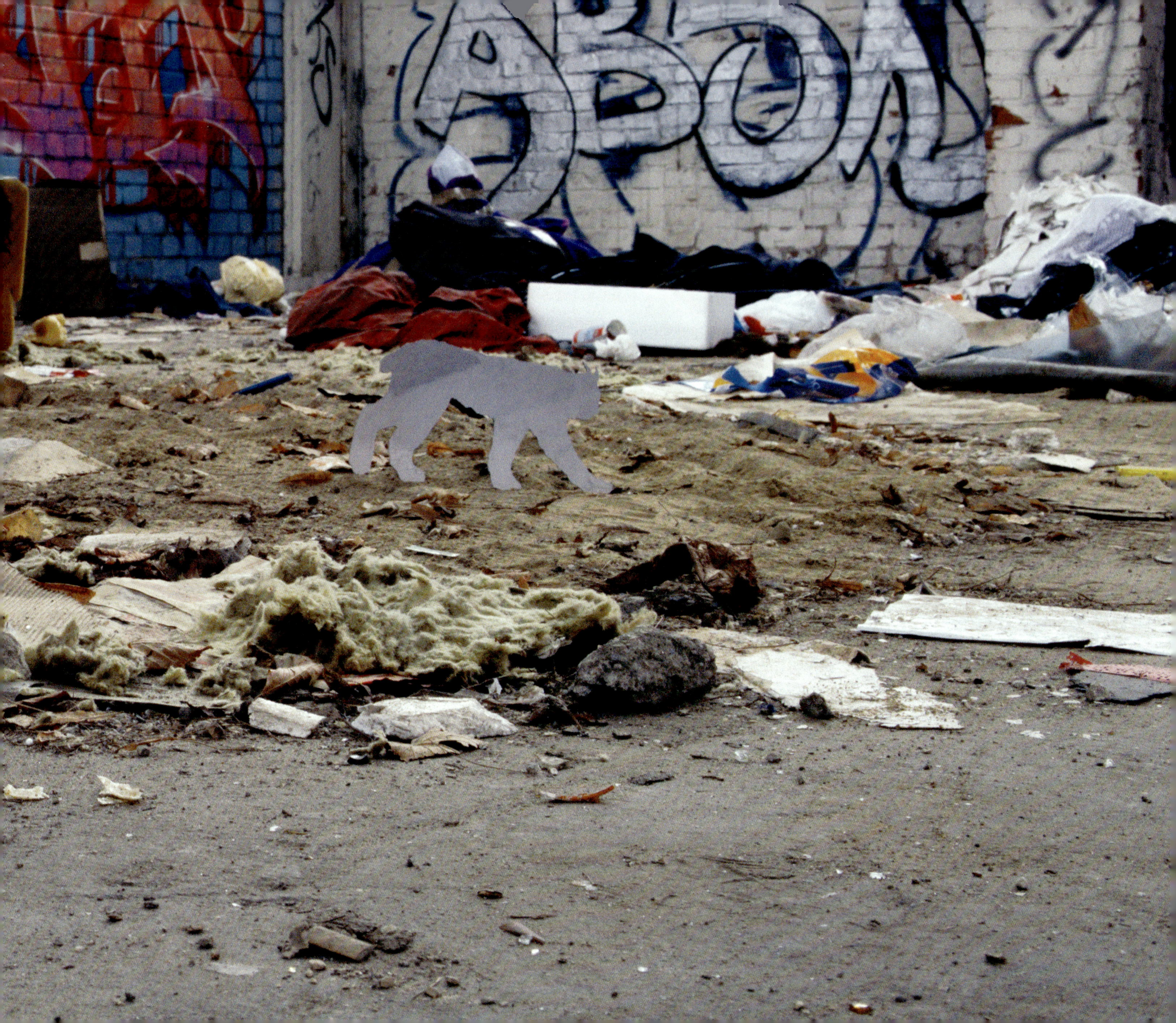

Eagle Owl - Reichstag - Berlin
鹰·猫头鹰—Reichstag—柏林

2007
Durst Lambda print
52x72см

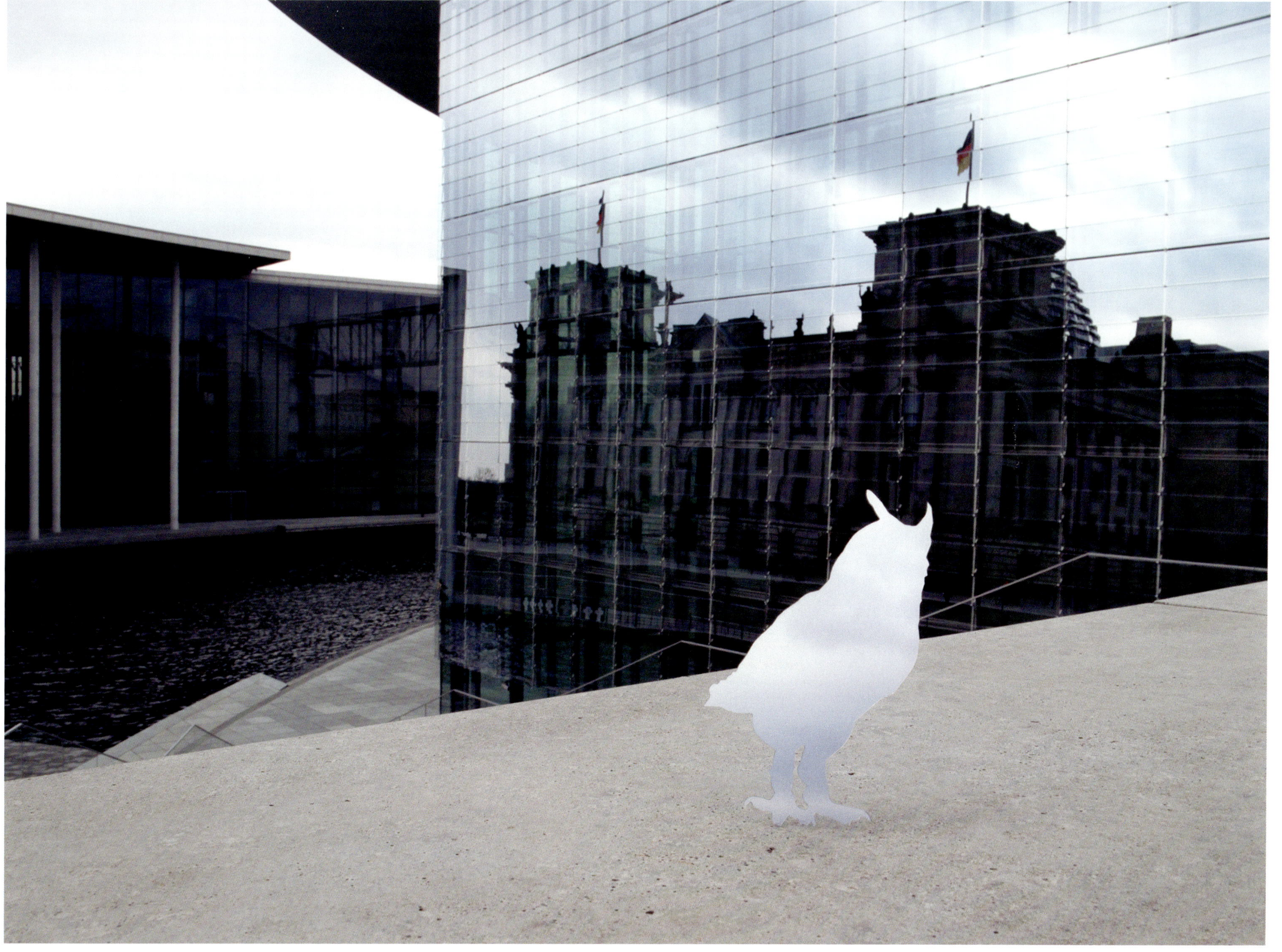

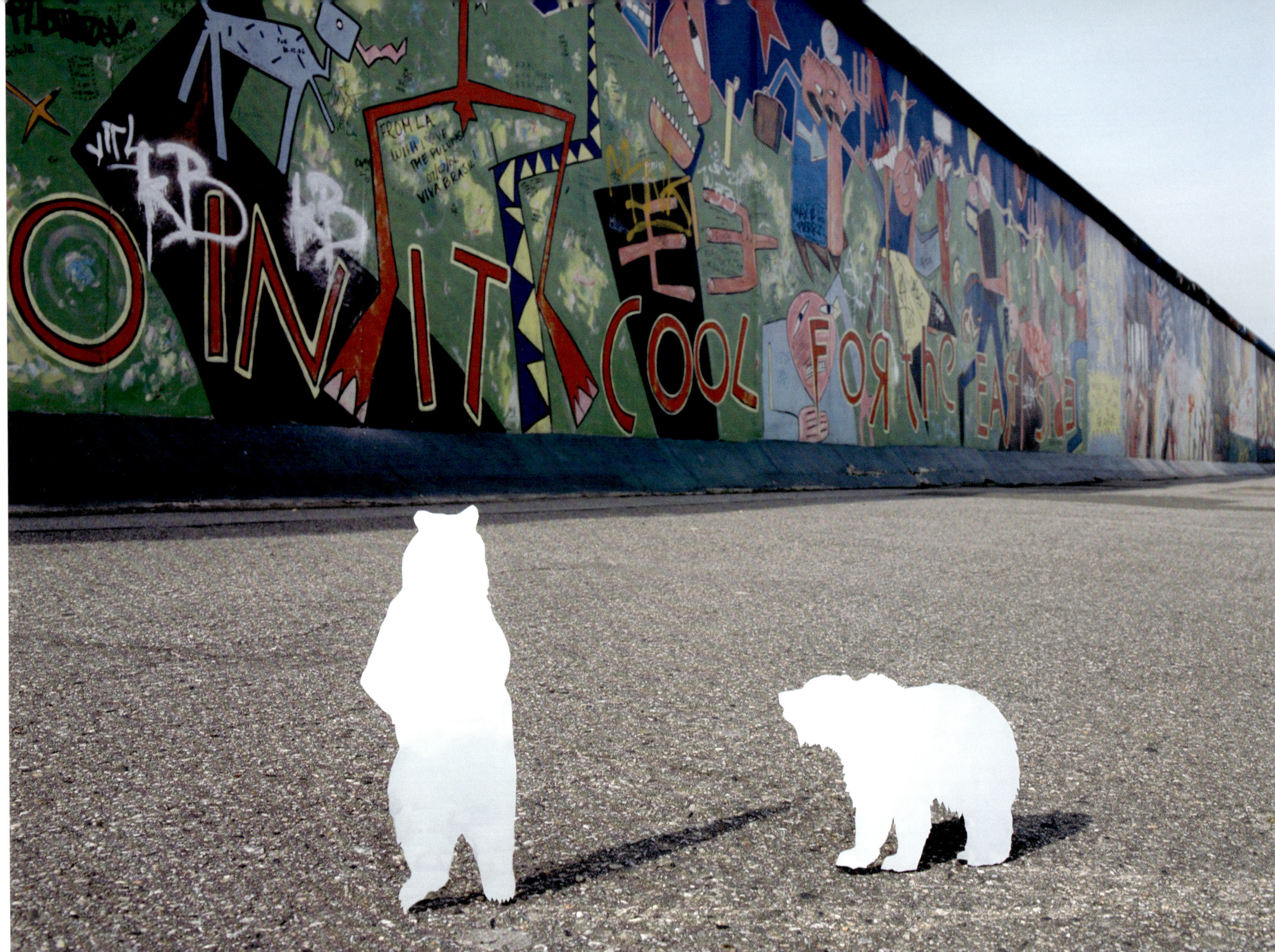
FROM LA
WITH LOVE
THE PULLING
VIVA BRASIL
IT COOL FOR THE EAST SIDE

European Brown Bear - The Wall - Berlin
欧洲棕熊—墙—柏林

2007
Durst Lambda print
52x72cm

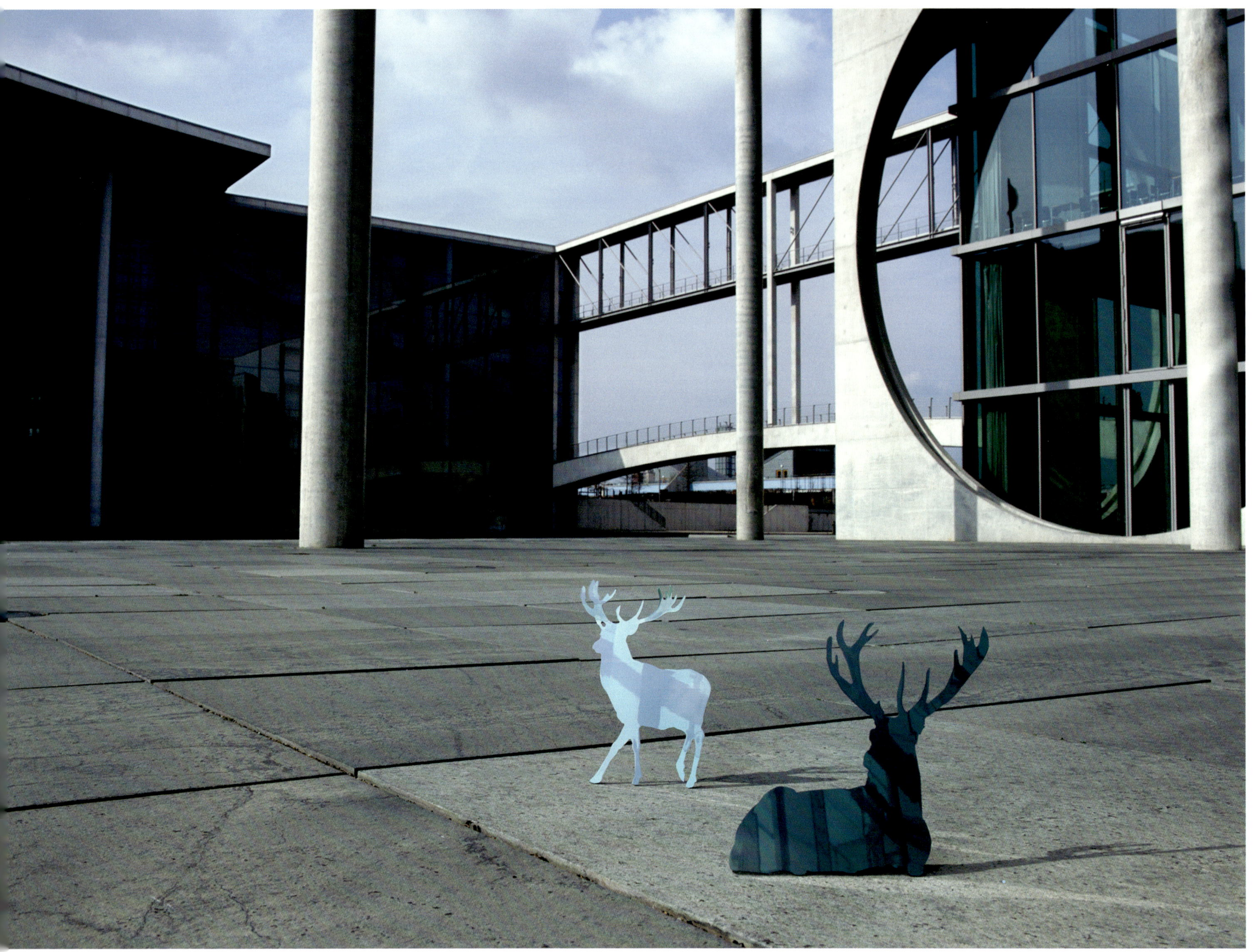

Red Deer - Bibliotheque German Parliament - Berlin
红鹿一德国议会图书馆一柏林

2007
Durst Lambda print
52x72cm

Lynx - Berliner Dom - Berlin
野山羊—柏林大教堂—柏林

2007
Durst Lambda print
52x72cm

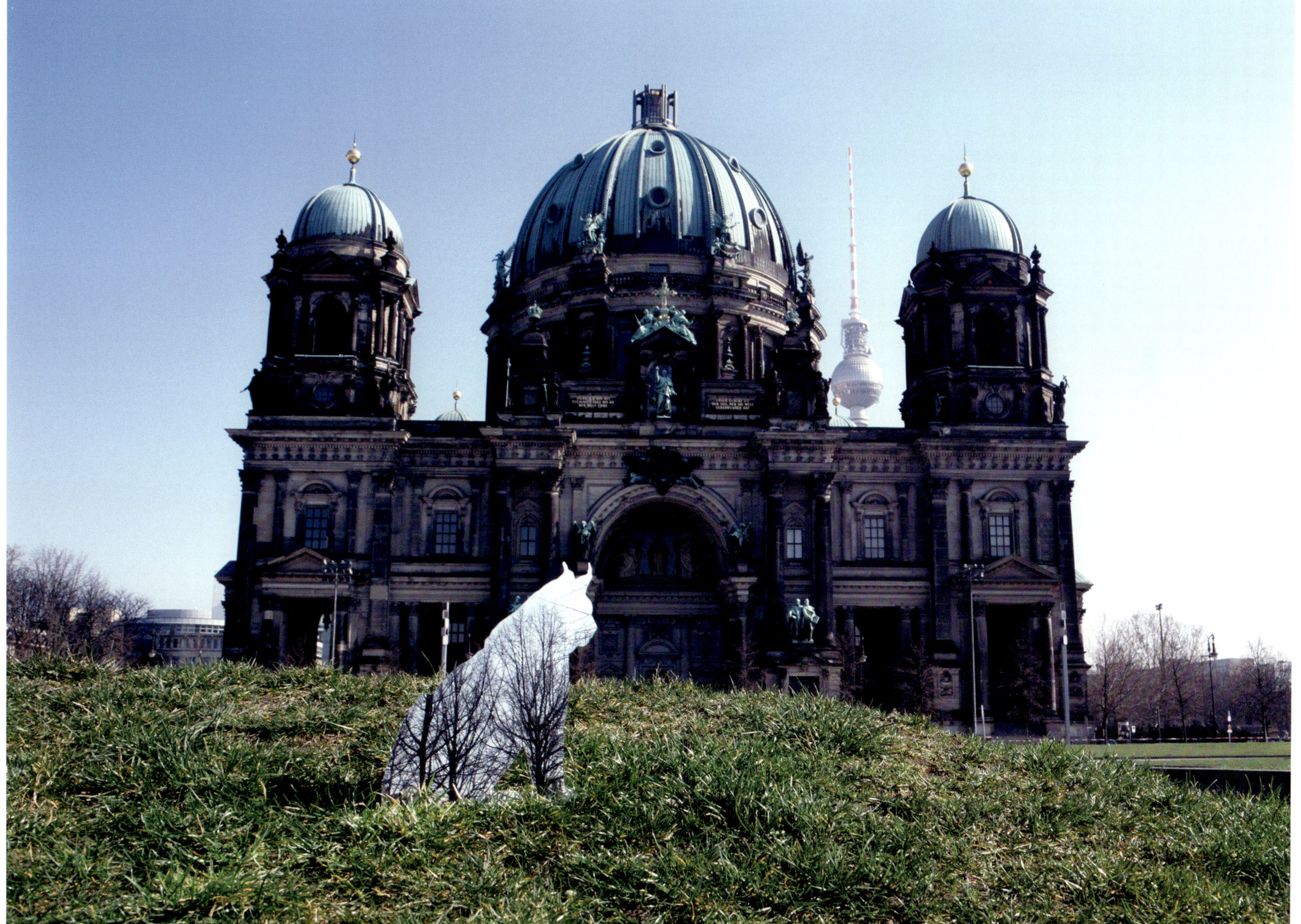

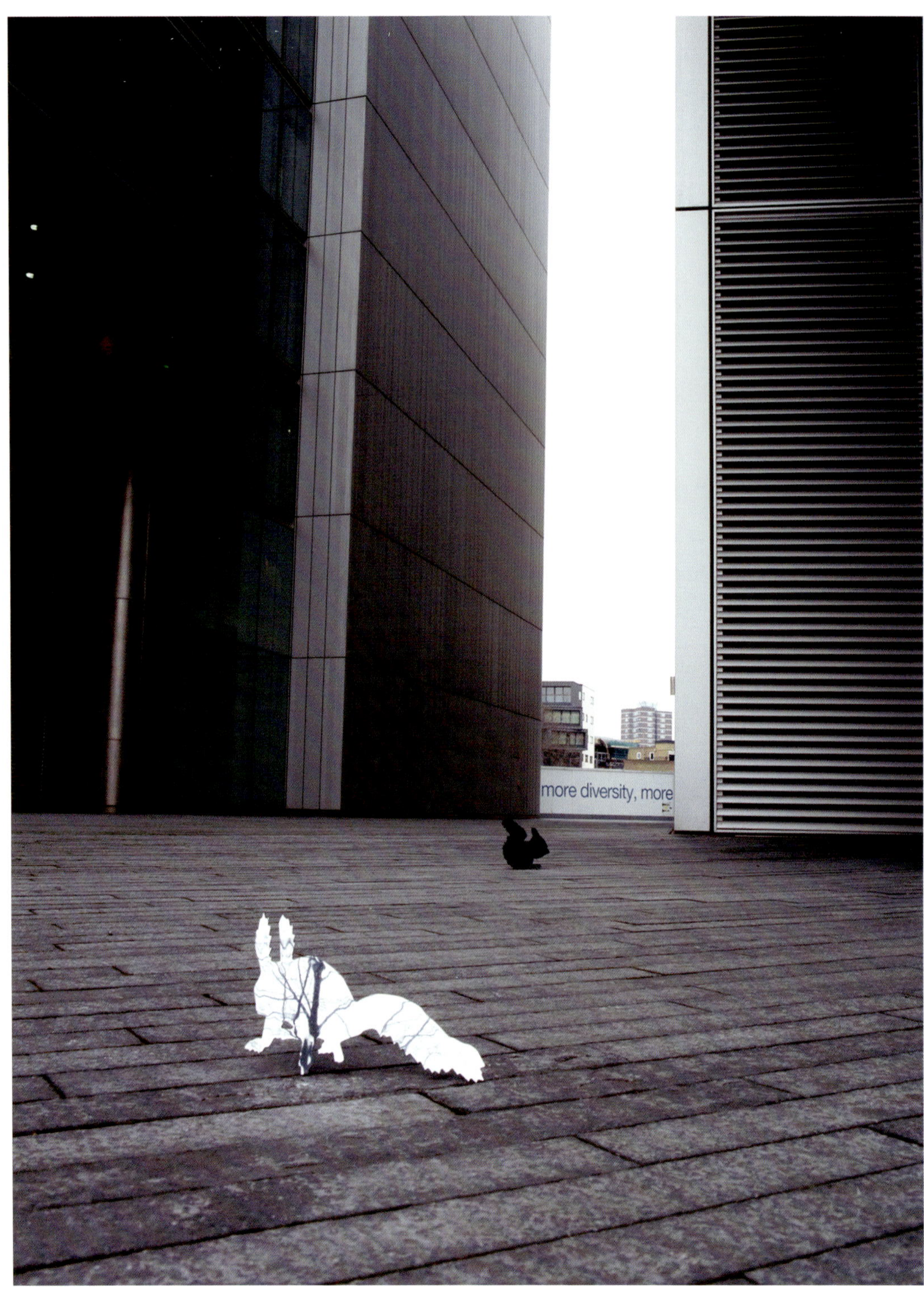

Red Squirrel - More - London
红松鼠—更多—伦敦

2007
Durst Lambda print
72x52cm

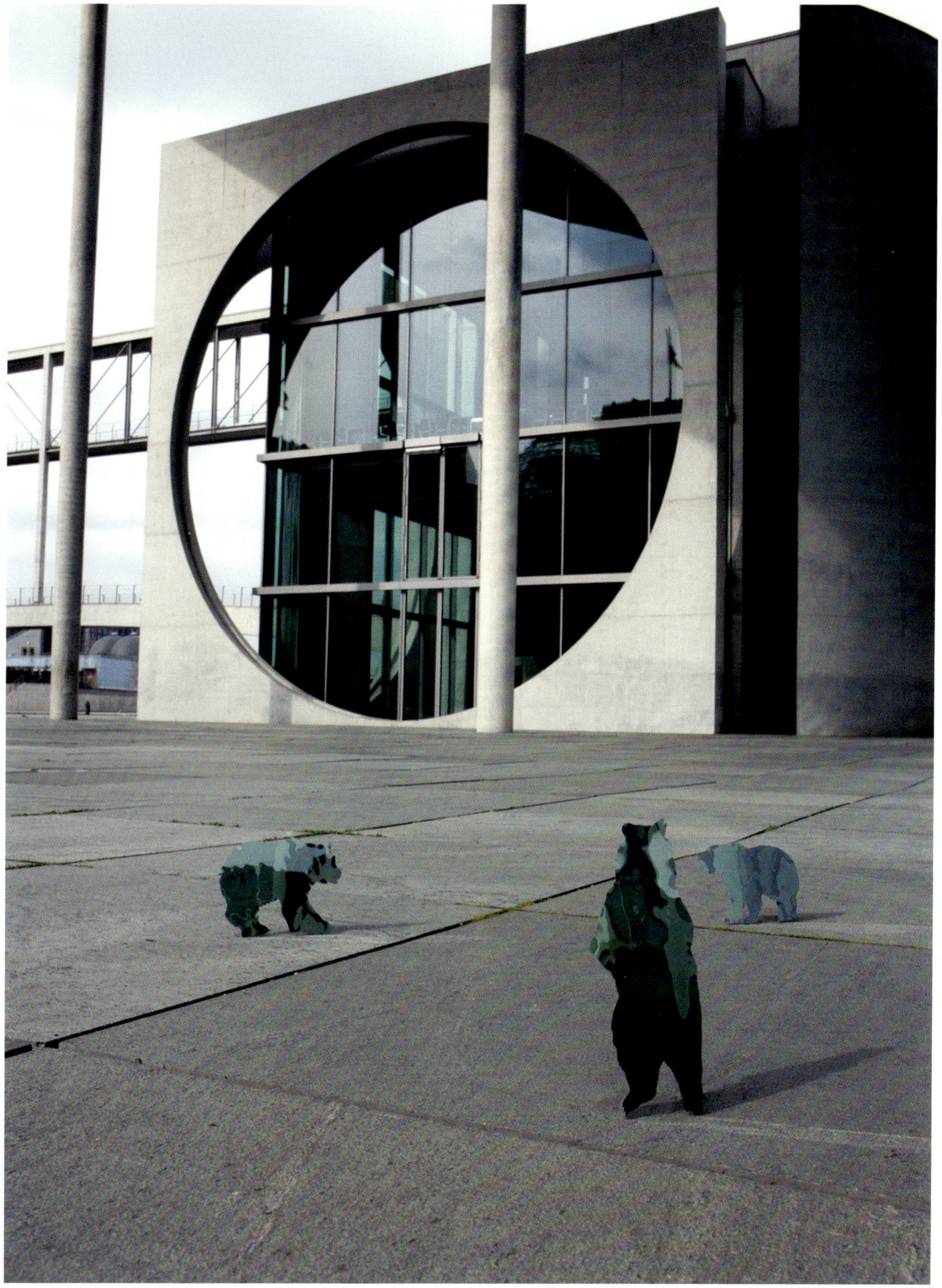

European Brown Bear - Bibliotheque German Parliament - Berlin 143
欧洲棕熊一德国议会图书馆一柏林

2007
Durst Lambda print
160x120cm

Roe Deer - Docklands - London I
狍鹿—Docklands—伦敦I

2007
Durst Lambda print
120x160см

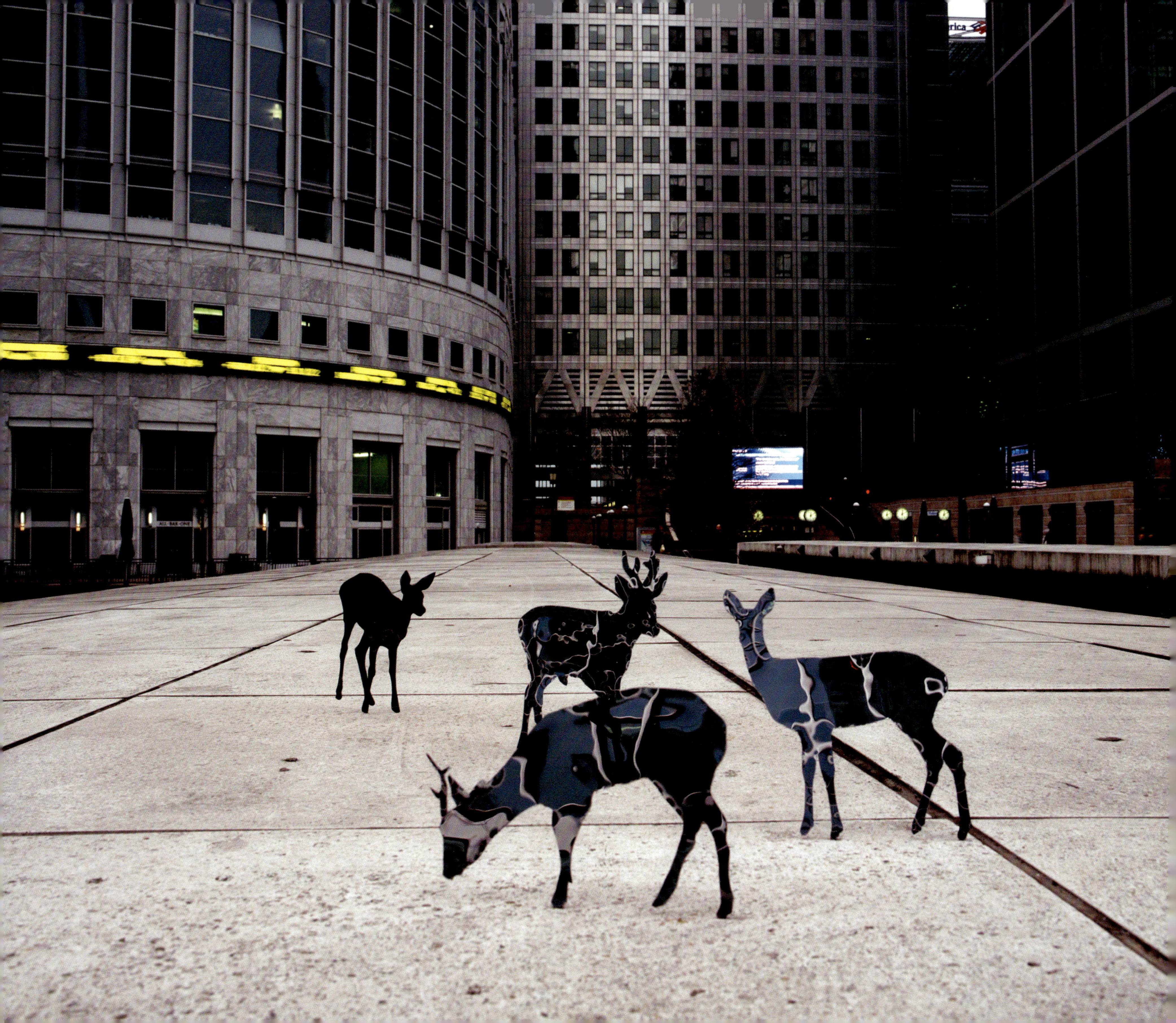

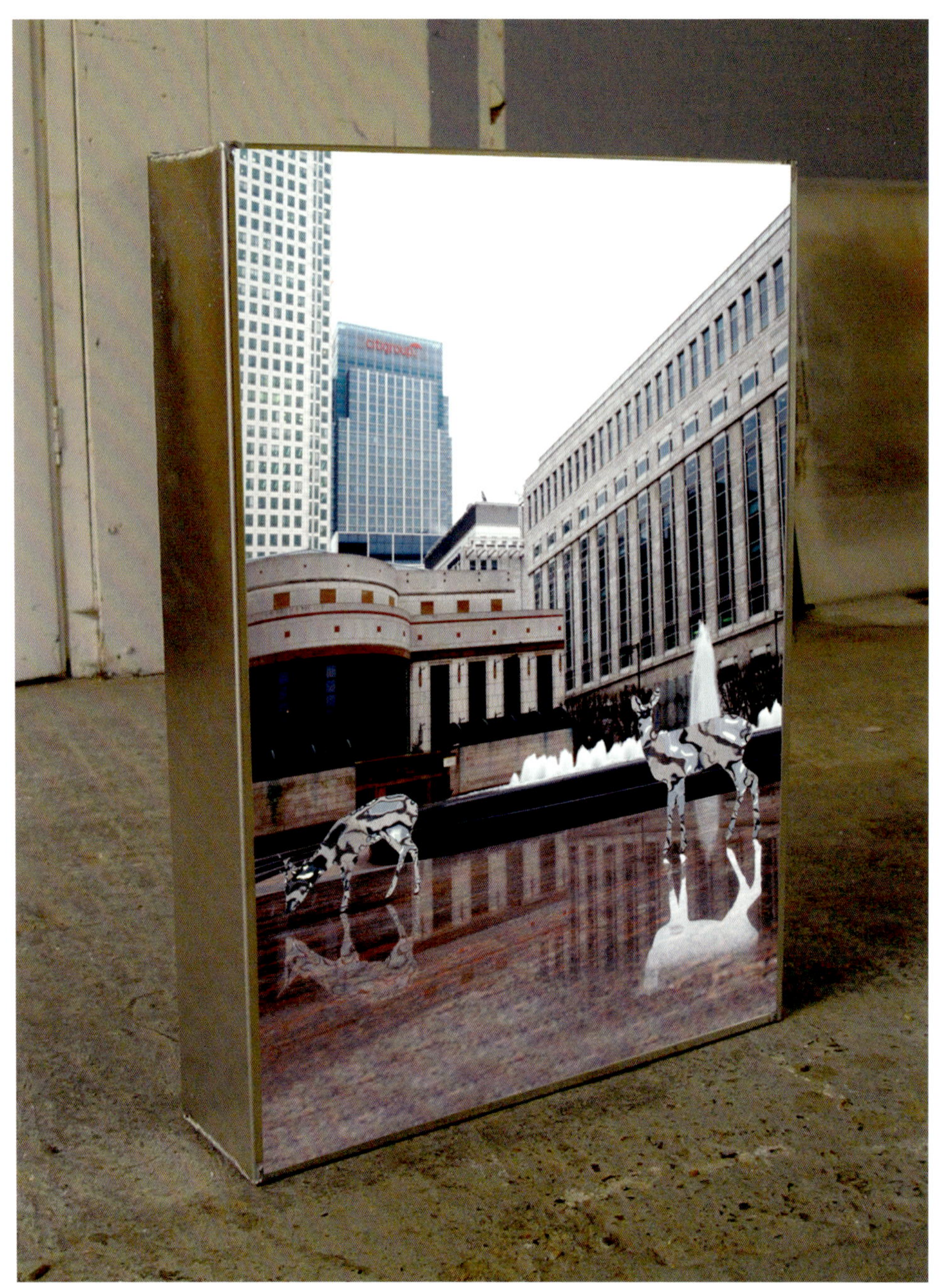

Roe Deer - Docklands - London II
狍鹿—Docklands—伦敦II

2007
Bespoke lightbox
定做的灯箱
74.4x54.4x11см

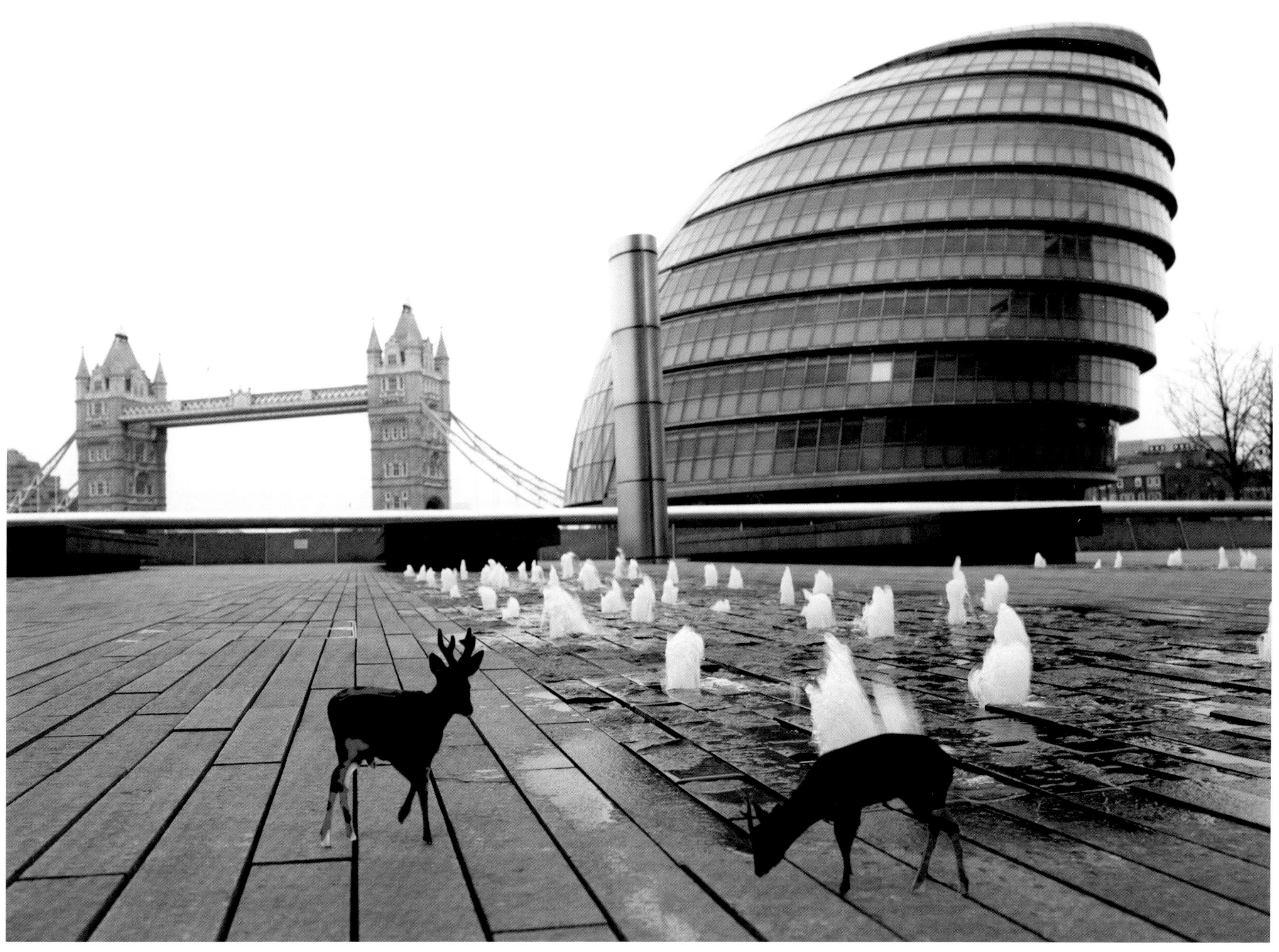

Roe Deer - City Hall - London III
狍鹿－市政厅－伦敦III
2007
Durst Lambda print
52x72cm

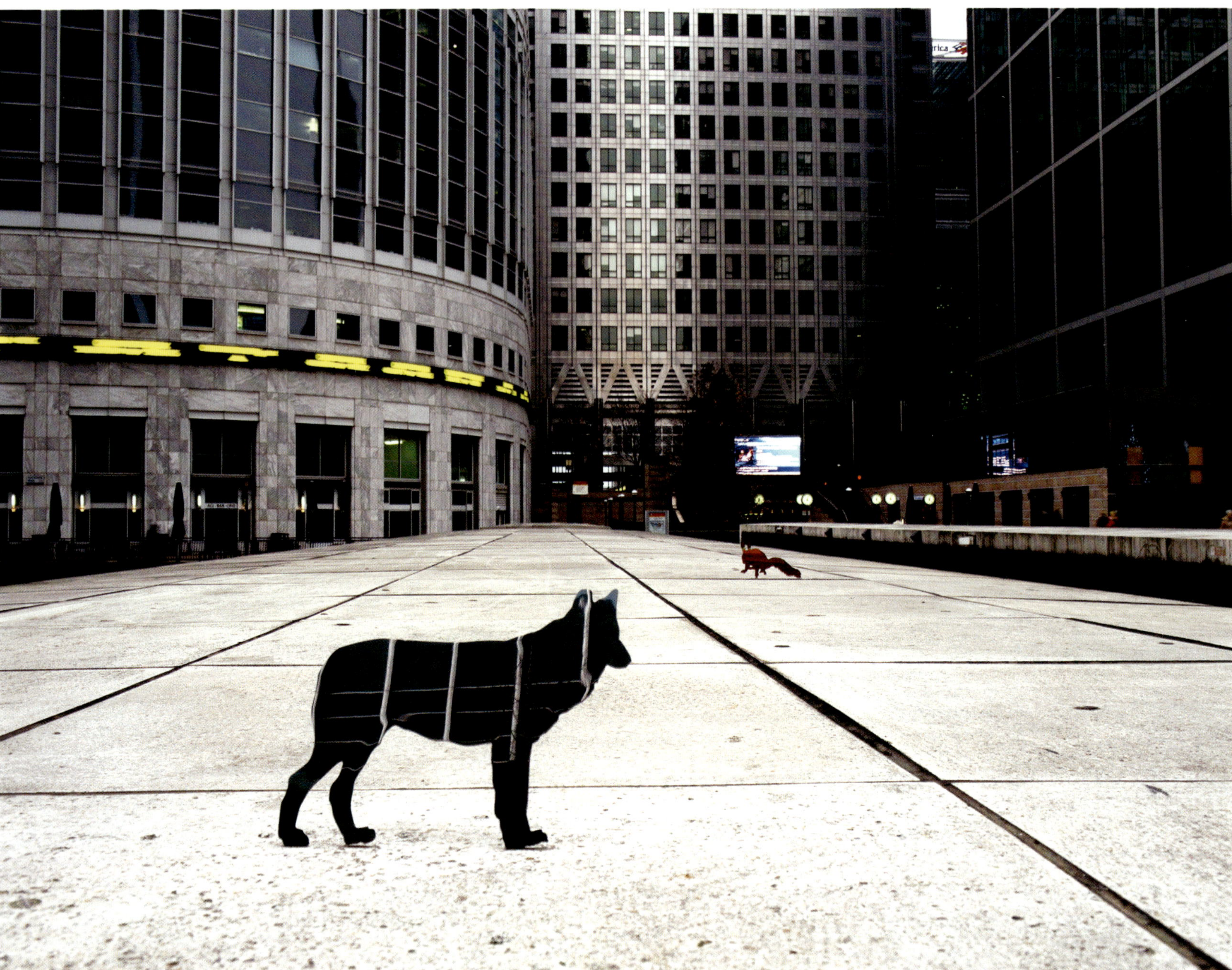

European Wolf Red Squirrel - Docklands - London
欧洲狼·红松鼠—Docklands—伦敦
2007
Recycled advertising lightbox
广告灯箱使用再生材料制作
131x190x16cm

INSTALLATION, SCULPTURE AND MIXED MEDIA

装置艺术、雕塑艺术以及混合媒体艺术

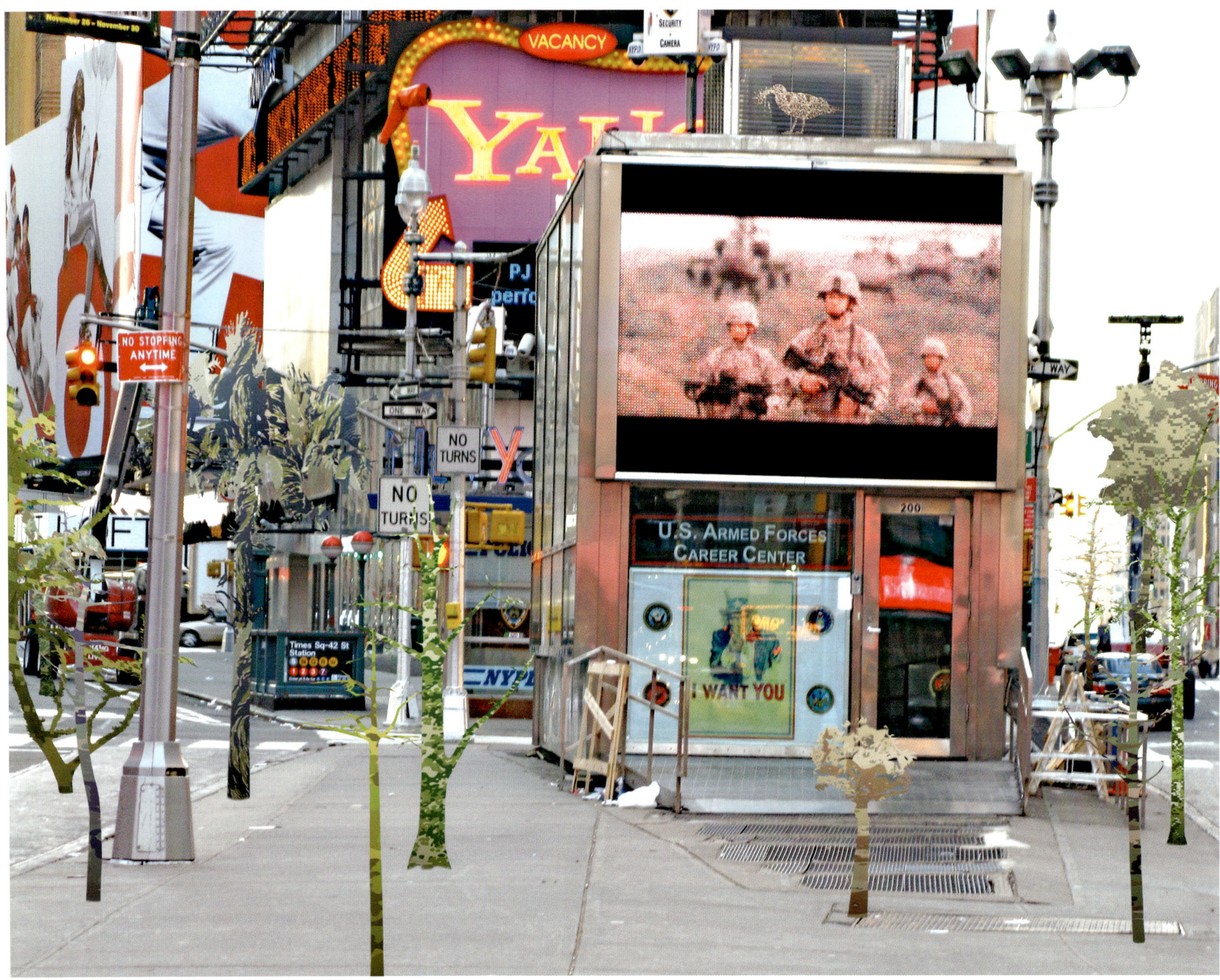

Because There Is Nothing On This Green Earth That Is Stronger Than No.3
因为这个绿色地球上没有更强的

2008
Durst Lambda print (from animation still)
46x60cm

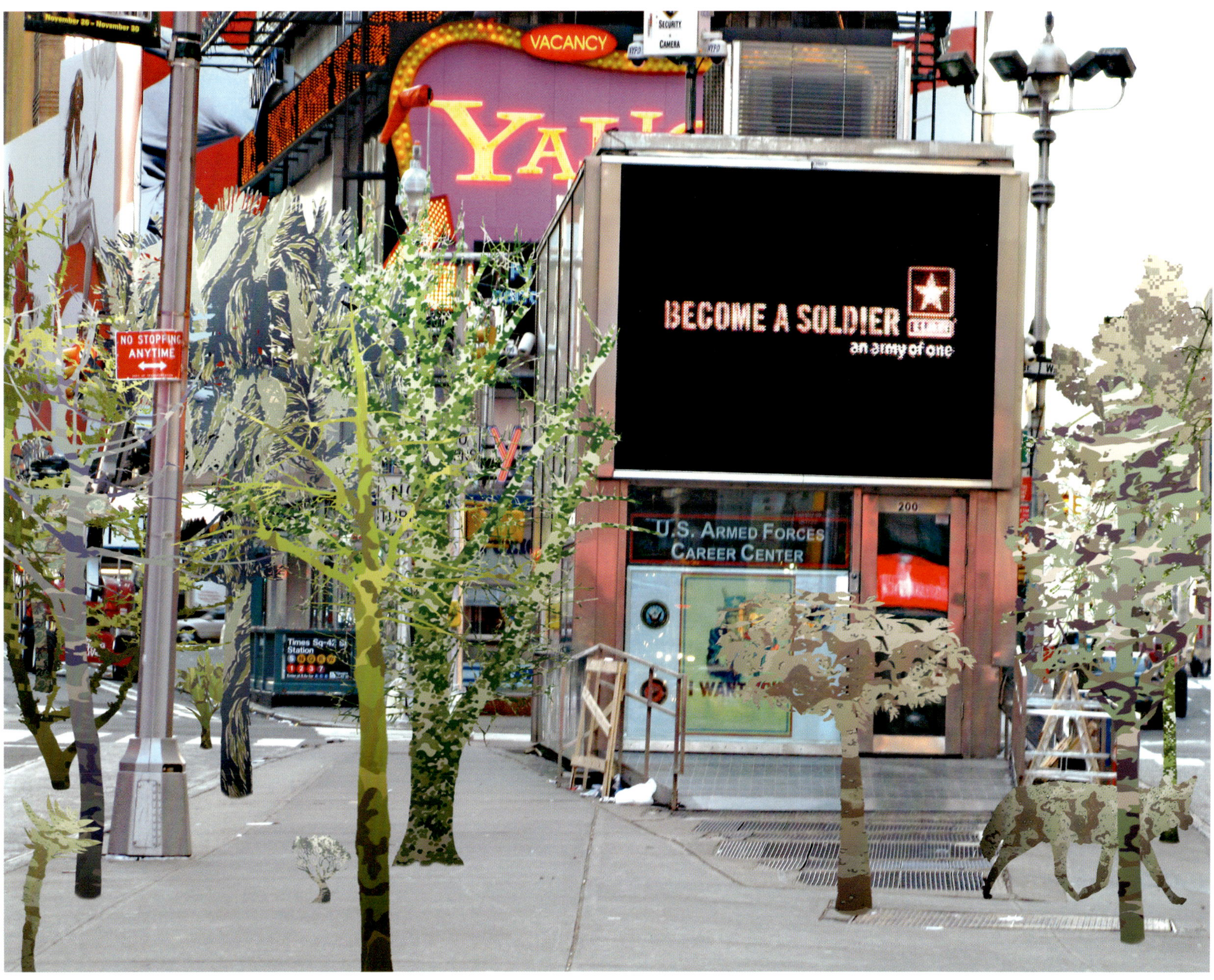

Because There Is Nothing On This Green Earth That Is Stronger Than No. 14
因为这个绿色地球上没有更强的

2008
Durst Lambda print (from animation still)
46x60см

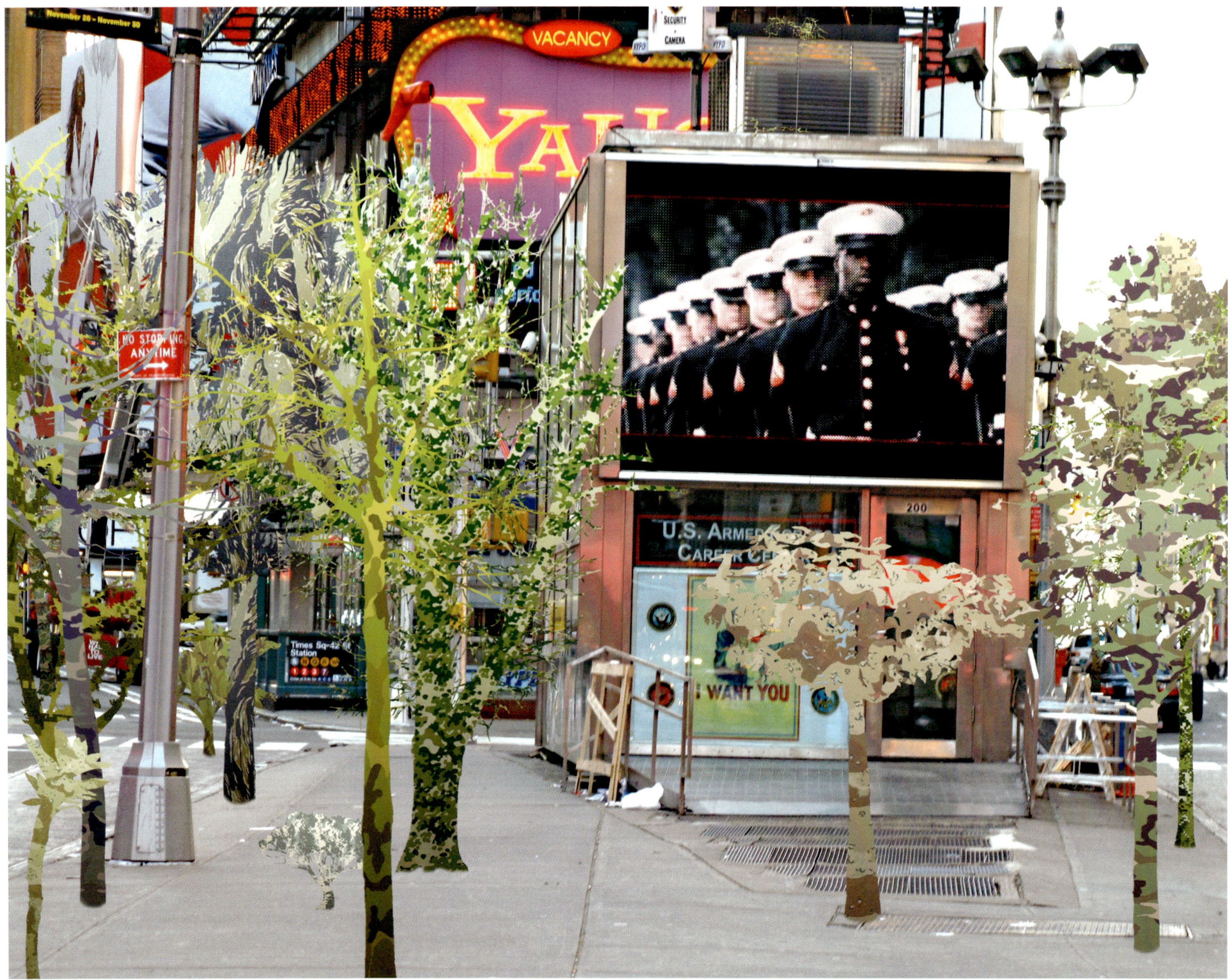

Because There Is Nothing On This Green Earth That Is Stronger Than No 20
因为这个绿色地球上没有更强的

2008
Durst Lambda print (from animation still)
46x60см

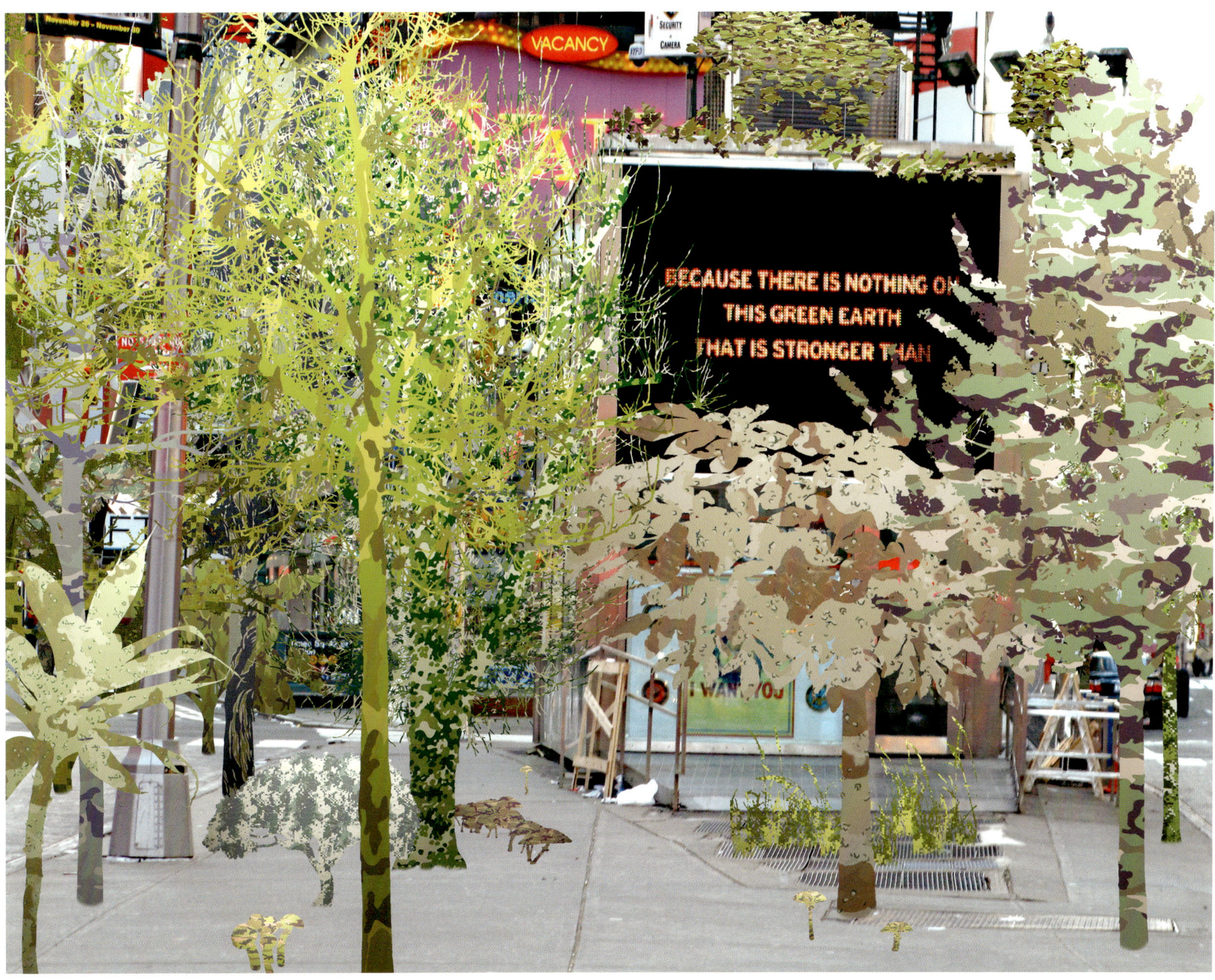

Because There Is Nothing On This Green Earth That Is Stronger Than No 36
因为这个绿色地球上没有更强的

2008
Durst Lambda print (from animation still)
46x60см

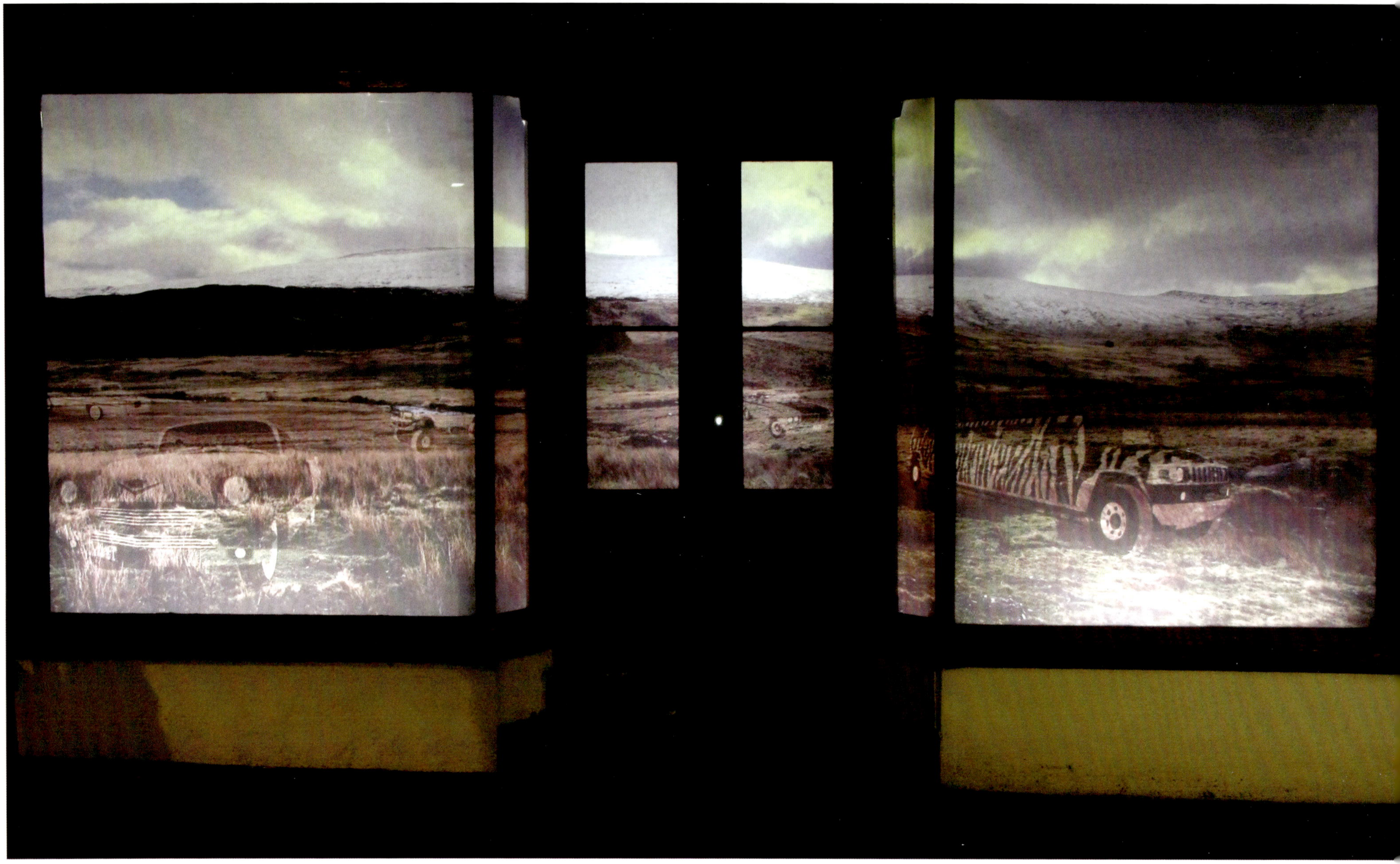

DETAIL ON FOLLOWING PAGE:
下页图片：

All Terrain
所有领域

2008
Dimensions variable
Installation: Print on backlit paper, lighting
Margate Rocks 08 Festival of Contemporary Visual Art
尺寸可以变动
装置材料：背光纸印刷、照明设备、
08玛尔格特岩石、当代视觉艺术节

All Terrain
所有领域

2008
Dimensions variable
Installation: Print on backlit paper, lighting
Margate Rocks 08 Festival of Contemporary Visual Art
尺寸可以变动
装置材料：背光纸印刷、照明设备、
08玛尔格特岩石、当代视觉艺术节

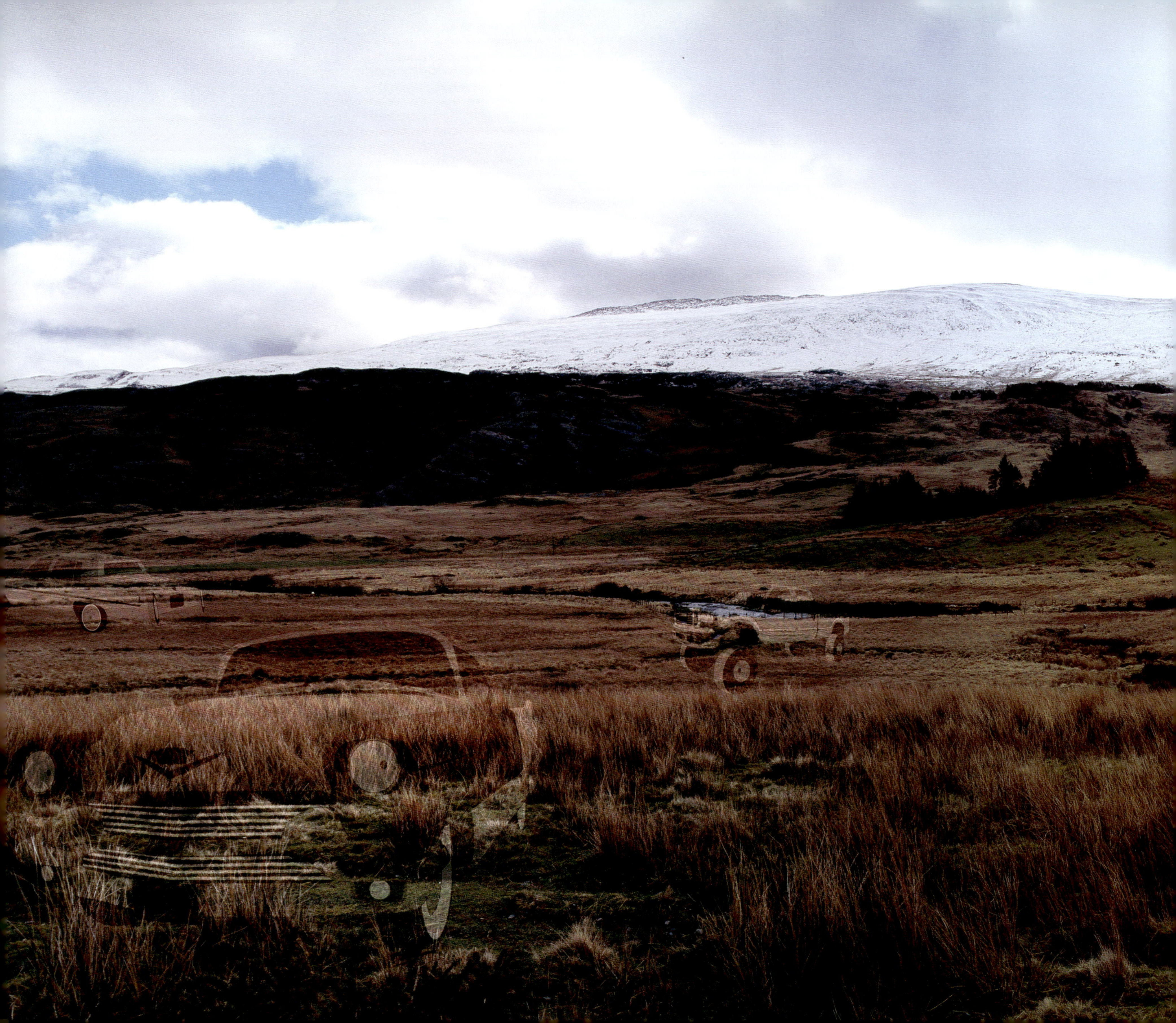

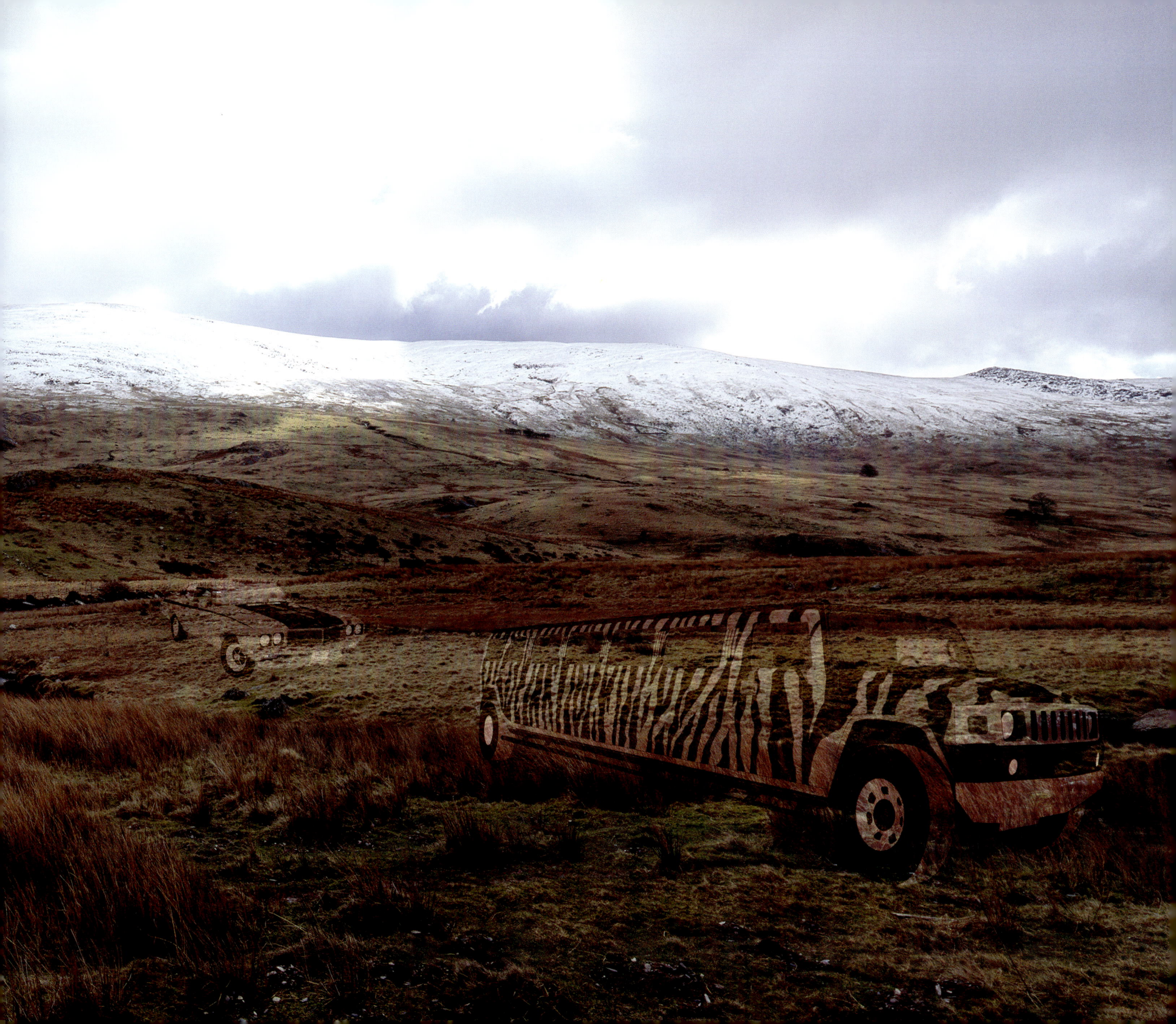

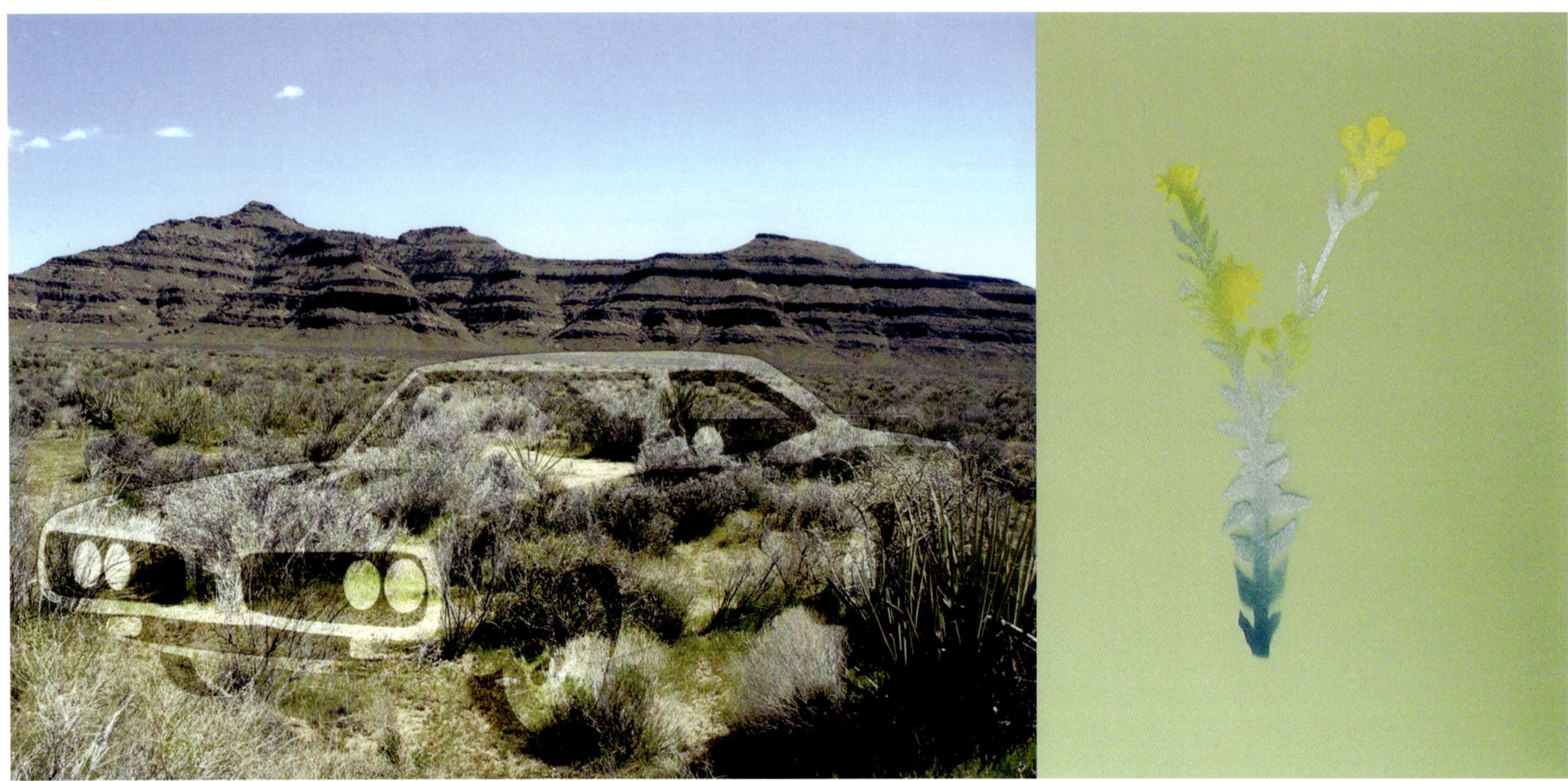

Endangered Americans - Florida Golden Aster
濒危的美国人—佛罗里达金菊

2007
Photographic hand-cut collage and metallic car
paint drawing
照片手刻拼贴画和金属汽车
颜料绘画
32x67cm

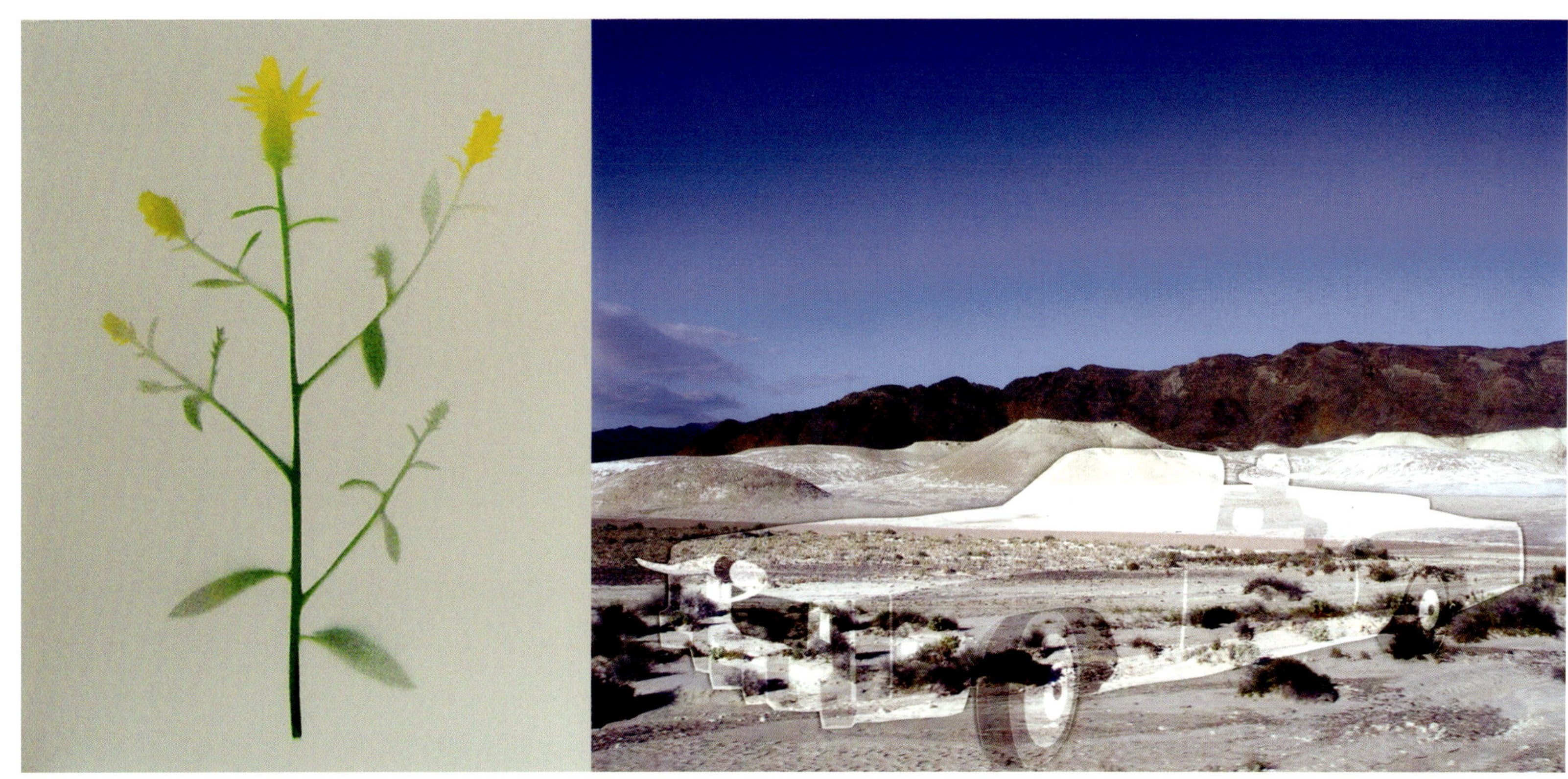

Endangered Americans - Way-side Aster
濒危的美国人—路边菊

2007
Photographic hand-cut collage and metallic car
paint drawing
照片手刻拼贴画和金属汽车
颜料绘画
32x67cm

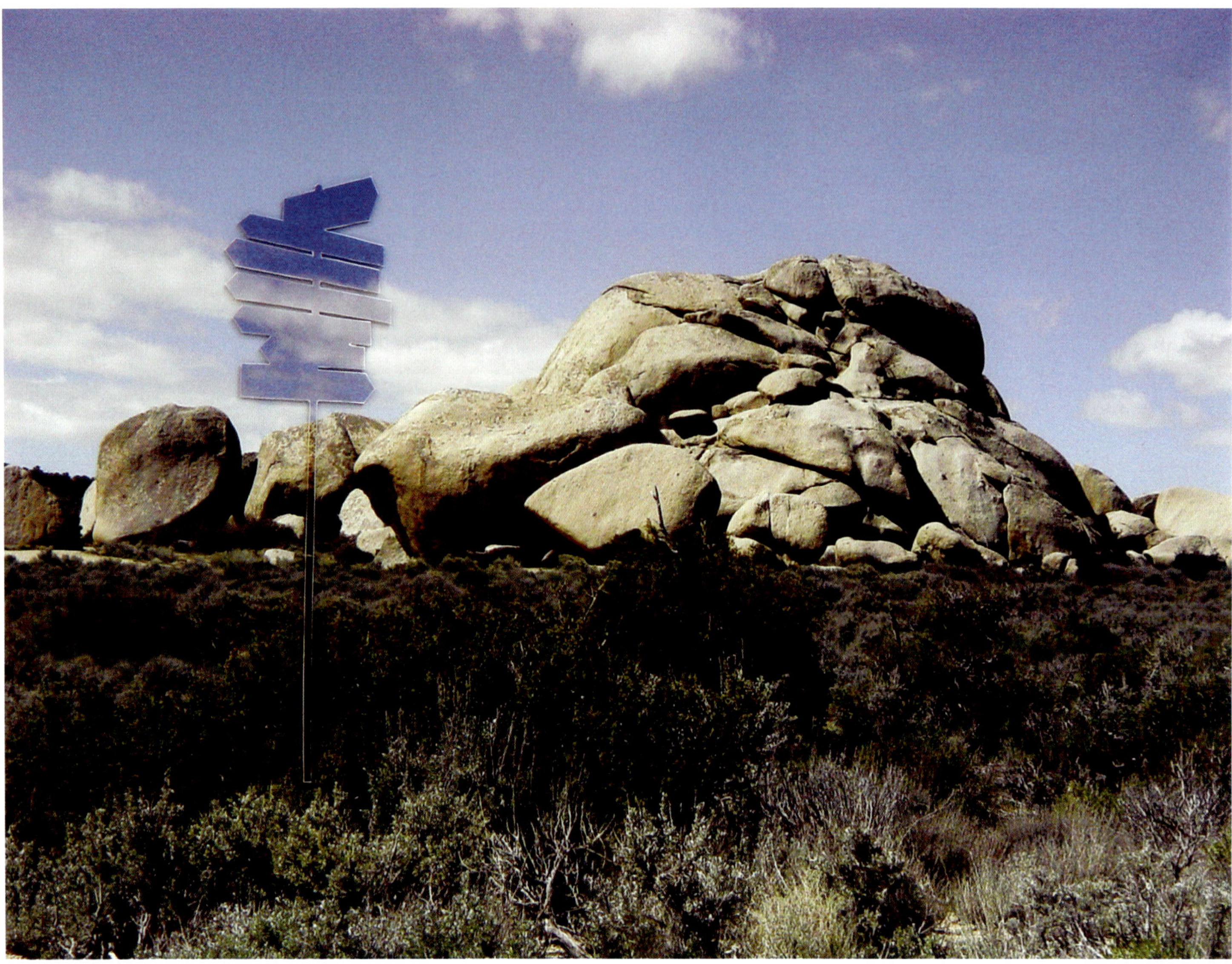

Under Construction I
施工中I

2007
Photographic hand-cut collage
照片手刻拼贴画
21x29.5cm

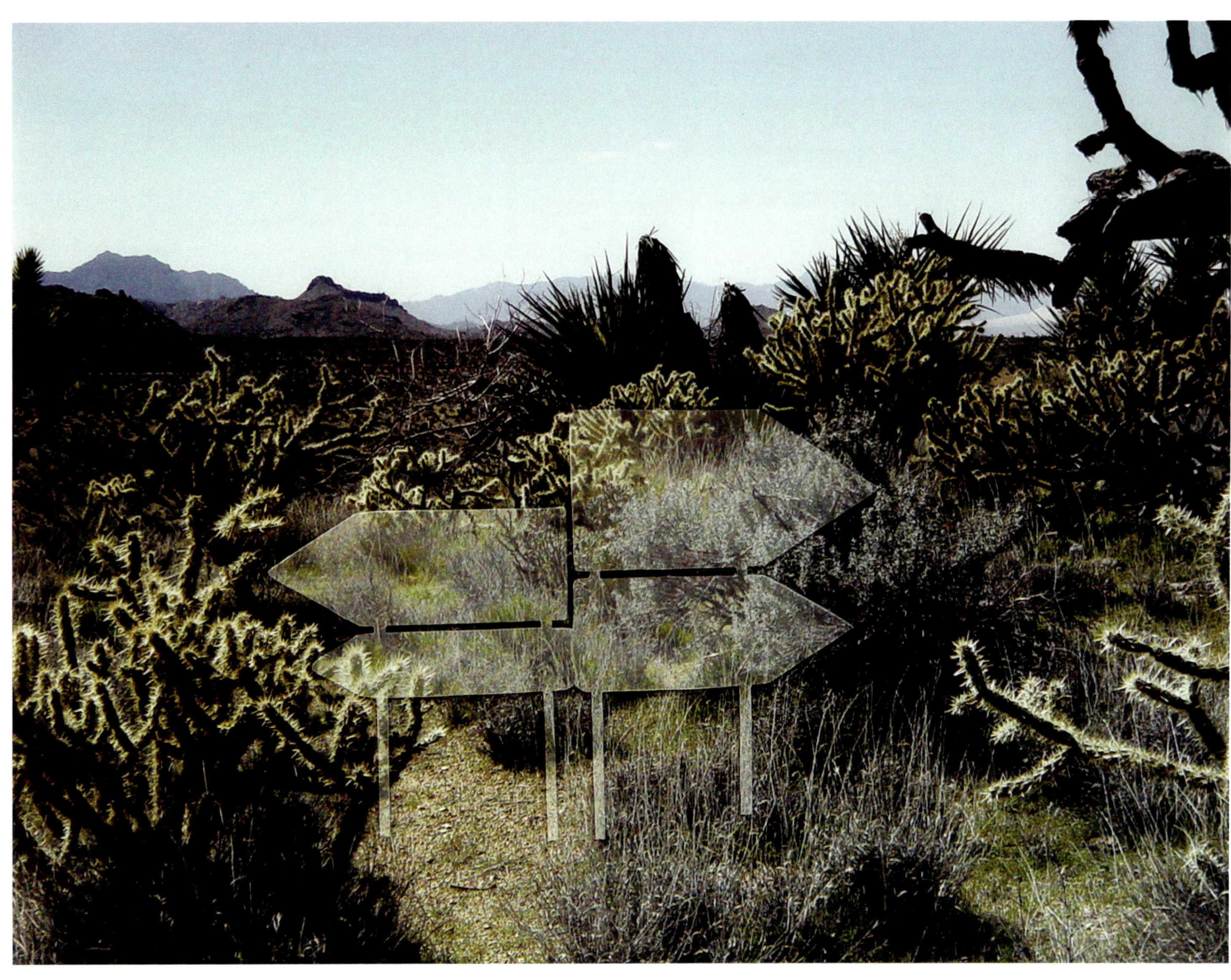

Under Construction II
施工中II

2007
Photographic hand-cut collage
照片手刻拼贴画
21x29.5cm

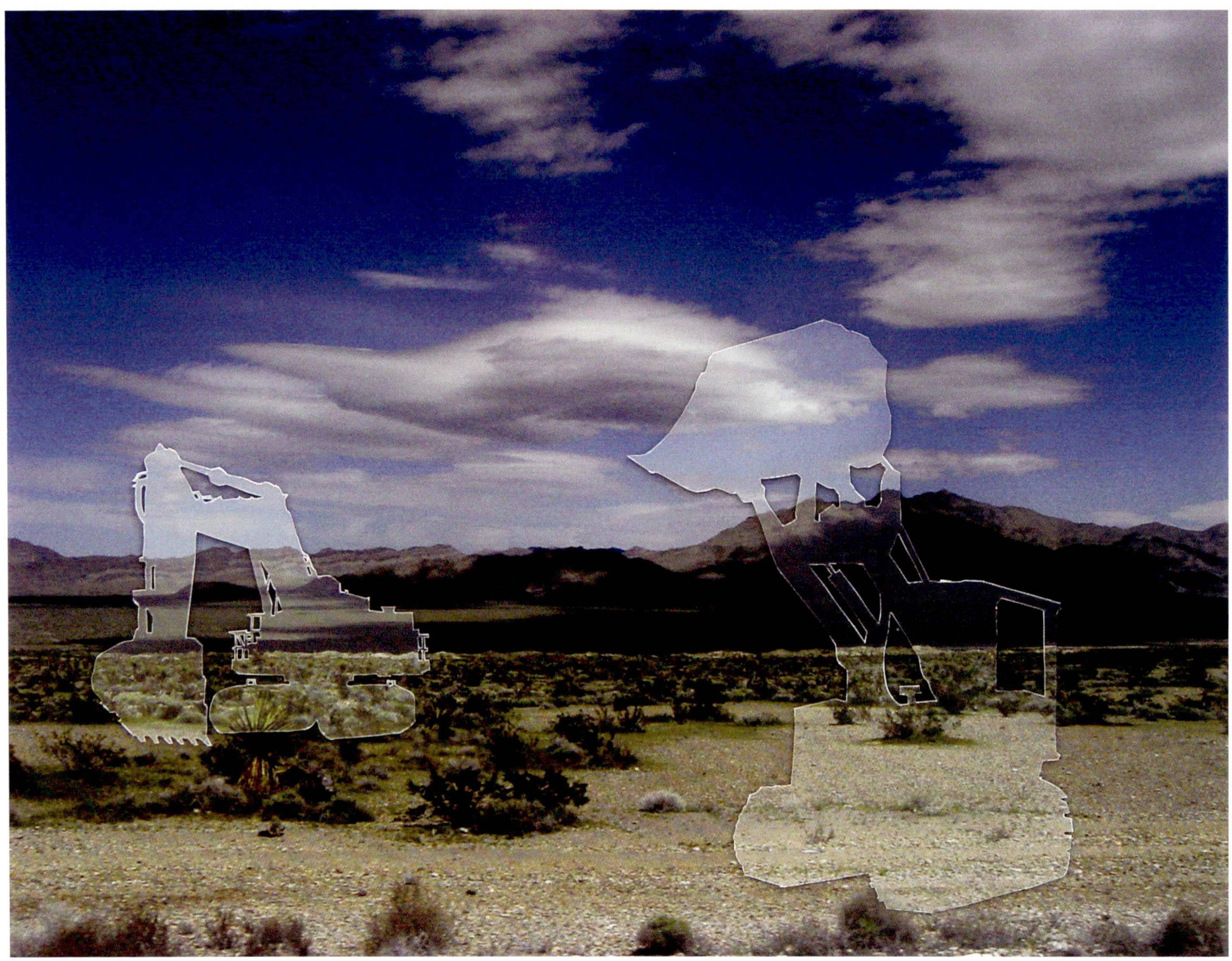

Under Construction III
施工中III

2007
Photographic hand-cut collage
照片手刻拼贴画
21x29.5cm

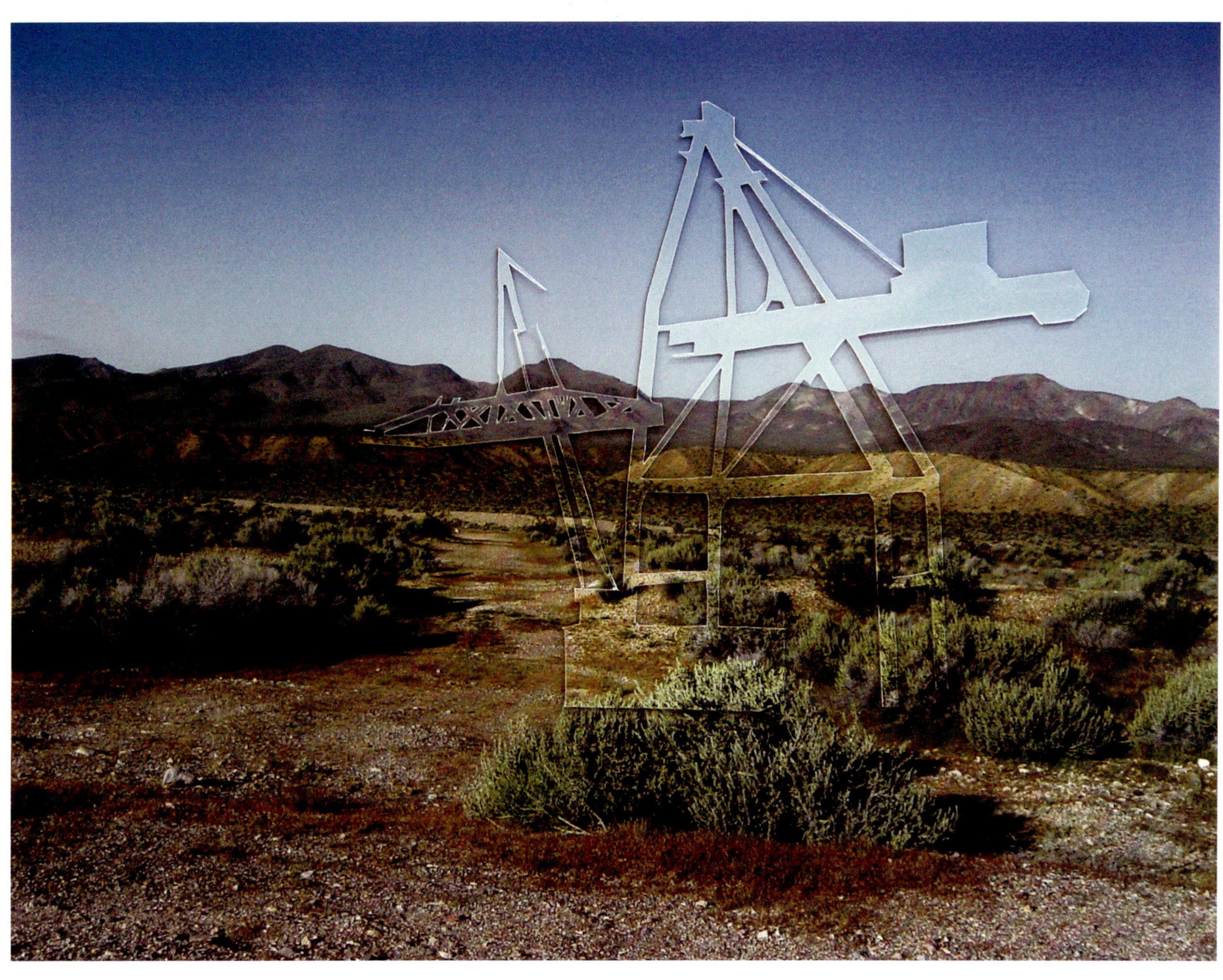

Under Construction IV
施工中 IV

2007
Photographic hand-cut collage
照片手刻拼贴画
21x29.5cm

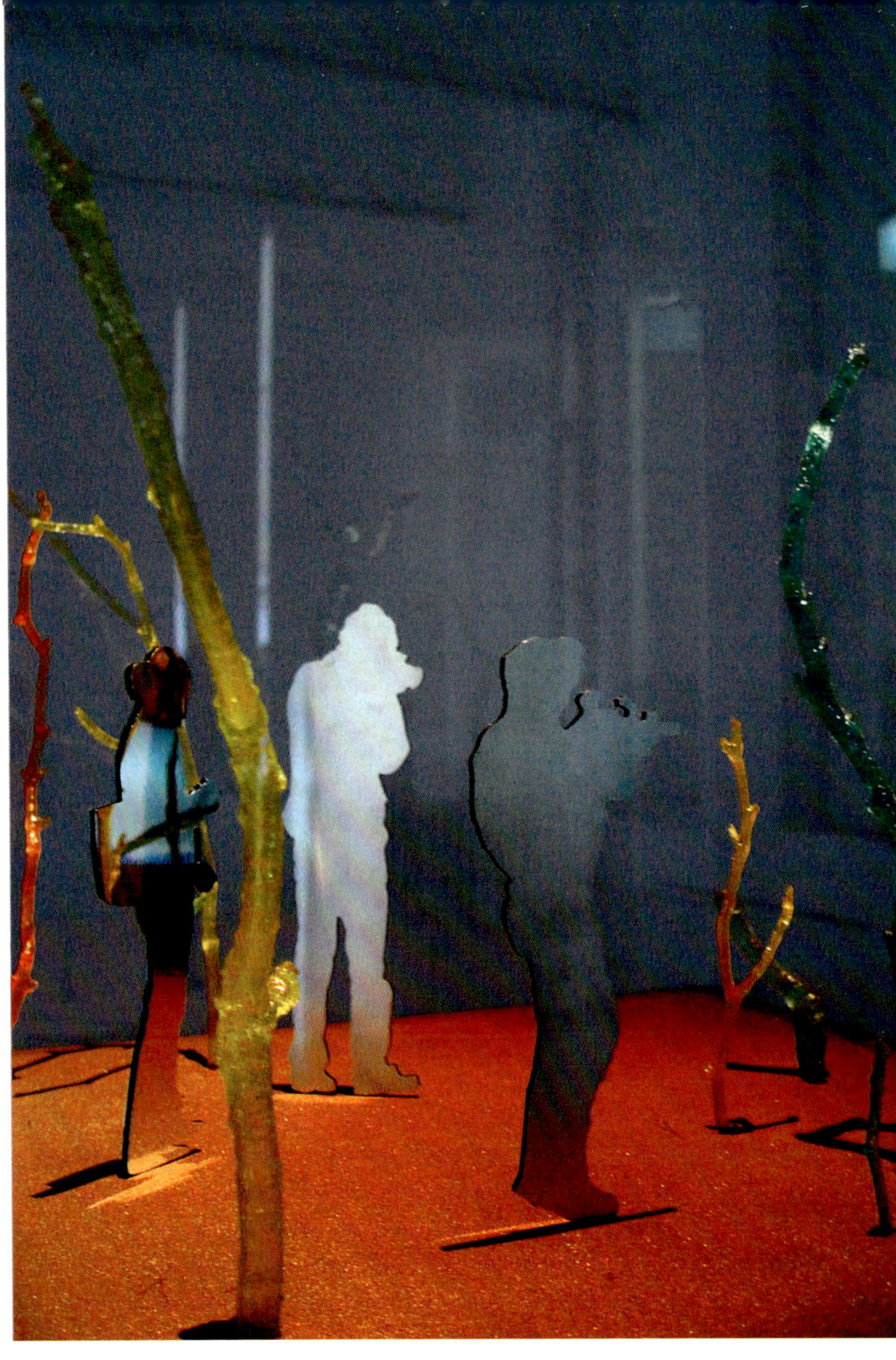

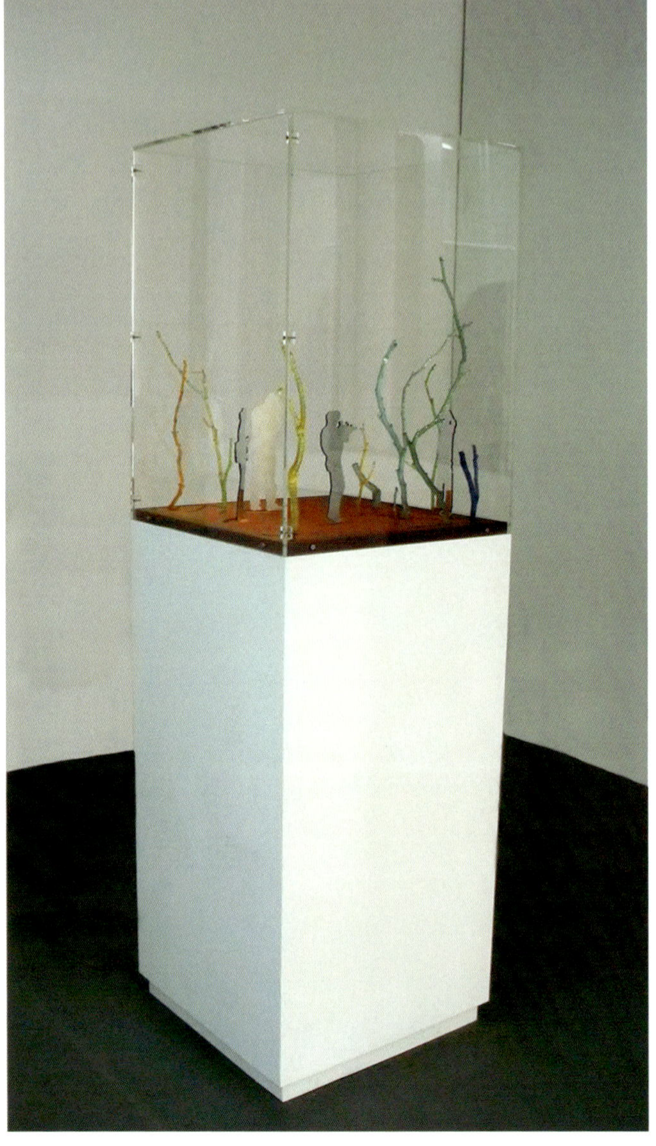

Capture
捕获

2006
Cast resin, aluminium figures, MDF and perspex plinth
雕塑材料：充填树脂、铝合金人体、
中密度纤维板以及透明塑胶底座
193x60x60cm

Pedestrian
步行者

2006
Sculpture: aluminium figures, artificial ferns, MDF
and perspex plinth
雕塑材料：铝合金人体、人造蕨类植物、
中密度纤维板以及透明塑胶底座
75x120x40cm

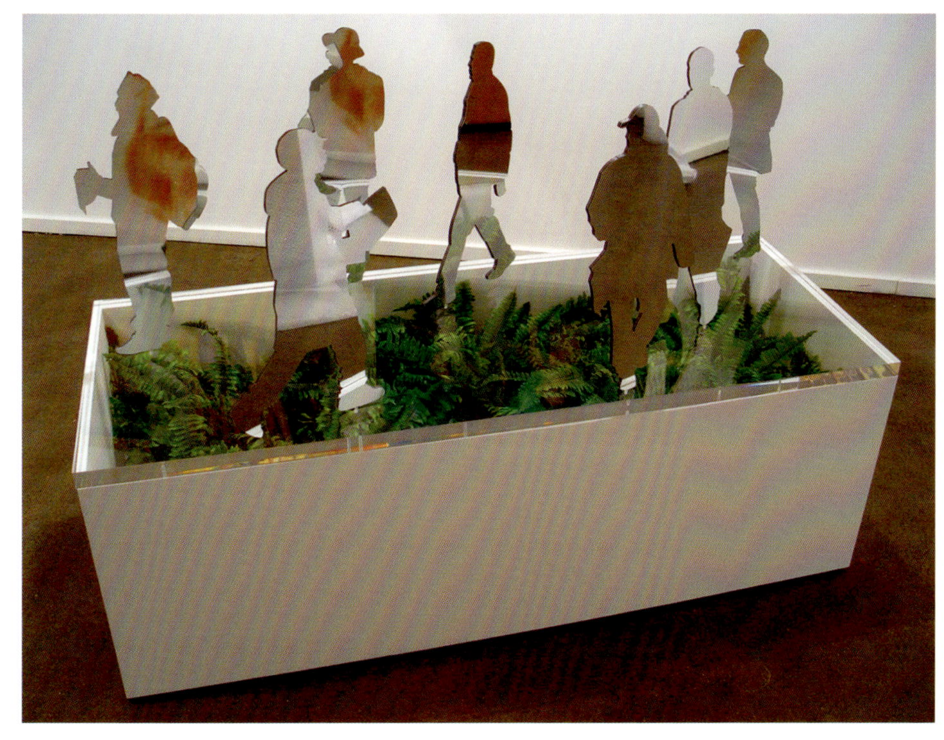

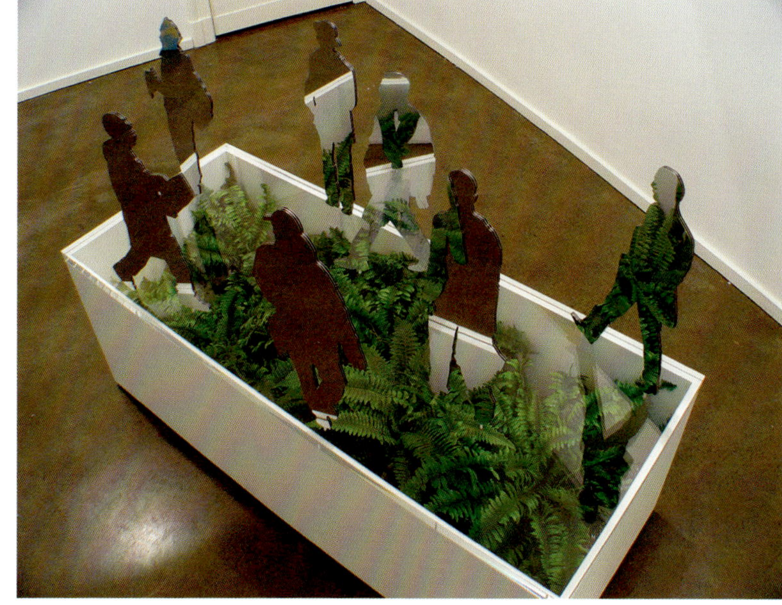

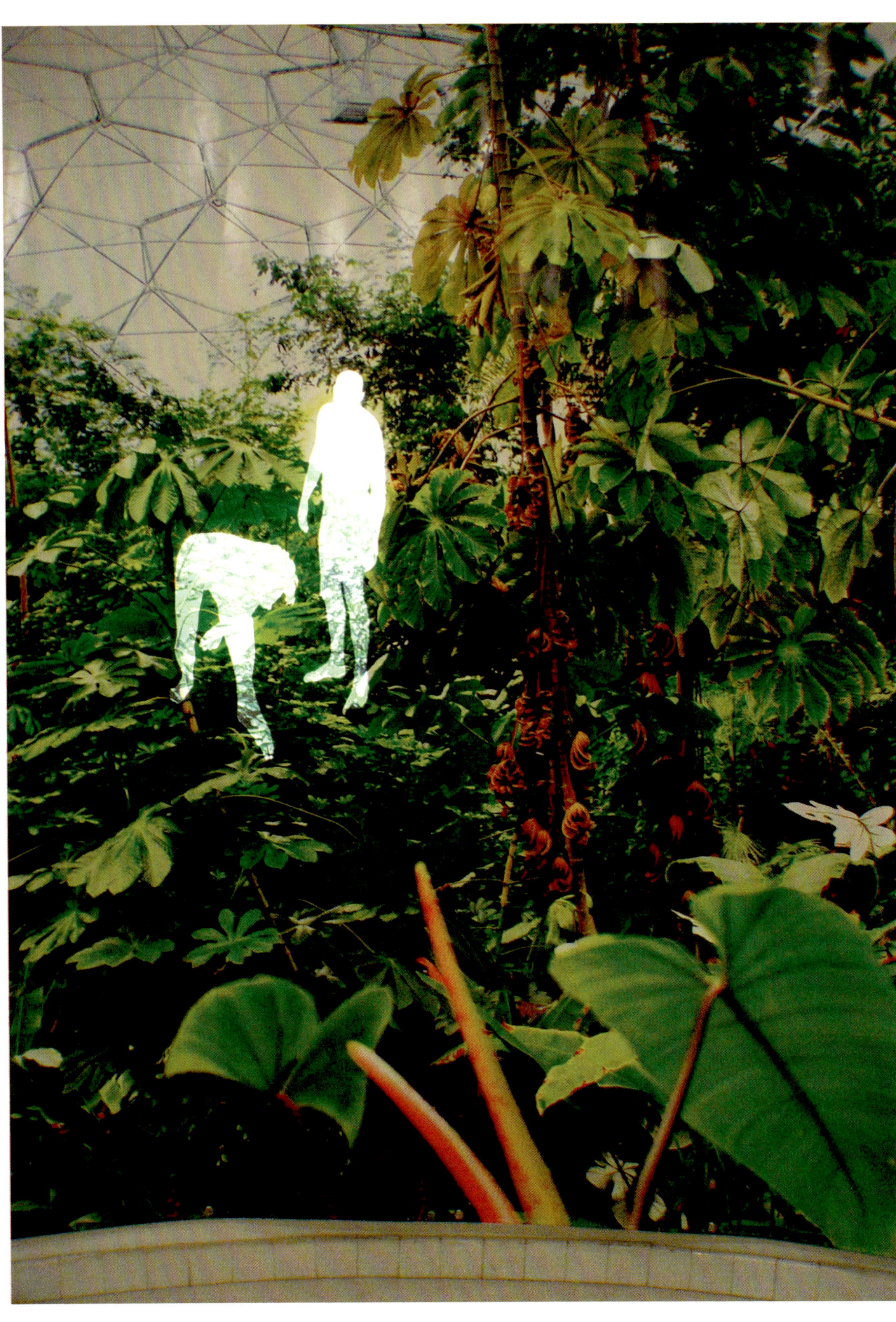

Past Is The Future (detail)
昔日映照未来

2004
Frissiras Museum Athens
Installation: panoramic photograph, moving gobo projections
展出地点：Frissiras博物馆，雅典
装置材料：全景照片、移动遮光投影
3x14м

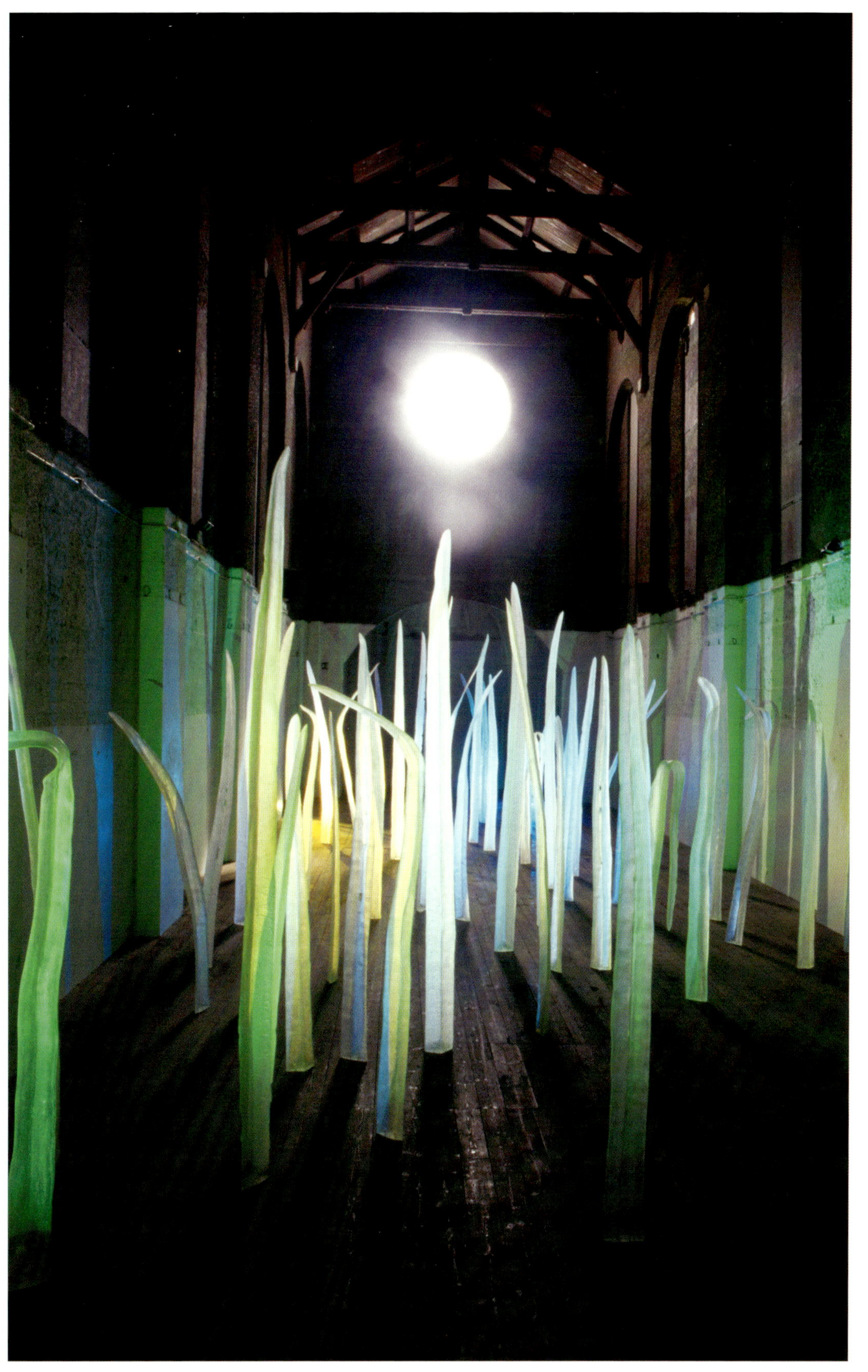

Drift
漂移

2001
Dilston Grove, London
Sculpture Installation: cast resin, light projectors
Sound by Tom Silvester
Tallest sculpture 3M
展出地点：Dilston Grove画廊，伦敦
雕塑装置材料：充填树脂、轻型投影灯
音效制作：Tom Silvester
高度：3米

Terra Incognita

2002
Artspace, Sydney
Cast resin, MDF, light projectors
Sound by Tom Silvester
Tallest sculpture 3m
展出地点：艺术空间，悉尼
雕塑装置材料：充填树脂、中密度纤维板、轻型投影灯
音效制作：Tom Silvester
高度：3米

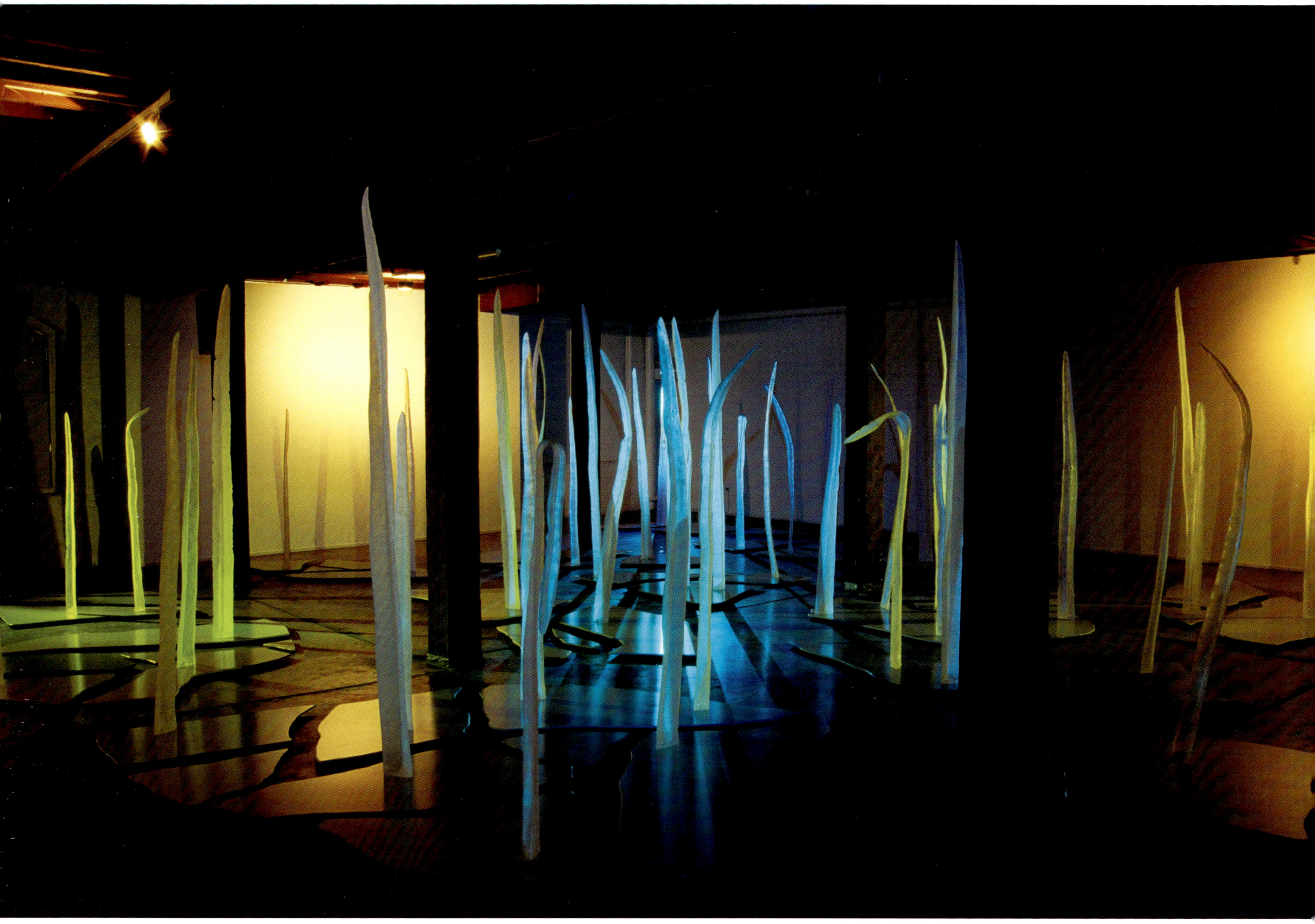

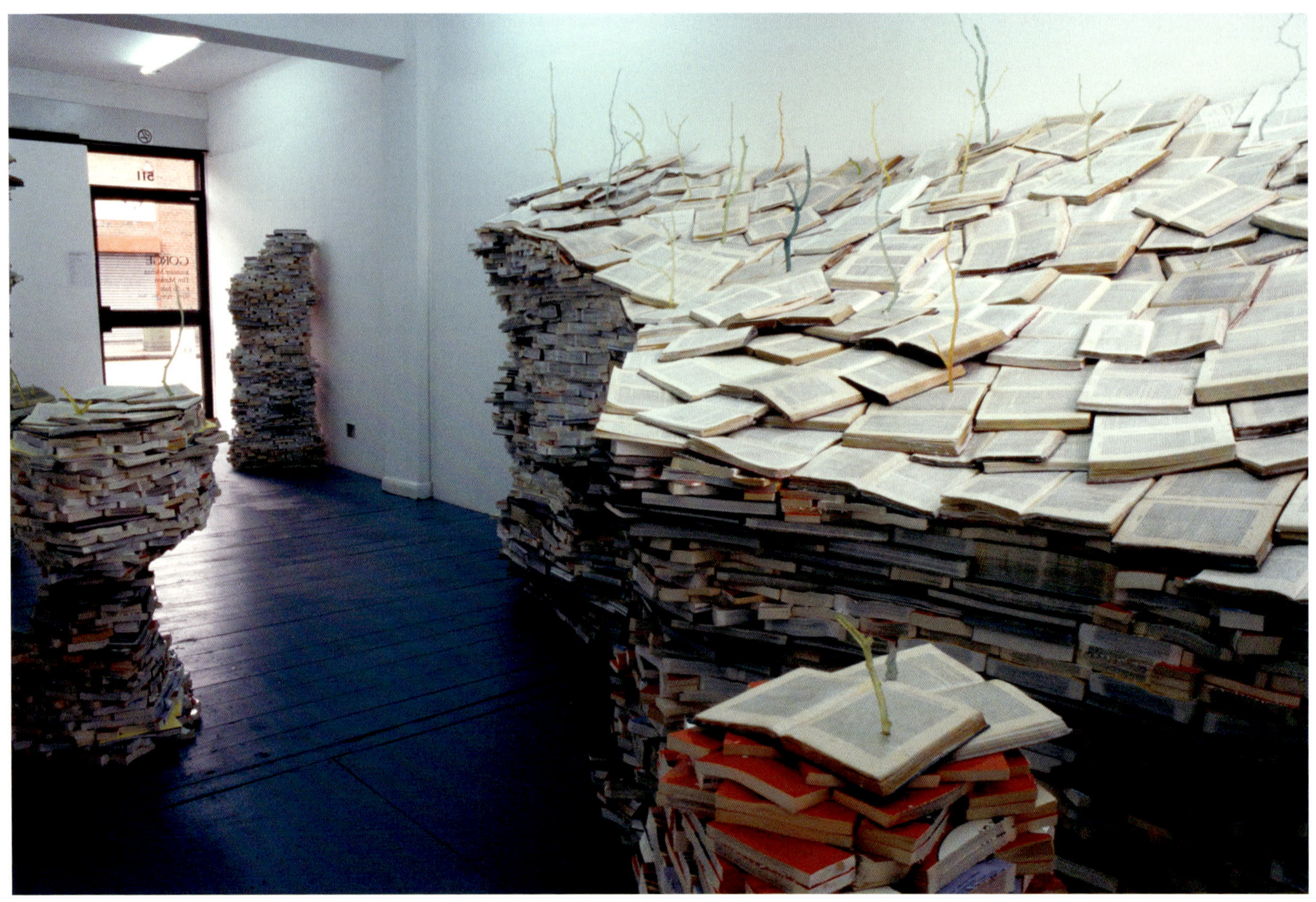

Gorge
峡谷

2000. VOID London
Sculpture Installation: recycled books, wax, cast resin plant forms
Tallest point 2.2m
展出地点：VOID 画廊，伦敦
雕塑装置材料：再生纸张印制的书籍、树腊、充填树脂、植株
高度：2.2米

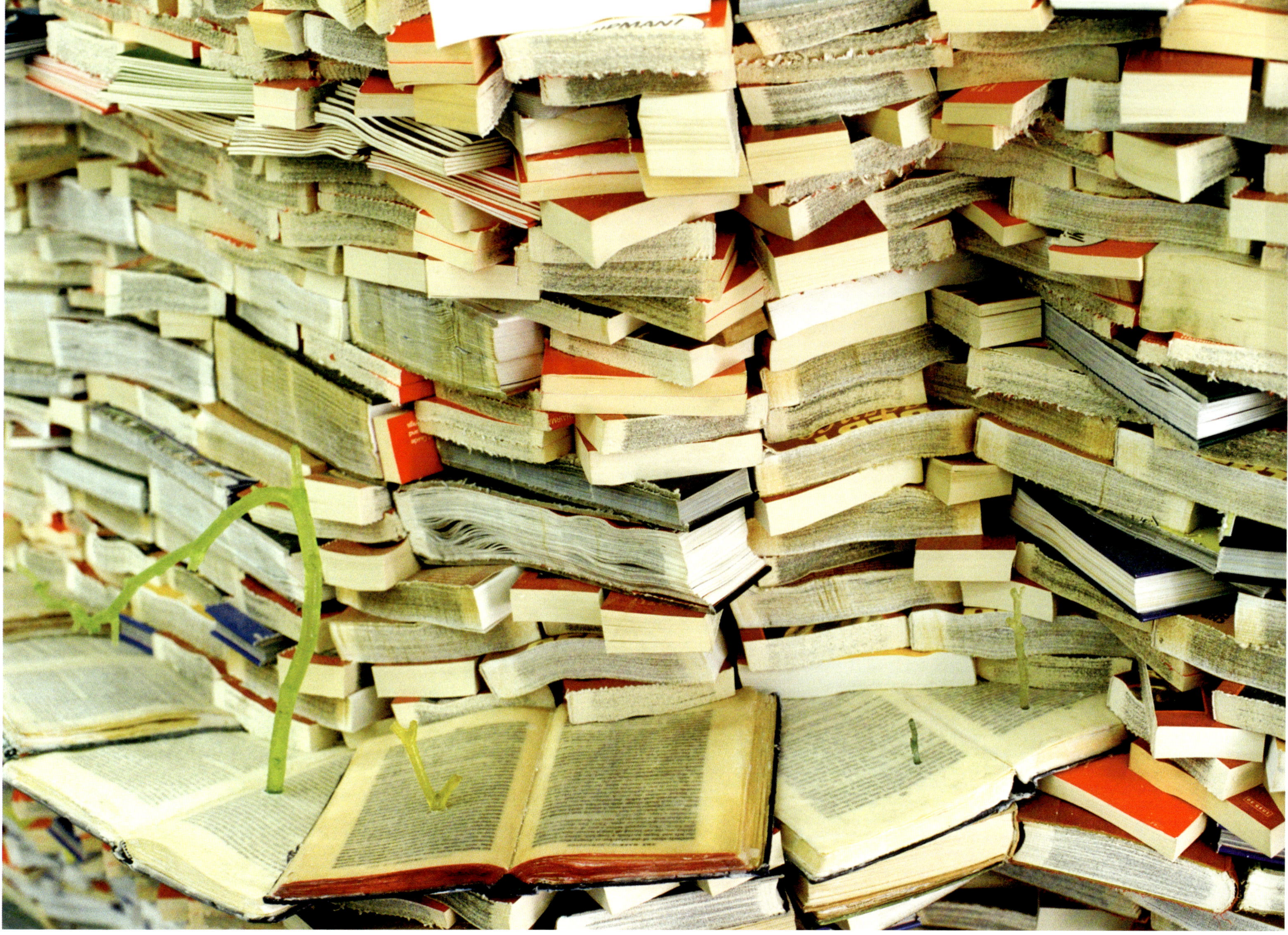

DETAIL: Gorge
局部: 峡谷

2000 VOID, London
展出地点：VOID 画廊，伦敦

作品展览年表
鸣谢
版本说明

EXHIBITION HISTORY
ACKNOWLEDGEMENTS
IMPRINT

MASLEN & MEHRA

Live and work in Europe

Tim Maslen

BORN: Perth Australia

EDUCATION: 1996-97 MA Fine Art, Goldsmiths University of London
1987-89 BA Fine Art, Curtin University, Perth, WA

Jennifer Mehra

BORN: London United Kingdom

EDUCATION: 1993-95 Fine Art, National Art School Sydney
1989-90 Foundation Fine Art, City Art Institute Sydney

SELECTED SOLO EXHIBITIONS

2009	Native, Galerie Caprice Horn/Berlin
2008	Shadow Lands, Priska C. Juschka Fine Art, New York
	Maslen & Mehra, MK Contemporary, Milton Keynes UK
	Two Worlds, Piramid Art Center, Istanbul
2007/8	Around, Maslen & Mehra / Federico Guida, First Gallery Rome
	Maslen & Mehra, Seven Dials Covent Garden, London
2006	Metropolis, Galerie Caprice Horn/Berlin
	Maslen & Mehra, Galería Sicart, Barcelona
	Maslen & Mehra, Lacen Galerie, Paris
2003	Phoenix, Perth International Arts Festival, Holmes à Court Gallery, Perth, WA
2002	Terra Incognita, Artspace, Sydney
2001	Drift film, 291 Gallery, London
	Drift, Dilston Grove, London
2000	Woodland, Downing Centre, Sydney
	Gorge, VOID, London

SELECTED GROUP EXHIBITIONS

2008	Light and Transition, Galerie Caprice Horn/Berlin
	Silver, Perth Institute Of Contemporary Art
	Margate Rocks 08, Festival of Contemporary Visual Art
	Grounded, Ellen Curlee Gallery, St Louis, USA
	Pulse New York, Priska Juschka Fine Art, New York
	Mexico Arte Contemporaneo, Galerie Caprice Horn/Berlin
	Mirror for the 21st Century, BECA, New Orleans
	European Month of Photography, Berlin
	Art Chicago, Galerie Caprice Horn/Berlin
	The Famous, the Infamous & the Really Quite Good, Decima Gallery, London
	Art Hong Kong, Galerie Caprice Horn/Berlin
	Palm Beach 3, Galerie Caprice Horn/Berlin
2007	Slow Space Fast Pace, Arttrail Cork, Ireland
	Photo Miami, Galerie Caprice Horn/Berlin
	Nature Scopes, Gongju National Museum South Korea
	Optical Titillations, Galerie Caprice Horn/Berlin
	ArteBA07, Buenos Aires, Galeria Sicart Barcelona
	Art Cologne, Galerie Caprice Horn/Berlin
	Urban Space, Art and Technology Institute, Oi Futuro, Foto Rio 2007/Wooloo, Rio De Janeiro & Berlin
	Urban Space, 7th Festival of Documentary Photography FOTOPUB, Slovenia
	Urban Space, 5th edition of Foto Arte Brasilia, Festival of Light
	Corpo Sociale, Galleria Pack, Milan
	Reality Bites, Galerie Caprice Horn/Berlin
	Modern 07, Munich, Galerie Caprice Horn/Berlin
	Slick, Paris, Galerie Lacen
	Photo London, Galerie Caprice Horn/Berlin
	Art LA, Los Angeles, Galerie Caprice Horn Berlin
	KIAF, Korea, Galerie Caprice Horn/Berlin
2006	Photo Miami, Galerie Caprice Horn/Berlin
	The Stars Down to Earth, Nunnery Gallery, London
	06'Vilafranca Contemporània, Galeria Sicart, Barcelona
	Life and Fiction, Galerie Caprice Horn/Berlin
	Harlem Art Project, Hosted by Philips de Pury & Company, Saatchi & Saatchi, New York
	Art Moscow, Central House of Artists, Moscow, Galerie Caprice Horn/Berlin
	Refraction, International Month Of Photography, Galerie Caprice Horn/Berlin
	Photo New York, Galerie Caprice Horn/Berlin
	Buenos Aires Photo, Galeria Sicart Barcelona
	06-07 Culture Bound, East Wing Collection No 7, Courtauld Institute, London
2005	About- From - For Nature, Old Police Station, Gongju, South Korea
	Urbanbodies, Brick Lane, London
	Western Biennale of Art: Art Tomorrow, John Natsoulas Center For The Arts, California, Curated by Edward Lucie-Smith
	Splendid, Shoreditch, London
2004	Tempered Ground, Museum Of Garden History, London
	Gods Becoming Men, Frissiras Museum, Athens, Curated by Edward Lucie-Smith
	The Garden Of Earthly Delights, Brockwell Park, London
	Art That Makes You Curious, Shoreditch Tabernacle Hall, London
	The Royal Road To The Unconscious, project by Dallas Seitz, Freud Museum London and Telephone Repeater Station, North Yorkshire
2003	Waterhouse Natural History Art Prize Exhibition, South Australian Museum
	Mirror II Nature, Mile End Art Pavillion, London
	Chairman's Choice, The Nunnery Gallery, London
2002	Chaos, Bishopsgate Goodsyard, London
2001	Five, Australia House, The Strand, London
	European Forum for Emerging Creation, Lyon, France

MASLEN & MEHRA

蒂姆·马斯伦 (Tim Maslen)
出生地：　澳大利亚佩思
学历：　　1987-89 年就读于西澳佩斯科廷大学，获美术学士学位
　　　　　1996-97 年就读于伦敦戈德史密斯大学，获美术硕士学位

詹妮弗·梅赫拉 (Jennifer Mehra)
出生地：　英国伦敦
学历：　　1989-90 年就读于悉尼城市艺术学院，美术预科班
　　　　　1993-95 年就读于悉尼国家艺术学院，美术专业

主要个展

2009　《本土》(Native)，Caprice Horn 画廊，柏林
2008　《影子地带》(Shadow Lands)，Priska C. Juschka 艺术画廊，纽约
　　　马斯伦 & 梅赫拉作品展，米尔顿凯恩斯现代艺术馆，米尔顿凯恩斯，英国
　　　《两个世界》(Two Worlds)，金字塔艺术中心，伊斯坦布尔
2007/8　《周边》(Around)，马斯伦 & 梅赫拉 / Federico Guida 作品展，第一画廊，罗马
　　　马斯伦 & 梅赫拉作品展，考文特花园七晷区 (Seven Dials Covent Garden)，伦敦
2006　《大都市》(Metropolis)，Caprice Horn 画廊，柏林
　　　马斯伦 & 梅赫拉作品展，Sicart画廊，巴塞罗那
　　　马斯伦 & 梅赫拉作品展，Lacen画廊，巴黎
2003　《凤凰》(Phoenix)，佩斯国际艺术节，Holmes à Court 画廊，佩斯，西澳
2002　《Terra Incognita》，艺术空间，悉尼
2001　《漂移》影片，291画廊，伦敦
　　　《漂移》(Drift)，Dilston Grove 画廊，伦敦
2000　《林地》(Woodland)，唐宁中心，悉尼
　　　《峡谷》(Gorge)，VOID 画廊，伦敦

主要联展

2008　《斗转星移》(Light and Transition)，Caprice Horn画廊 / 柏林
　　　《银色》(Silver)，佩斯当代艺术学院
　　　《08玛格里特岩石》(Margate Rocks 08)，当代视觉艺术节
　　　《根基》(Grounded)，Ellen Curlee 画廊，圣路易斯，美国
　　　《脉动纽约》(Pulse New York) Priska Juschka 美术馆，纽约
　　　墨西哥当代艺术展，Caprice Horn 画廊 / 柏林
　　　《二十一世纪写真》(Mirror for the 21st Century)，BECA 画廊，新奥尔良
　　　欧洲摄影月，柏林
　　　芝加哥艺术展，Caprice Horn 画廊 / 柏林
　　　《极致·低劣·上乘》(The Famous, the Infamous & the Really Quite Good)，
　　　Decima 画廊，伦敦
　　　香港艺术展，Caprice Horn 画廊 / 柏林
　　　《棕榈树·沙滩3》(Palm Beach 3)，Caprice Horn 画廊 / 柏林

2007　《慢空间·快节奏》(Slow Space Fast Pace)，科克Arttrail画廊，爱尔兰
　　　迈阿密摄影展，Caprice Horn 画廊，柏林
　　　《自然·视野》(Nature Scopes)，公州国家博物馆，韩国
　　　《光的激发》(Optical Titilations)，Caprice Horn画廊 / 柏林
　　　07 巴塞罗那艺术展，Buenos 艺术展，Sicart 画廊，巴塞罗那
　　　科隆艺术展，Caprice Horn 画廊 / 柏林
　　　《城市空间》(Urban Space)，艺术与技术学院，Oi Futuro, 2007 摄影 / Wooloo
　　　画廊，里约热内卢和柏林
　　　《城市空间》，第七届 FOTOPUB 纪实摄影展，斯洛文尼亚
　　　《城市空间》，第五届巴西利亚摄影艺术节，灯光节
　　　《Corpo Sociale》，Pack 画廊，米兰
　　　《现实的刺痛》(Reality Bites)，Caprice Horn 画廊 / 柏林
　　　07 现代艺术展，慕尼黑，Caprice Horn 画廊 / 柏林
　　　《Slick》当代艺术博览会，巴黎，Lacen 画廊
　　　伦敦摄影展，Caprice Horn 画廊 / 柏林
　　　洛杉矶艺术展，洛杉矶，Caprice Horn 画廊 / 柏林
　　　韩国国际艺术博览会 (KIAF)，朝鲜，Caprice Horn 画廊 / 柏林
　　　迈阿密摄影展，Caprice Horn 画廊 / 柏林
2006　《明星荟萃》(The Stars Down to Earth)，Nunnery 画廊，伦敦
　　　06 Vilafranca当代艺术展，Sicart 画廊，巴塞罗那
　　　《现实与幻想》(Life and Fiction)，Caprice Horn画廊 / 柏林
　　　哈莱姆艺术项目(Harlem Art Project)，Philips de Pury 公司主办，Saatchi & Saatchi
　　　萨奇画廊，纽约
　　　莫斯科艺术展，艺术家中心，莫斯科，Caprice Horn 画廊 / 柏林
　　　《折射》(Refraction)，国际摄影月，Caprice Horn 画廊 / 柏林
　　　纽约摄影展，Caprice Horn 画廊 / 柏林
　　　Buenos 摄影艺术展，Sicart 画廊，巴塞罗那
06-07　《文化局限》(Culture Bound)，东翼收藏画廊7号，考陶尔德艺术学院，伦敦
2005　《关于·来自·为了自然》(About- From - For Nature)，老警察局，公州，韩国
　　　《城市素描》(Urbanbodies)，Brick Lane 画廊，伦敦
　　　西方艺术双年展：未来艺术，John Natsoulas 艺术中心，加利福尼亚，
　　　爱德华·路希一史 密斯策展
　　　《辉煌》(Splendid)，Shoreditch 画廊，伦敦
2004　《大地的脾性》(Tempered Ground)，花园历史博物馆，伦敦
　　　《上帝走下圣坛》(Gods Becoming Men)，Frissiras博物馆，雅典，爱德华·路希一史密斯策展
　　　《地球的后花园》(The Garden Of Earthly Delights)，Brockwell公园，伦敦
　　　《艺术的魅力》(Art That Makes You Curious)，Shoreditch Tabernacle 会馆，伦敦
　　　《走向未知世界的王者之路》(The Royal Road To The Unconscious)，Dallas Seitz 资助
　　　项目，伦敦弗洛伊德博物馆和电话中继站，北约克郡
2003　《水房》(Waterhouse)，自然历史艺术大奖赛，南澳博物馆
　　　《镜像II·自然》(Mirror II Nature)，Mile End 艺术分馆，伦敦
　　　《司仪的选择》(Chairman's Choice)，Nunnery画廊，伦敦
2002　《浑沌》(Chaos)，Bishopsgate Goodsyard 画廊，伦敦
2001　五人展，澳大利亚馆，河滨马路(The Strand)，伦敦
　　　欧洲新锐论坛，里昂，法国

2008   Lettre International magazine, special edition, The Way We Live, p. 74,246.
Ayşegül Sönmez, Interview, *Radikal newspaper*, Turkey, p. 23.
Cumhuriyet newspaper, Feature - Kultur section, Turkey, p. 15.
Maslen & Mehra, *Carte D'arte Internazionale magazine*, Italy, Feature.
Mirror for the 21st Century, *BECA*, New Orleans catalogue.
Jenny Kendler, *Wunderkammer*, A Journal of Environmental Art Maslen & Mehra,
Alix Rule, Critics Choice, *Saatchi online*, (Published 16 Feb).
This Week in New York, Shadow Lands, (Published 6 Feb).
Robert Clark, preview, Maslen & Mehra/MK Contemporary,
The Guardian Guide, (12 Jan).
New works section, *Aesthetica Cultural Arts Magazine*, (Feb/Mar), p. 18.
Maslen & Mehra/ MK Contemporary, catalogue.
Galerie Caprice Horn/Berlin, Gallery catalogue.

2007   *Karnival Magazine*, Recognition and Alienation by Elaine O'Sullivan, p. 14-15,17,23.
Slow Space Fast Pace, Cork, Ireland, catalogue.
Geumgang Nature Art Pre- Biennale, *Nature Scopes*, South Korea, catalogue, pp. 112-113.
BBC2, London, interview Summer Exhibition series, (22 June 7pm).
Art es magazine, cover and sixteen page project, pp. 47-63.
Kunst Magazine, Berlin, cover.

2006   Philip Gefter, Reflections in a Molten Eye, *New York Times*, half page feature,
International Edition, (31 Dec).
Le Parisien, newspaper review of Lacen Galerie solo exhibition, (29 Nov).
Art Monthly Australia, preview Paris solo exhibiton, (Oct), p. 42.
06'Vilafranca Contemporània, Spain, catalogue, pp. 14-15.
Charles Rump, Kunstmarkt, *Die Welt Newspaper*, (22 April).
NY Arts Magazine, Stars Down to Earth exhibition by Andrew Hunt, (Sept), p. 70.
Vanessa Desclaux, Stars Down to Earth, *AN Magazine*, (Sept), p. 7.
The Nunnery Gallery, *Stars Down to Earth Catalogue*, London, pp. 5,14.
Australian Art Review Magazine, Two Up, feature by Victoria Hynes, June pp. 54-55.
Culture Bound, East Wing Collection no. 7, Courtauld Institute online catalogue.
Exberliner, Berlin magazine, March, p. 40.
Origina Magazine Mexico no. 154, Maslen & Mehra pp. 62-69.
Art & Architecture Journal [UK], Maslen & Mehra, no. 63, p. 57.

2005   *Sydney Morning Herald*, Celebrating the Surreal is Only Natural by Valerie Lawson, (6 April).
Art Monthly UK, Urbanbodies by Amna Malik, (April), pp. 30-31.
AN Magazine UK, Urbanbodies by Kelly O'Reilley, p. 6.
Western Biennale of Art, catalogue, published California, pp. 62-63.
Sacramento Bee, Western Biennale review by Victoria Dalkey, California, (27 Feb).
California Aggie, Western Biennale review by Elizabeth Marxen, (10 March).
Art & Architecture Journal UK, Maslen & Mehra: Past is the Future, (February) no. 61, p. 56.
Light,magazine, cover image, (March).

2004   World Sculpture News Hong Kong, Gods Becoming Men Athens,
spring vol. 10 no. 2, pp. 12,14,18.
International Art Newspaper, What's On in Europe, (July/August) no. 149.
ERT Greek National Television, interview, (July).
New Zealand Art Monthly, events section, (July).
The Frissiras Museum Athens, *Gods Becoming Men*, catalogue.
Tempered Ground, catalogue, Parabola, London.
Gods Becoming Men, *Art & Australia Magazine*, vol. 42 no.1, pp. 54-55.
Maslen & Mehra / Gods Becoming Men, *Qantas inflight magazine*, (August).

2003   The Nunnery Gallery, *Chairmans Choice*, catalogue, London.
The Waterhouse Natural History Art Prize catalogue, South Australian Museum, (August).
Simon Blond, Partners in Provocative Art, *The West Australian Newspaper*, (8 Feb) p. 12.
Ted Snell, Perth Festival,*The Australian Newspaper*, (7 Feb).

2002   Edward Lucie-Smith, *Art Tomorrow*, book, pp. 231,228.
Simon Rees, *Art & Australia magazine*, feature, (December) pp. 232-233.
Paul McGillick, *Indesign magazine*, feature, (Aug), p. 30.
Paul McGillick, *Artlink magazine*, feature, (June), pp. 34-35.
Terra Incognita, *Qantas inflight magazine*, feature, (April), p. 19.
Victoria Hynes, *Sydney Morning Herald*, Metro Section, feature, (19 April).
Jeroen Bergmans, The Agenda, *Wallpaper magazine*, (April).
Bruce James, *Radio National Australia*, interview, (16 April).
2SER, Interview re 'Terra Incognita', (27 March).
Light magazine, cover image, (March).

2001   Nightlife, documentary, *London Weekend Television*, 'Drift' Exhibition and interviews,
Channel 4 UK, (28 Sept).
Bill Overton, *BBC London Live Radio*, interview regarding 'Drift' project, (29 Aug), 10pm.
Metro Newspaper, Art Review by Fisun Guner, Drift exhibition, (4 Sept).
Jessica Lack, *The Guardian Guide*, preview 'Drift', (25 September).
The Guardian, Going Out, Picks of the week, 'Drift' exhibition.
Gillian Nichol, preview Drift, *AN Magazine*, (Sept).
Richard Dorment, Art Critic London, review 'Drift', *The Telegraph*.
Architect Journal, preview, Drift, (Sept).
Blueprint Magazine, Diary recommended exhibitions 'Drift', (Sept).
Building Design, preview 'Drift', (Sept).
Stephen Mitchell, Going Out Guide, *Evening Standard*,
recommended exhibition, (28 Aug).
What's On Magazine, review 'Drift', (12 Sept).
Sydney Morning Herald, Spotlight, preview 'Drift', (23 Aug).

2000   What's On London, review 'Gorge' installation, (12 July), p. 26.
Flash Art International, News, (Summer), p. 52.
Visiting Arts International Diary, (Summer), p. 1.
Profiles, *Art Almanac Australia*, (September), p. 101.
The Sydney Morning Herald, Metro Section, critic's pick by Courtney Kidd, (22 Sept), p. 23.
Catherine Keenan, Olympic Spotlight, *The Sydney Morning Herald*, (26 Sept), p. 13.
Exhibitions to watch, 'Woodland', *Artlink magazine*, p. 78.
Living Art, *Vogue Living*, Australia, (Oct/Nov) p. 36.
Ron Banks, Instilled With Ambition, *The West Australian newspaper*, (5 October), p. 6.
Art & Australia magazine, 'Gorge' installation, Vol 38, p. 291.

SELECTED AWARDS AND RESIDENCIES

2007   Arts Council Of England, award for the publication: Maslen & Mehra - Mirrored
2007   Nominee in Fine Art Professional, International Color Awards,
Masters of Colour Photography
2004   Arts Council Of England, new work award
2003   The Eden Project, residency
2002   Artspace, residency, Sydney
2001   Artswa, award for residency/exhibition Sydney
2001   The Henry Moore Foundation, award for Drift project
2001   London Arts, award for Drift project

2008　土耳其《自由报》，阿瑟库·森梅兹（Ayşegül Sönmez）采访报道，第23页
土耳其《共和国报》，特写，文化版，第15页
马斯伦 & 梅赫拉，意大利《Carte D'arte Internazionale》杂志，特写
《二十一世纪写真》联展，BECA 画廊，新奥尔良目录
《环境艺术》期刊，百宝箱：马斯伦 & 梅赫拉，詹妮·肯德勒（Jenny Kendler）撰稿
萨奇在线（Saatchi online）文章：评论家的选择，作者：亚历克斯·鲁尔（Alix Rule），2月16日出版
《本周纽约》（This Week in New York），作品：《影子地带》，2月6日出版
《英国卫报导读》（The Guardian Guide UK），马斯伦 & 梅赫拉作品 / MK 当代艺术馆预告，罗伯特·克拉克（Robert Clark）撰稿，1月12日
《文化艺术审美》杂志（Aesthetica Cultural Arts），《新作品》栏目。2/3月，第18页
马斯伦 & 梅赫拉作品 / MK当代艺术馆，目录
Caprice Horn 画廊 / 柏林美术馆，目录

2007　《Karnival》杂志文章：认可与疏远，作者：艾琳·欧沙利文（Elaine O'Sullivan），第14-15、17、23页
《慢空间·快节奏》，科克，爱尔兰，目录
《自然·视野》，金刚自然艺术双年展，韩国，目录，第112 - 113页
伦敦 BBC2 台，夏季展览会系列专访，6月22日，晚7时
西班牙《艺术》杂志，封面及16页项目，第47 - 63页
柏林《艺术家》杂志，封面

2006　《纽约时报》文章：熔眼的思考，菲利普·吉夫特（Philip Gefter）撰稿，1/2 页，特写，12月31日，国际版
《巴黎人报》（Le Parisien）述评：Lacen画廊个人展览，11月29日
《澳大利亚艺术》月刊（Art Monthly Australia），巴黎个展预告，10月，第42页
《06'Vilafranca Contemporània》，西班牙，目录，第14 - 15页
《世界报》（Die Welt）文章：艺术市场，作者：查尔斯·鲁姆普（Charles Rump），4月22日
《纽约艺术》杂志（NY Arts）文章：《明星荟萃》艺术展，安德鲁·亨特（Andrew Hunt）撰稿，9月，第70页
英国《AN》杂志文章：《明星荟萃》艺术展，范奈萨·德斯克劳斯（Vanessa Desclaux）撰稿，9月，第7页
《明星荟萃》艺术展目录，Nunnery 画廊，伦敦，第5、14页
澳大利亚《艺术评论》杂志文章：Two Up，特写，维多利亚·海因斯（Victoria Hynes）撰稿，6月，第54 - 55页
《文化局限》艺术展，东翼收藏画廊7号，考陶尔德艺术学院在线目录
柏林《Exberline》杂志，3月，第40页
墨西哥《Origina》杂志，第154期，马斯伦 & 梅赫拉，第62 - 69页
英国《艺术与建筑》期刊，马斯伦 & 梅赫拉，第63期，第57页

2005　《悉尼先驱晨报》（Sydney Morning Herald）文章：朴实地赞美超现实，作者：瓦雷利·劳森（Valerie Lawson），4月6日
《英国艺术月刊》（Art Monthly UK）文章：《城市素描》，作者：埃米纳·马利克（Amna Malik），4月，第30 - 31页
英国《AN》杂志文章：《城市素描》，作者：凯利·奥莱利（Kelly O'Reilley），第6页
《西方艺术双年展》目录，加利福尼亚出版，第62 - 63页
《萨克拉门托蜜蜂》（Sacramento Bee）评论文章：《西方艺术双年展》，维多利亚·达尔凯（Victoria Dalkey）撰稿，加利福尼亚，2月27日
《加州农大》（California Aggie）评论文章：《西方艺术双年展》，伊丽莎白·马克森（Elizabeth Marxen）撰稿，3月10日
英国《艺术与建筑》期刊，马斯伦 & 梅赫拉作品：《昔日映照未来》，2月，第61期，第56页

2004　《世界雕塑》，香港新闻：《上帝走下圣坛》艺术展，雅典，春季卷第10卷第2期，第12、14、18页
《世界艺术》报刊文章：欧洲时讯，7/8月，第149期
希腊国家 ERT 电视台，专访，7月
《新西兰艺术月刊》，时事版，7月
雅典Frissiras博物馆，《上帝走下圣坛》艺术展，目录
《大地的脾性》艺术展，目录，Parabola画廊，伦敦
《艺术与澳大利亚》杂志，《上帝走下圣坛》艺术展，第42卷第1期，第54 - 55页
澳大利亚《Qantas inflight》杂志，马斯伦 & 梅赫拉 /《上帝走下圣坛》艺术展，8月

2003　《司仪的选择》艺术展，目录，Nunnery 画廊，伦敦
《水房·自然历史艺术大奖展》目录，南澳博物馆，8月
《西澳报》文章：挑鲜艺术的合作伙伴，作者：西蒙·布朗德（Simon Blond），2月8日，第12页
《澳大利亚》文章：佩斯文化节，作者：特德·斯内尔（Ted Snell），2月7日

2002　《未来艺术》（Art Tomorrow），爱德华·路希—史密斯著，第八章，第228、231页
《艺术与澳大利亚》杂志，特写，西蒙·里斯（Simon Rees）撰稿，12月，第232 - 233页
《设计》杂志，特写，保罗·麦克格里克（Paul McGillick）撰稿，8月，第30页
澳大利亚《Artlink》艺术季刊，特写，保罗·麦克格里克（Paul McGillick）撰稿，6月，第34 - 35页
澳大利亚《Qantas inflight》杂志，特写，关于《Terra Incognita》，4月，第19页
《悉尼先驱晨报》，都市版，特写，维多利亚·海因斯（Victoria Hynes）撰稿，4月19日
《墙纸》（Wallpaper），记事册，乔洛恩·伯格曼斯（Jeroen Bergmans）撰稿，4月
澳大利亚国家广播电台，访谈节目，布鲁斯·詹姆斯（Bruce James）主持，晚8.30，4月16日
澳大利亚 2SER 广播电台，作品专访：《Terra Incognita》，3月27日
《光线》杂志（L(ight)，封面图片，3月

2001　《夜生活》，《人物纪实》栏目，伦敦周末电视节目，《漂移》展览访谈，9月28日，4 频道，英国
BBC 伦敦在线广播，采访：《漂移》项目，比尔·奥弗顿（Bill Overton）主持，8月29日，晚10时
《地铁报》（Metro）艺术评论：《漂移》个人展览，作者：费桑·冈纳（Fisun Guner），9月4日
《英国卫报导读》，《漂移》预告，杰西卡·莱克（Jessica Lack）撰稿，9月25日
《卫报》，《走出去》栏目，一周要闻：《漂移》个展作品
英国《AN》杂志，《漂移》预告，吉琳·尼科尔（Gillian Nichol）撰稿，9月
伦敦艺术评论家：《每日电讯报》，《漂移》述评，理查德·多曼特（Richard Dorment）撰稿
《建筑师》期刊，《漂移》预告，9月
《蓝图》杂志（Blueprint）《九月日记》展览推荐，《漂移》
《建筑设计》，《漂移》预告，9月
《标准晚报》（Evening Standard），《走出去》栏目导读：展览推荐，斯蒂芬·米切尔（Stephen Mitchell）撰稿，8月28日
《快讯杂志》（What's On Magazine），《漂移》述评，9月12日
《悉尼先驱晨报》，《聚光灯》栏目，《漂移》预告，8月23日

2000　《伦敦快讯》，关于《山峡》装置艺术，7月12日，第26页
《国际闪现艺术》（Flash Art International），新闻报道，2000 年夏季版，第52页
英国访问艺术署（Visiting Arts）的《国际日志》（International Diary），夏季版，第1页
《澳大利亚艺术年鉴》（Art Almanac Australia），人物简介，9月，第101页
《悉尼先驱晨报》，都市版文章：评论家文摘，考特内·基德（Courtney Kidd）撰稿，9月22日，第23页
《悉尼先驱晨报》文章：奥林匹克聚光灯，凯瑟琳·凯南（Catherine Keenan）撰稿，9月26日，第13页
澳大利亚《Artlink》艺术季刊，作品展讯：《林地》，第78页
澳大利亚《时尚生活》（Vogue Living），艺术生活，10/11月，第36页
《西澳大利亚州》报刊文章：蓄势待发，朗·班克斯（Ron Banks）撰稿，10月5日，第6页
《艺术与澳大利亚》杂志，作品：《山峡》装置艺术，第38卷，第291页

主要奖项和资助

2007　英格兰艺术委员会，出版奖：马斯伦 & 梅赫拉——《镜像》组照
2007　美术专业提名奖，国际色彩协会奖，彩色摄影大奖
2004　英格兰艺术委员会，作品创新奖
2003　英国《伊甸园》项目，访问邀请
2002　艺术空间，访问邀请，悉尼
2001　西澳艺术，访问邀请 / 展览邀请，悉尼
2001　Henry Moore 基金会，《漂移》项目资助
2001　伦敦艺术大学，《漂移》项目资助

THE ARTISTS WOULD LIKE TO THANK:
两位艺术家特别在此表示衷心的感谢:

Caprice Horn
Edward Lucie-Smith
Eugen Blume
Carl Middleton
Arts Council England
National Lottery
Bow Arts Trust
Priska C. Juschka Fine Art, New York
Milton Keynes Contemporary
Factory Settings
Other Peoples Sculpture
Sam Forster
Artspace Sydney
Cafe Gallery Projects London/Dilston Grove
Bedri Baykam
Adeline Loh, Page One Publishing, Singapore
Phil & Marg Maslen
Mike & Annie Cannon
Jeffrey & Jocleyn Kirby
Tom Silvester & Michelle Kemp + Grace
Linh Tran & Paul Harvey
Alison Raimes
The Feldman-Wallace family
Elizabeth Wardle
Daria Price

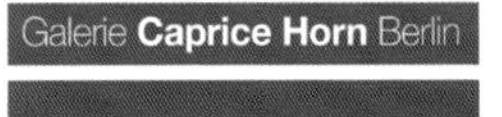
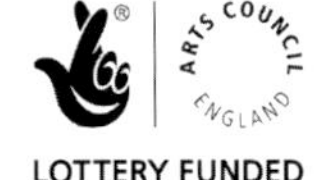
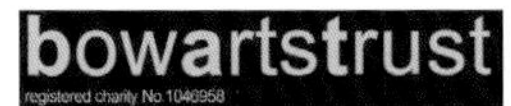

IMPRINT

版本说明

Bibliographic information published by
The Deutsche Nationalbibliothek
The Deutsche Nationalbibliothek lists this
publication in the Deutsche Nationalbibliografie;
detailed bibliographic data are available in the
Internet at http://dnb.d-nb.de.

书目信息由
德国国家图书馆公布，
本书的在版信息已列入德国国家文献目录；
详细编目数据可以通过互联网获得：
http://dnb.d-nb.de

Distributed in the United Kingdom
Cornerhouse Publications
70 Oxford Street
Manchester M1 5 NH
United Kingdom
Phone: +44-161-200 15 03
Fax: +44-161-200 15 04

英国国内发行单位：
Cornerhouse 出版社
70 Oxford Street
Manchester M1 5 NH
United Kingdom
电话： +44-161-200 15 03
传真： +44-161-200 15 04

Distributed outside Europe
D.A.P. Distributed Art Publishers, Inc.
155 Sixth Avenue
2nd Floor
New York NY 10013
USA
phone +1-212-627 19 99
fax +1-212-627 94 84

欧洲以外发行单位：
D.A.P.艺术出版发行公司
155 Sixth Avenue
2nd Floor
New York NY 10013
USA
电话： +1-212-627 19 99
传真： +1-212-627 94 84

EDITOR: Dr. Caprice Horn
Galerie Caprice Horn/ Berlin
Kochstraße 60
D - 10969 Berlin
Germany
www.capricehorn.com

编辑： Caprice Horn 博士
Caprice Horn 画廊 / 柏林
Kochstraße 60
D - 10969 Berlin
Germany
网址： www.capricehorn.com

TEXTS: Edward Lucie-Smith
Eugen Blume

撰稿： 爱德华·路希—史密斯 (Edward Lucie-Smith)
尤金·布卢姆 (Eugen Blume)

TRANSLATION: Accent Consultants
PHOTO CREDITS: Maslen & Mehra

翻译： Accent Consultants 顾问咨询公司
照片来源： 马斯伦 & 梅赫拉

BOOK DESIGN: Carl Middleton for Neat
www.neatdesign.org

装帧设计： 卡尔·米德尔顿 (Carl Middleton for Neat)
网址： www.neatdesign.org

TYPEFACE: Din and Whitney
PAPER: MAXIsatin 170gsm
REPROGRAPHICS: DZA Satz und Bild GmbH
Altenburg
PRINT / BINDING: DZA Druckerei zu Altenburg GmbH
Altenburg

版面设计： Din & Whitney
纸张： MAXIsatin 纸重： 170gsm
翻印： DZA Satz und Bild GmbH
Altenburg
印刷 / 装订： DZA Druckerei zu Altenburg GmbH
Altenburg

All rights reserved. Printed in Gemany.

版权所有，德国印制

© Nürnberg 2008, Verlag für moderne Kunst
Nürnberg, Maslen & Mehra, the authors

出版单位：©现代艺术家出版社，纽伦堡，2008年，版权所有。
作者： 马斯伦 & 梅赫拉，纽伦堡

www.vfmk.de
ISBN 978-3-940748-42-3

网址： www.vfmk.de
国际书号： ISBN 978-3-940748-42-3

184

COVER IMAGE, FRONT: European Wolf Red Squirrel - Docklands - London, 2007
BACK: Inferno Crater Waimangu New Zealand, 2006

封面图片，封面: 欧洲狼·红松鼠 - Docklands - 伦敦，2007
封底: Inferno Crater, Waimangu, 新西兰，2006